So exotic, so homemade

MANCHESTER
1824

Manchester University Press

The Critical Image

This series explores the historical and contemporary uses of photography. It aims to develop photographic history and criticism and investigates practice. The publications draw on methods and theories widely used in art history, literature, film and cultural studies.

Series editor John Taylor
Department of History of Art and Design
Manchester Metropolitan University

Already published

Jane Brettle and Sally Rice (eds) *Public bodies – private states: new views on photography, representation and gender*

David Brittain (ed.) *Creative Camera – thirty years of writing*

Sarah Kember *Virtual anxiety: photography, new technologies and subjectivity*

Peter Kennard *Domesday Book: photopoem*

Roberta McGrath *Seeing her sex: medical archives and the female body*

Peter D. Osborne *Travelling light: photography, travel and visual culture*

John Roberts *The art of interruption: realism, photography and the everyday*

Lindsay Smith *The politics of focus: women, children and nineteenth-century photography*

John Taylor *A dream of England: landscape, photography and the tourist's imagination*

John Taylor *Body horror: photojournalism, catastrophe and war*

Ian Walker *City gorged with dreams: Surrealism and documentary photography in interwar Paris*

So exotic, so homemade

Surrealism, Englishness and documentary photography

Ian Walker

MANCHESTER UNIVERSITY PRESS
Manchester and New York

distributed exclusively in the USA by Palgrave

Published by Manchester University Press
Oxford Road, Manchester M13 9NR, UK
and Room 400, 175 Fifth Avenue, New York, NY 10010, USA
www.manchesteruniversitypress.co.uk

Distributed exclusively in the USA by
Palgrave, 175 Fifth Avenue, New York,
NY 10010, USA

Distributed exclusively in Canada by
UBC Press, University of British Columbia, 2029 West Mall,
Vancouver, BC, Canada V6T 1Z2

British Library Cataloguing-in-Publication Data
A catalogue record for this book is available from the British Library

Library of Congress Cataloging-in-Publication Data applied for

ISBN 978 0 7190 7340 3 *hardback*

First published 2007

16 15 14 13 12 11 10 09 08 07 10 9 8 7 6 5 4 3 2 1

Typeset in Sabon and Trade Gothic Display by
Koinonia, Manchester
Printed in Great Britain by
Biddles Ltd, King's Lynn, Norfolk

Arts & Humanities
Research Council

Contents

List of figures

Acknowledgements

The acknowledgements for my previous book *City Gorged with Dreams* were extensive, thanking many people who had helped either directly or indirectly with its development. All those thanks still stand for this volume; here I will be more specific.

I was able to talk with a number of participants in this book before they died and their voices can be heard here – Eileen Agar, Roland Penrose, Bill Brandt and Humphrey Spender. I wasn't able to discuss this project with Ian Breakwell before his death in 2005, but it has certainly benefited from previous conversations. Other artists whose work appears in the last chapter – John Davies, Susan Hiller, Patrick Keiller, Martin Parr - have also been very helpful and informative. I am especially grateful to Patrick Keiller for allowing me to use the phrase 'So exotic, so homemade' from his film *London* as the title of this book.

For their help in various ways, I would also like to thank Yves Abrioux, Dawn Ades, Kate Best, David Briers, Jeremy Deller, Mary Fedden, Matthew Gale, Paul Hammond, Annette Jemison, Charlotte Jennings, Mary-Lou Legg, Sandra Lummis, Neil Matheson, David Mellor, Andrew Murray, Antony Penrose, Russell Roberts, Wolf Suschitzky, Julia Winckler and Victoria Worsley. For their assistance with illustrations, I also thank John Flahive at the British Film Institute, the Lisson Gallery, the Mayor Gallery, the Anthony Reynolds Gallery and the Timothy Taylor Gallery as well as the archives listed below.

Two chapters in the book have been developed out of conference papers. A paper on Eileen Agar's photographs was delivered at the fourth International Symposium on Surrealism: *Surrealism Laid Bare, Anew*, at West Dean, Sussex in 2005; subsequently, it was published (in a more detailed version than has been possible here) in *Tate Papers*, 4 (November 2005). My thanks to Jennifer Mundy for that invitation. Second, a paper on Humphrey Jennings was presented at the conference *Mass-Observation, Surrealism and the Everyday* at the Manchester Museum, 2005. It was a very stimulating day, for which I want to especially thank the conference's organisers Anna Dezeuze and Steven Gartside.

A project like this requires time and money to undertake. The School of Art, Media and Design at the University of Wales, Newport, generously funded the expenses of the primary research for this book. The final concentrated period of writing was made possible by a sabbatical supported by a Research Leave Grant from the Arts and Humanities Research Council. I am also particularly grateful for the support I have received from my colleagues in photography at Newport (particularly Ken Grant and Celia Jackson, who took over many of my responsibilities during that sabbatical). Finally, my thanks go also to the Kraszna-Krausz Foundation who have part funded the production costs of the illustrations, which are such an important part of the book.

One of the ways in which this project has differed from *City Gorged with Dreams* has been in its use of primary materials. It has been an extraordinary experience going round Britain to visit the archives and collections where the material I have discussed is held and it has made me very aware of how the physical experience of the archive is bound up with one's sense of the material found there. Descending into the darkened space of the Insight Research Centre below the National Museum in Bradford, one's voice drops to a whisper. The Lee Miller Archives, on the other hand, are housed in an old farmhouse in Sussex and one can look up from one's work to gaze across the South Downs. (Probably the strangest experience was in the Library of Trinity College, Cambridge, designed by Sir Christopher Wren. Among the papers of Julian Trevelyan deposited there are letters and postcards written to him by Tom Harrisson from the Mass-Observation headquarters at 85 Davenport Street, Bolton. As I read them, the space between that run-down terrace house and Wren's magnificently intimidating space seemed to exemplify the structures of English culture which threads through this book.)

Formally then, I would like to thank the staff of Tate Archives (especially Dominic Persad, Tim Pate and Adrian Glew); Ann Simpson in the archive of the Scottish National Museum of Modern Art, Edinburgh; Carole Callow and Arabella Hayes at the Lee Miller Archive, Sussex; Fiona Salvesen and Perry Bonewell at Bolton Museums and Art Gallery; Katy Whitaker at the National Monuments Record Centre, Swindon, and Sue Daly in Sotheby's Picture Library, London. Also the staff of the Imperial War Museum Collection; the Insight Research Centre at the National Museum of Photography, Film and Television, Bradford; the Mass-Observation Archive, University of Sussex, and the Wren Library, Trinity College, Cambridge.

Somewhat ironically, this book was largely written in Wales – albeit only 15 miles from the English border. But I am finishing it while staying at Dungeness, a place which, while it does not otherwise feature in this book, nevertheless, seems very symbolically placed – a relic, almost, of a disappearing England which is just another 25 miles from France. My thanks to Susan Trangmar for facilitating my stay there and to everyone else who helped me explore the sites where the photographs in this book were made. In Lancaster, Fiona and Barry Howarth were, as ever, hospitable. (And thank you in particular to Barry for his insistence that we had to visit Blackpool when the illuminations were up. They *were* wonderful.) In Swanage, Tim Edgar and Kate McGrail made my stay both enjoyable and profitable. Russell Roberts gave me precise directions for finding

Brandt's 'Snicket' in Halifax and, on a visit to Ploumanac'h in Brittany, Susan Butler insisted that, having come this far, we shouldn't let the walls of bramble prevent us from discovering Eileen Agar's viewpoints.

And, as always, my greatest thanks go to Susan, without whose support and editing prowess this book would not have happened.

Introduction

The camera is gazing at Tower Bridge as it slowly opens and a giant cruise liner manoeuvres its way through into the Pool of London. It is 11 January 1992, and the narrator tells us he has been away for seven years working as a ship's photographer, but has now returned to 'Dirty Old Blighty'. A coruscating description of Britain follows, culminating in the words: 'It's so exotic, so … homemade'. This phrase, from Patrick Keiller's film *London*, evokes the complex and paradoxical sense that this country is at the same time both very familiar and rather strange.

Sixty years earlier, in 1932, Paul Nash had written a short article in which he had remarked: 'Whether it is possible to "Go Modern" and still "Be British" is a question vexing quite a few people today.'[1] Could one, Nash asked, be both British and modern – to cherish traditional culture while also embracing the ideas of international modernism? This juxtaposition resonates with the one posed by Keiller. British *or* modern, exotic *and* homemade. What is the modern, what is the exotic and where are they located? Are they already here, embedded in our culture, waiting to be recognised, or are they imported from elsewhere? But then again, where is 'home'?

I have decided to examine these questions by concentrating on the intersection of three concepts – Englishness, Surrealism and Documentary. But why bring these terms together and how is each of them being used here? Initially, there is most to say about Englishness. Straightaway, I should make it clear that my choice of Englishness rather than Britishness is quite deliberate. The two terms have often been used as synonyms – indeed, I think that Nash meant 'Being English' rather than British – and we need to be careful about which we are referring to. But Englishness is, I think, a term that is more specific in its implications.

In the 1980s, there were several major studies exploring the nature of being English; these included books by Martin J. Wiener, Patrick Wright, Robert Colls and Philip Dodd.[2] There have been others since. It is presumably no coincidence that this has been a period when the relationship of Englishness to Britishness has become increasingly problematic, but if the understanding of contemporary Englishness is fraught, so too has been the attempt to look back to discover where 'Englishness' came from. In his magisterial study, *The Making of English Identity*, Krishan Kumar searched though English history to discover where the concept of an English nation takes hold, but failed to find it in any developed form until quite late – towards the end of the nineteenth century. This is the moment that Colls and Dodd had also identified; Kumar calls it 'the moment of Englishness'.[3]

This is somewhat strange, since it was also the high point of the *British* Empire, but it seems at that very moment, the English themselves started to question where it had all come from. Even more paradoxically, the most highly developed industrial nation in the world looked for its essence in the rural landscape – to be specific, in the countryside of southern England – and not in the cities where most of the population lived. As Jeremy Paxman has remarked, this is 'not the country in which the English actually live, but the place they *imagine* they are living in'.[4] In 1985, Patrick Wright coined the phrase that came to sum up this sense of nationalism: 'Deep England'.[5] This was, Alan Howkins wrote, 'the evocation or even the invention of the idea that within rural England especially there is something, in the view of this invented myth, "incommunicable" or "indivisible" in the national heritage'.[6]

There has been a tendency to characterise this identification of Englishness with landscape as deeply nostalgic and conservative. Often it was, and many studies quote from the same string of sources. There is the Prime Minister Stanley Baldwin, giving an after-dinner speech in 1924: 'To me, England is the country and the country is England.'[7] There is H. V. Morton, whose book *In Search of England*, published in 1927, went through many subsequent reprintings (I am looking here at the twenty-sixth edition from 1939). Morton found the essential England nestling in a country churchyard: 'as long as one English field lies against another there is something left in the world for a man to love'.[8] There is H. J. Massingham, 'a townie who had escaped to the Chilterns', who 'produced book after book (his own score was forty in thirty years) telling the English people that the Industrial Revolution had "destroyed the true England", while the countryside was "a source of our daily bread and the indispensable foundation of our national well-being".'[9]

And so on. But this mythologisation of the English countryside was never a simple process – is Hardy's writing or Elgar's music simple? – and indeed other writers have questioned just how extensive it was. Peter Mandler for example has argued that this retrospection was limited to the upper-middle classes, while Alex Potts has analysed the differences between earlier versions of ruralism and that of the interwar years.[10] (Here, the development of Neo-Romanticism in the 1930s, which I briefly reference in the first chapter, would be one marker.) David Matless, in his book *Landscape and Englishness*, developed a complex argument that, between the wars, there existed 'a movement for the planning and preservation of landscape which sought to ally preservation and progress, tradition and modernity, city and country in order to define Englishness as orderly and modern'.[11]

Of course, it has always been misleading to think of Englishness as any one thing and the most subtle writers of the period would have concurred with J. B. Priestley, when, at the end of his 1934 book *English Journey*, he quickly altered the confident assertion 'I had seen England' to the less monolithic 'I had seen a lot of Englands'.[12] England was always a multifarious place, with contradictions and ambiguities threaded through its identity. But we can try to identify several particular landscapes that will appear here – landscapes of difference and opposition, often, but also of connection – landscapes which stand apart yet merge. To do this, I look first at texts by two of the major writers of the 1930s.

Graham Greene subtitled his 1936 novel *A Gun for Sale* 'an entertainment', to distinguish it from the serious books he wrote. But its underlying subject was serious enough – the threat of war in Europe. At the end of the book, when that war has been averted (at least for another three years), the heroine Anne and her fiancé, the policeman Mather, travel by train from the provincial town Nottwich back to London. As they pull out of Nottwich (which clues in the text tell us is Nottingham), 'the dusk came up from the dark wounded ground and the glow of furnaces became visible beyond the long black ridge of slag-heaps'.[13] Soon though the train passes into the countryside. As the countryman Mather looks out, 'A small lit village came up besides his window ... he had just time to notice the grey English church squatted among the yews and graves, the thick deaths of centuries, like an old dog who will not leave his corner.' Eventually the train reaches London and now it is the turn of Anne (the Londoner) to gaze on 'a great viaduct under which the small bright shabby streets ran off like the rays of a star with their sweet shops, their Methodist chapels, their messages chalked on the paving stones ... "Oh," she said with a sigh of unshadowed happiness, "we're home."'

All three landscapes – industrial, rural and metropolitan – appear in this book. We visit the southern rural landscape in the work of Paul Nash, though we find that it is a more fraught place than we might have thought. We travel north with Mass-Observation to a landscape of slag-heaps – indeed, much further north than Nottingham, which after all is only in the Midlands. (I might also add that I am myself from the Midlands, the place which Ian Breakwell – born in Derby – called a 'nowhere land' which, seen from the north, is in the south, and from the south, is in the north.[14] That might grant this study a little neutrality.) And then we come to London, the capital, the metropolis against which all the rest of the country is set. Already then, a series of shifting dichotomies is forming – the north set against the south, the urban against the rural, London against the rest.

The poet Louis MacNeice recounted that, as an Oxford undergraduate in the summer of 1927, he and his friends would hire a canoe: 'instead of going up the Cherwell as was the custom, we used to paddle along the evil-smelling canal through the slums or up the Isis past the gas-drums'. (The influence of Eliot's *The Waste Land* is evident here.)

> One May morning we were on this stretch of the Isis watching a dragonfly among the cow-parsley ... when a goods train came over the railway bridge and we made a chant out of the names on the trucks – Hickleton, Hickleton, Hickleton, Lunt, Hickleton, Longbotham. This incantation of names at once became vastly symbolic ... a sense of things worn out, scrap iron and refuse, the shadow of the gas-drum, this England ... The placid dotage of a great industrial country.[15]

What is interesting here is that we not only have the rural and the industrial juxtaposed, with the south (Oxford) meeting the north (Hickleton is near Barnsley and Lunt is north of Liverpool, so it's a curiously made-up train they watch go past). But, moreover, the two elements have come together and merged into a total effect. And that, for once, it has been caused by the north encroaching on the south. (The movement in the 1930s will usually be the other way round, but perhaps the most potent moment when the north came south was when the hunger marchers walked through rural England on their way to London. It was apparently the shock of seeing those men marching through Cambridge that turned another young student, Charles Madge, to Communism.)[16]

MacNeice was from Northern Ireland, which gives his concluding observation about 'this England' an additional twist. But he shared with many of his English contemporaries a desire to escape: 'For the foreign was calling strongly ... I did not want placidity, or dotage, or industry; I wanted certain new worlds which really meant old worlds ... Travel! Travel must be "experience" at its highest.'[17] This sets up another 'other' – abroad as opposed to the home of England. This took many forms in the travel writing of the interwar years, but as we will see with Eileen Agar in Brittany and Roland Penrose in the Balkans, the desire to escape Englishness could sometimes tie in with a more positive attraction – in their case to the exoticism of Surrealism. (Something of the reverse happened when artists came from abroad – Bill Brandt from Germany and Lee Miller from the United States – bringing their experience of Parisian Surrealism to bear on their engagement with England.)

One of the arguments about Surrealism when it arrived in England in the 1930s was whether it was a force that had come from abroad to challenge the stale local culture or whether it was in fact a reassertion of certain traditions that had always existed within English culture. We return to this argument later, but it is worth noting here that the two artists who brought Englishness and Surrealism together in the most challenging fashion – Paul Nash and Humphrey Jennings – held opposing views on this subject. Nash was interested in the ways that Surrealism connected with English traditions of romanticism; Jennings was excited by the challenge that it posed to them. Yet there were intriguing parallels in their work as well as radical divergences.

This seems to be what E. L. T. Mesens was getting at when he juxtaposed pictures by Nash and Jennings in the *London Bulletin*, the main mouthpiece for Surrealism in Britain. In June 1938, Mesens (who was himself Belgian) placed together images by these two members of the British Surrealist group under the heading 'English Landscapes': a painting by Nash above a photograph by Jennings (figure 1).[18] At first it is the difference that is striking. Nash's *Nocturnal Landscape* is one of a series of paintings based on the megaliths of Avebury while Jennings' photograph is of an industrial scene. Nash's painting has a southern, rural source while Jennings' photograph is (presumably) northern. And, of course, they are in contrasting media; a painting in the tradition of English landscape art and a photograph in the social documentary mode of the 1930s.

Yet, provoked by the pictures' juxtaposition, one notes how similar the biomorphic forms with which Nash peoples his landscape are to the two white ghosts in the Persil advert. How the fence in the photograph is echoed by a fence-like form in the painting, and the vertical chimney paralleled by two of the megaliths, which seem also to thrust upwards. These are largely formal parallels, but their resonance suggests that there may be others of a broader cultural nature. Nash and Jennings were at the opposite poles of English Surrealism, but Mesens' juxtaposition subtly proposes that their positions are connected as much as they are opposed.

It is also worth noting that, alongside the overt dyad of north/south, the earlier triad south/north/London is also in operation here, albeit by implication. The *London Bulletin* was, of course, published in London by the London Gallery (which Mesens also ran). And at the time their pictures were published here, both Nash and Jennings – despite the strong attachment they felt for rural England – were living in London. Yet it is intriguing how little the image of London actually features in English Surrealism in the 1930s, compared to, say, the central presence of Paris and Prague in French and Czech Surrealism. English Surrealism, it seems, was always looking elsewhere, away from London. Only in the early 1940s and because of external forces, would there be an engagement between Surrealism and the city.

This book has grown from two previous projects, which looked at different aspects of Surrealism. Most immediately, there is my previous book *City Gorged with Dreams*, to which this volume forms something of a sequel.[19] As its subtitle indicated, that looked at the relationship between 'Surrealism and documentary photography in interwar Paris'. It seemed to me that there was a glaring discrepancy in the way that Surrealist photography had been discussed up to that point, in that the photographic document and its cousin documentary photography had been left out the picture. Many of the central ideas discussed there – particularly concerning a Surrealist understanding and exploitation of photographic indexicality – are equally relevant here.

It would be impossible to claim that Surrealism in England can rival Surrealism in Paris (or indeed in Prague or Brussels). But what I think is more intriguing – and has been discussed very little – is how Surrealism related to other cultural forces in interwar England, for much of the most interesting work was made not within categories, but between them. This is why I have chosen to look not at

ENGLISH LANDSCAPES

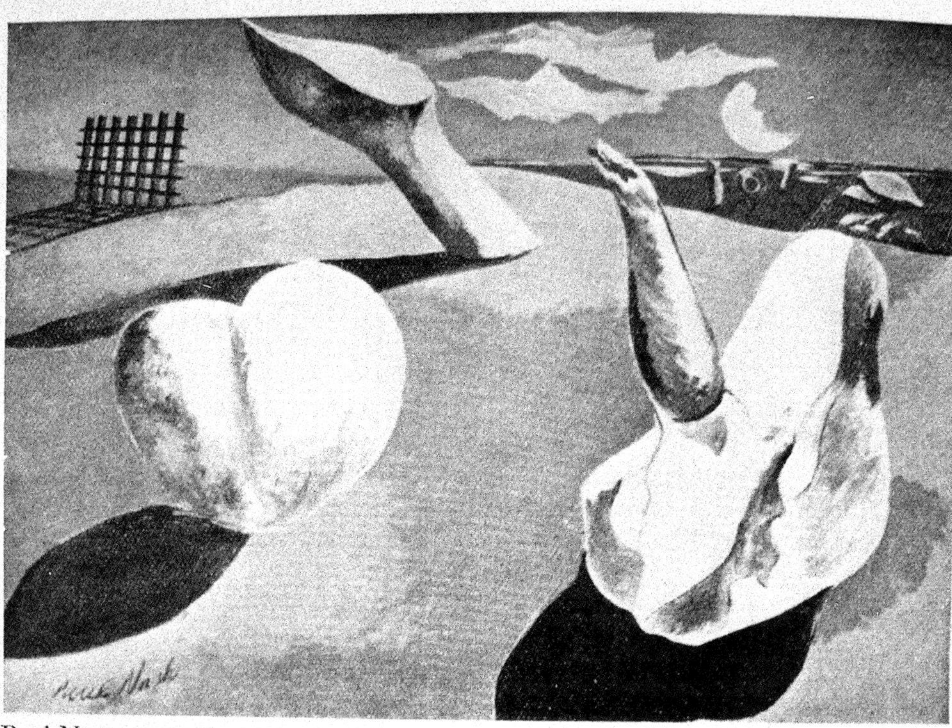

Paul NASH

Nocturnal Landscape

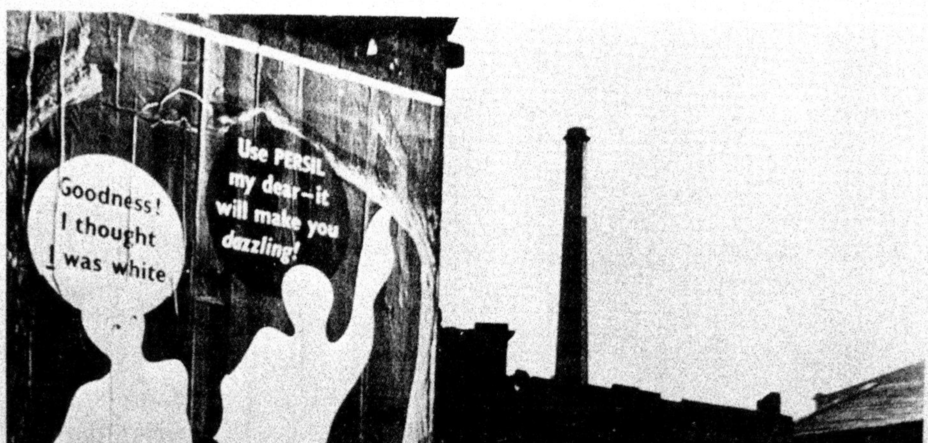

Photograph by Humphrey Jennings

Fig 1 'English Landscapes', *London Bulletin*, 3 (June 1938). Painting by Paul Nash, *Nocturnal Landscape*. © Tate, London 2005; photograph by Humphrey Jennings. © DACS 2006.

a defined category called 'English Surrealist photography', but rather to look at the relation *between* Englishness, Surrealism and photography. What happens when Surrealism encounters an English sense of place – be it the rural landscape, the industrial town or the seaside resort – is something unique and only rarely paralleled in Surrealism as it developed elsewhere.

Of course, there is a problem looming here, for surely this emphasis upon the Englishness of English Surrealism runs quite counter to the insistence of Surrealists themselves that their movement is internationalist and has no truck with nationalism. Yet at a greater distance, it seems undeniable that there is something Spanish about the work of Buñuel and something Czech about the work of Švankmajer. Is it possible for an outsider to care about Catholicism the way that Buñuel does or understand the puppet theatre as Švankmajer does? But, as I discuss below with the work of Nash, elements which come out of an individual's immediate cultural background are joined with elements from elsewhere and both are transformed in the process. And it is in this process of hybridisation that the work of Jennings, Nash (and others) continues to resonate.

The other project which has fed into this book (over a much longer period of time) is an exhibition I curated in 1986 for the Glynn Vivian Gallery in Swansea: *Contrariwise: Surrealism and Britain 1930–1986*.[20] This was one of several exhibitions mounted for the fiftieth anniversary of the International Surrealism Exhibition in London, which aimed to reassess the movement's success in Britain.[21] (I spoke of Britain then, because, after all, the exhibition was being staged in the home town of Ceri Richards, Dylan Thomas and Neddy Seagoon.) Unlike the other 1986 exhibitions, *Contrariwise* did not restrict itself to the 1930s but extended to what was then the present day. For it seemed to me that one of the interesting things about Surrealism in England/Britain was the influence it had within both art and the broader culture in the second half of the twentieth century (though of course, as always, one must be careful what one calls 'surrealist').

I want to develop that here. So where the first chapters of this book are monographic, focusing on case studies of particular works, the chapters on 'the North' and 'the Blitz' start to look more broadly at the relationship between Surrealism and culture. This leads to the final chapter, which explores how the three elements of Englishness, Surrealism and documentary intersected in the second half of the twentieth century. (The concentration on broader issues in these chapters has in turn affected how the work of individual artists has been discussed – the photography of Bill Brandt, in particular, is fragmented across several chapters. This is not to downplay the importance of Brandt, but there have been several monographic studies of his work and it seems more interesting here to place it in a broader context.)

Finally, there is the third term, 'documentary', which may seem like the simplest of the three but isn't. It is a usage which developed through the interwar years that I discuss here, and in Britain it was usually prefixed by another word: 'social'. The tradition of documentary in Britain was essentially realist and concerned with a rather narrow range of subject matter: industrialisation, urban poverty, working-class life. That is an honourable tradition, but it is not my subject as such and I use the term 'documentary' in a much broader way – Chapter 1, for instance, is on Nash's photographs of stones and trees. Documentary here includes landscape photography and the personal snapshot as well as scenes of industrial blight, and the reasons for making it are equally broad – personal and poetic as well as social. In addition, while my focus is on documentary photography, I have wanted at several points to look at parallel developments in film. It could hardly be any other way with the work of Jennings, but films by Lindsay Anderson and Patrick Keiller are key works in the final chapter.

I use the term 'documentary' in ways that have become more common in recent years, as a genre that is broader and more ambiguous than has often been acknowledged in the past. Of course, it begins in the 'real' world – that world through which we move and which is exterior to us – and it always wants to say something about that. But it recognises that our relationship with the world is complex and often unstable. Introducing *City Gorged with Dreams*, I wrote that we must be careful of transposing our sense of 'documentary' back to work made in the 1930s, and that remains true here. Certainly, figures like Roland Penrose, Eileen Agar and even Paul Nash did not think about photography as a later generation would; even artists whose creative identity was more centred on the medium, like Bill Brandt, Lee Miller or Humphrey Spender, were operating in a different context. (It is a slightly unsettling moment when we see Brandt winning two guineas as runner-up in a 'Holiday Surrealism' competition.) Nevertheless, I think we can still see that they were all working, in different ways, between the factual and the poetic, the found and the constructed, the objective and the subjective.

This book sets out to complicate notions of English identity by asking what happened when it came into contact with Surrealism. It explores the ways in which the fundamental qualities of Surrealism were in turn affected by their transposition to England. And it investigates the ways in which the dominant realism of English Documentary was shifted, even subverted by Surrealism. It is a story that travels from Avebury to Blackpool, from the heart of 'Deep England' to the other side of Europe. And in the process, we will hopefully discover how it is that the exotic can be so homemade and the homemade so exotic.

Notes

1 Paul Nash, '"Going Modern" and "Being British"', *The Week-end Review* (12 March 1932), 322.

2 Martin J. Wiener, *English Culture and the Decline of the Industrial Spirit 1850–1980* (Cambridge: Cambridge University Press, 1981); Patrick Wright, *On Living in an Old Country* (London: Verso, 1985); Robert Colls and Philip Dodd (eds), *Englishness: Politics and Culture 1880–1920* (London: Croom Helm, 1986).

3 Krishan Kumar, *The Making of English Identity* (Cambridge: Cambridge University Press, 2003), Chapter 7, pp. 175–225.

4 Jeremy Paxman, *The English* (Harmondsworth: Penguin, 1999), p. 144.

5 Wright, *On Living in an Old Country*, especially pp. 81–7.

6 Alun Howkins, 'Rurality and English Identity', in David Morley and Kevin Robins (eds), *British Cultural Studies* (Oxford: Oxford University Press, 2001), p. 148.

7 Stanley Baldwin, *On England* (London: Philip Allan, 1926), p. 6.

8 H. V. Morton, *In Search of England* (London: Methuen, 1939), p. 280. Morton's case was actually more complex than this; see Michael Bartholomew, *In Search of H. V. Morton* (London: Methuen, 2004).

9 Paxman, *The English*, p. 147, quoting from H. J. Massingham, *Chiltern Country* (London: Batsford, 1940), p. 27. For a positive view of Massingham as a green radical, see Edward Abelson (ed.), *A Mirror for England: An Anthology of the Writings of H. J. Massingham 1888–1952* (Bideford: Green Books, 1989).

10 Peter Mandler, 'Against Englishness: English Culture and the Limits to Rural Nostalgia 1850–1940', *Transactions of the Royal Historical Society*, 6:7 (1997), 155–75; Alex Potts, '"Constable Country" Between the Wars', in Raphael Samuel (ed.), *Patriotism, Volume III: National Fictions* (London: Routledge, 1989), pp. 60–86.

11 David Matless, *Landscape and Englishness* (London: Reaktion, 1998), p. 14.

12 J. B. Priestley, *English Journey* (London: William Heinemann, 1934), p. 397. There were many later editions of this book, but one that is worth noting was the Fiftieth Anniversary Edition (London: Book Club Associates, 1984), which featured relevant photographs by Humphrey Spender, Bill Brandt and Edwin Smith. On Priestley, see John Baxendale, '"I had seen a Lot of Englands": J. B. Priestley, Englishness and the People', *History Workshop Journal*, 51 (2001), 87–111.

13 Graham Greene, *A Gun for Sale* (London: Vintage, 2005), p. 178.

14 Quoted by Victoria Worsley, 'Ian Breakwell (1943–2005)', *Henry Moore Institute Newsletter*, 63 (December 2005/January 2006), unpaginated, from her interview with Breakwell for the National Life Story Collection's Artist's Lives Project.

15 Louis MacNeice, *The Strings are False* (London: Faber, 1966), p. 108. This autobiographical text was probably written in 1941 and published posthumously.

16 Kathleen Raine, *The Land Unknown* (London: Hamish Hamilton, 1975), p. 80.

17 MacNeice, *The Strings are False,* pp. 234–5. This is from a later draft of his autobiography.

18 *London Bulletin*, 3 (June 1938), 14.

19 Ian Walker, *City Gorged with Dreams: Surrealism and Documentary Photography in Interwar Paris* (Manchester: Manchester University Press, 2002).

20 Ian Walker (ed.), *Contrariwise* (Swansea: Glynn Vivian Art Gallery, 1986).

21 See James Birch, Jonathan Blond and Jeremy Theophilus (eds), *A Salute to British Surrealism, 1930–1950* (Colchester: The Minories, 1985); Alexander Robertson (ed.) *Surrealism in Britain in the Thirties* (Leeds: Leeds City Art Gallery, 1986); Toni del Renzio and Duncan Scott (eds), *Surrealism in England: 1936 and After* (Canterbury: Canterbury College of Art, 1986); Andrew Murray (ed.), *British Surrealism – Fifty Years On* (London: Mayor Gallery, 1986). All these catalogues contained essays by Michel Remy, who subsequently produced the fullest book on the subject: *Surrealism in Britain* (Aldershot: Ashgate, 1999). In addition, on the role of photography within English Surrealism, see Neil Matheson, 'The Phantom of Surrealism: Photography, Cultural Identity and the Reception of Surrealism in England', *History of Photography* 29:2 (Summer 2005), 149–62.

England that is, in Dai Vaughan's words, 'cryptic with time-scarred signs'.[11]

This fluid sense of place was central to Nash's work, and it enabled a set of meanings that were both personal and cultural. Nash's first title for the autobiography he began writing in 1940 was *Genius Loci*. For the Romans, the *genius loci* was an actual god or spirit presiding over a particular place. By the time the phrase was in common use in English, in the seventeenth century, it more vaguely meant 'the body of associations connected with or inspirations that may be derived from' a place.[12] This concept was paramount for Nash; his autobiography, he said would be 'concerned mainly with my encounters with places rather than people – the effects places have had on me and I on places'.[13]

When Nash's autobiography was eventually published, posthumously, as *Outline*, it included his eloquent account of his early feelings for the 'Bird Garden' at the family home, an account which can stand for his sense of many subsequent 'elective places':

> its magic lay within itself, implicated in its own design and its relationship to its surroundings. In addition, it seemed to respond in a dramatic way to the influence of light. There were moments when, through this agency, the place took on a startling beauty, a beauty to my eyes wholly unreal. It was this 'unreality' or rather this reality of another aspect of the accepted world, this mystery of clarity which was at once so elusive and so positive, that I now began to pursue and which from that moment drew me into itself and absorbed my life.[14]

This account contains many traditional aspects and, in his essay for *Unit One* in 1934, Nash defined *genius loci* as a prime constituent of 'Englishness' in art.[15] It is also a visual account, with an artist's emphasis on form and light. But here I want to stress Nash's subtle shift between 'unreality' and 'reality'. Nash always remembered a phrase of his early mentor Gordon Bottomley that 'the greatest mystery comes of the greatest definiteness'.[16] His emphasis on the 'reality of another aspect of the accepted world' and his desire to pursue this with 'clarity' connects with Surrealist thought, and it is interesting to put Nash's testament alongside Louis Aragon writing about the Passage de l'Opéra in Paris: 'The disquieting atmosphere of places contains ... locks which cannot be bolted fast against infinity. Wherever the living pursue particularly ambiguous activities, the inanimate may sometimes assume the reflection of their most secret motives.'[17]

There are crucial differences of course; the Surrealists' early sites were specifically (if ambiguously) urban and Aragon's desired 'mythology' was 'modern' (even though, the Surrealists' relationship with modernity was also problematic). Nonetheless, one may still see Nash's sense of place as running parallel to Surrealist concerns. The landscapes found in Surrealist painting in France (by Ernst, Tanguy, Miró and Dalí) were allusive but generalised. What Nash did was to make visual images of particular landscapes, thus paralleling the evocation of particular urban sites in Surrealist texts such as Aragon's *Le Paysan de Paris* and Breton's *Nadja*.

This was also where photography became important for Nash. If one were to compare him with other Surrealist painter/photographers, his position would fall somewhere between René Magritte and Jindřich Štyrský. Like Magritte, Nash was working with an amateur camera: a pocket Kodak given to him by his wife for their journey to the USA in 1931. As with Magritte, this gives his photography an unpretentious air which can be a positive asset in drawing out the marvellous from the mundane. (It can also result in images that are simply mundane.) As Cardinal suggests, Nash's purpose was akin to Magritte's desire to 'put the real world on trial', and their inartistic photographic practices provided one route to that goal.[18] The Czech Surrealist Jindřich Štyrský, on the other hand, devoted himself for two years to photography, acquiring a professional camera (a Rolleiflex 6 x 6 cm.) and exhibiting his photographs in extensive cycles.[19] Nash did not go that far, but he did take his photographs seriously; he exhibited and published them and their relationship with his paintings and writings is crucial to a full understanding of his work.

In the late 1930s, Nash produced a number of articles illustrated with a mix of paintings and photographs. (One suspects he often did his own layout as well.) His favoured sitings for these texts were in two journals, the *Architectural Review* and *Country Life*, and it can be startling to come across one of Nash's articles surrounded in the first case by eulogistic analyses of modernist buildings and, in the second, by tales of hunting, polo and country house balls. In these situations, Nash's work almost takes on the appearance of what would now be called an 'artist's intervention'. The Nash of these essays is not just a painter writing – though it was his reputation in that field which got his articles published – but rather an artist working between writing, painting, photography and the found object in rich and provocative ways.

There have been two posthumous publications of Nash's photographs. In 1951, Nash's widow Margaret edited a selection of photographs under the title *Fertile Image*,[20] and in 1973, Andrew Causey curated an exhibition *Paul Nash's Photographs* at the Tate Gallery with an accompanying catalogue.[21] In *Fertile Image*, the images do not run in chronological order (indeed, they are undated) but are laid out to create juxtapositions; two Avebury pictures sit opposite two Stonehenge pictures, for example. The 1973 catalogue is more measured, proceeding in chronological order to provide an even overall view, where Margaret Nash is engaged but very selective. (She includes none of the pictures from Swanage.) The two volumes are complementary, but both are retrospective and partial – between them, they show only about 140 of the 1061 photographs by Nash now deposited in Tate Archives.

The photos that have most commonly been referred to as 'surrealist' have been individual pictures. In *Fertile Image*, Margaret Nash reproduced a few of these, commenting that they were 'photographic experiments made in connection with a passing interest in Surrealism'.[22] (Generally, she plays down the

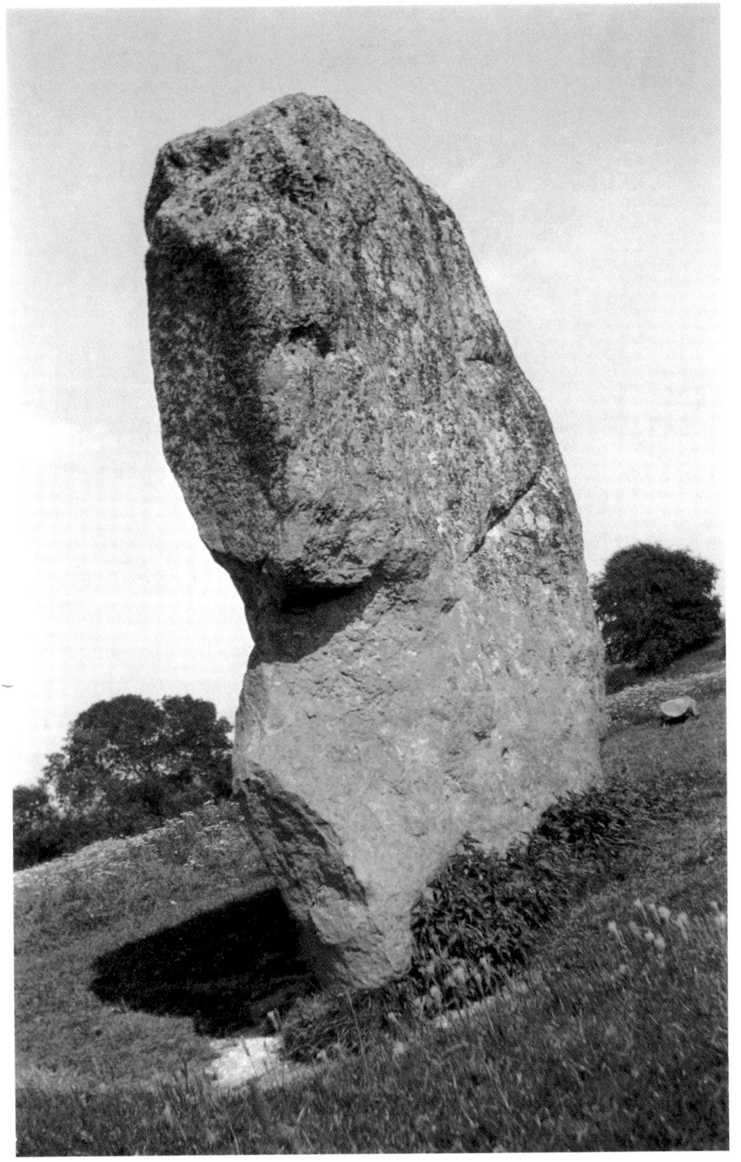

Fig 4 Paul Nash, *Avebury Sentinel*, 1933. © Tate, London 2005.

of the site fades, and the *landscape* asserts itself with all the force of its triumphant fusion of natural and artificial design.'[32] He accompanied the essay with a photograph of the horse seen at an extreme angle so that the rise and fall of its shape becomes paramount (figure 3). While aerial photography maintained its panoptic, distanced view, Nash typically got in low and close. Yet both images, in different ways, suggest that the horse is quite at home on its hillside and also an addition that is strange and startling – both ancient and somehow alien, almost modern.

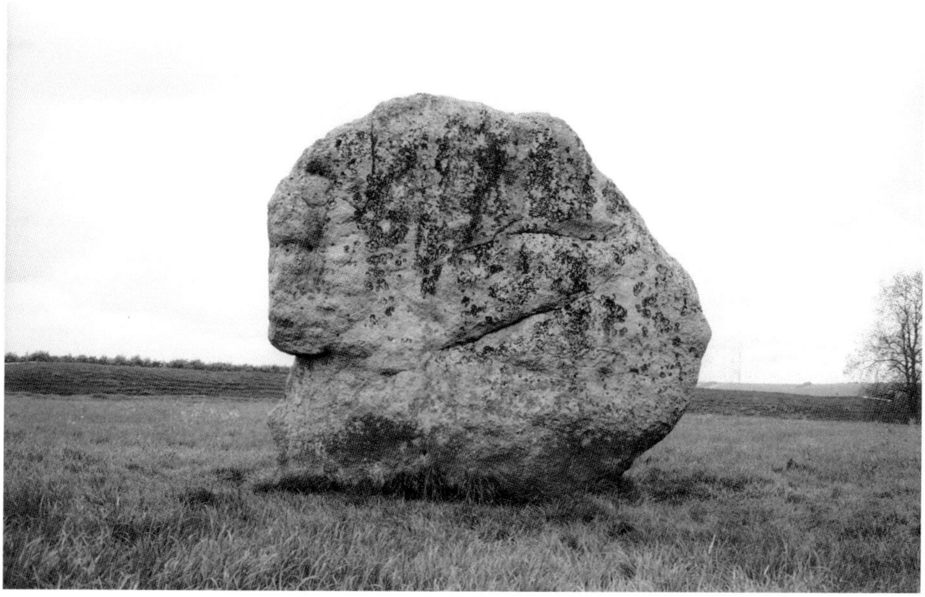

Fig 5 Ian Walker, *Stone 201, Avebury*, 2006. © Ian Walker.

Nash had also visited other prehistoric sites; in 1923, he saw the Rollright Stones in Oxfordshire and he knew Stonehenge, though he rather disliked its popularity. But none of these affected him as much as his visit to Avebury in July 1933. Nash would, of course, have known what Avebury was before he went there. He would have surely have read H. J. Massingham's popular book *Downland Man*, published in 1926, which opens with a grand evocation of Avebury as 'The First Capital of Europe'.[33] But, as every visitor discovers, no amount of knowledge will prepare one for the first view as the road turns through the great henge and past the enormous stones.

However, the Avebury that Nash saw in 1933 was very different from today for this was just before Alexander Keiller began the massive job of clearing the site and reinstating some of the fallen stones.[34] Nash had suffered a bad attack of asthma and gone to stay with a close friend Ruth Clark, who lived at Marlborough. One day they took a local bus to Avebury. 'Suddenly we saw on the left great stones standing up in a field. Paul was excited and fascinated', Clark remembered. 'His sensitiveness to magic and the sinister beauty of monsters was stirred, and he long contemplated the great mass of their forms, their aloofness, their majesty, the shadows they cast on the grass, the loveliness of their harsh surfaces and the tenderness of their colouring'.[35] Nash himself also later described his response: 'The great stones were then in their wild state, so to speak. Some were half-covered by the grass, others stood in cornfields or were entangled and overgrown in the copses, some were buried under the turf. But they were wonderful and disquieting, and as I saw them then, I shall always remember them'.[36]

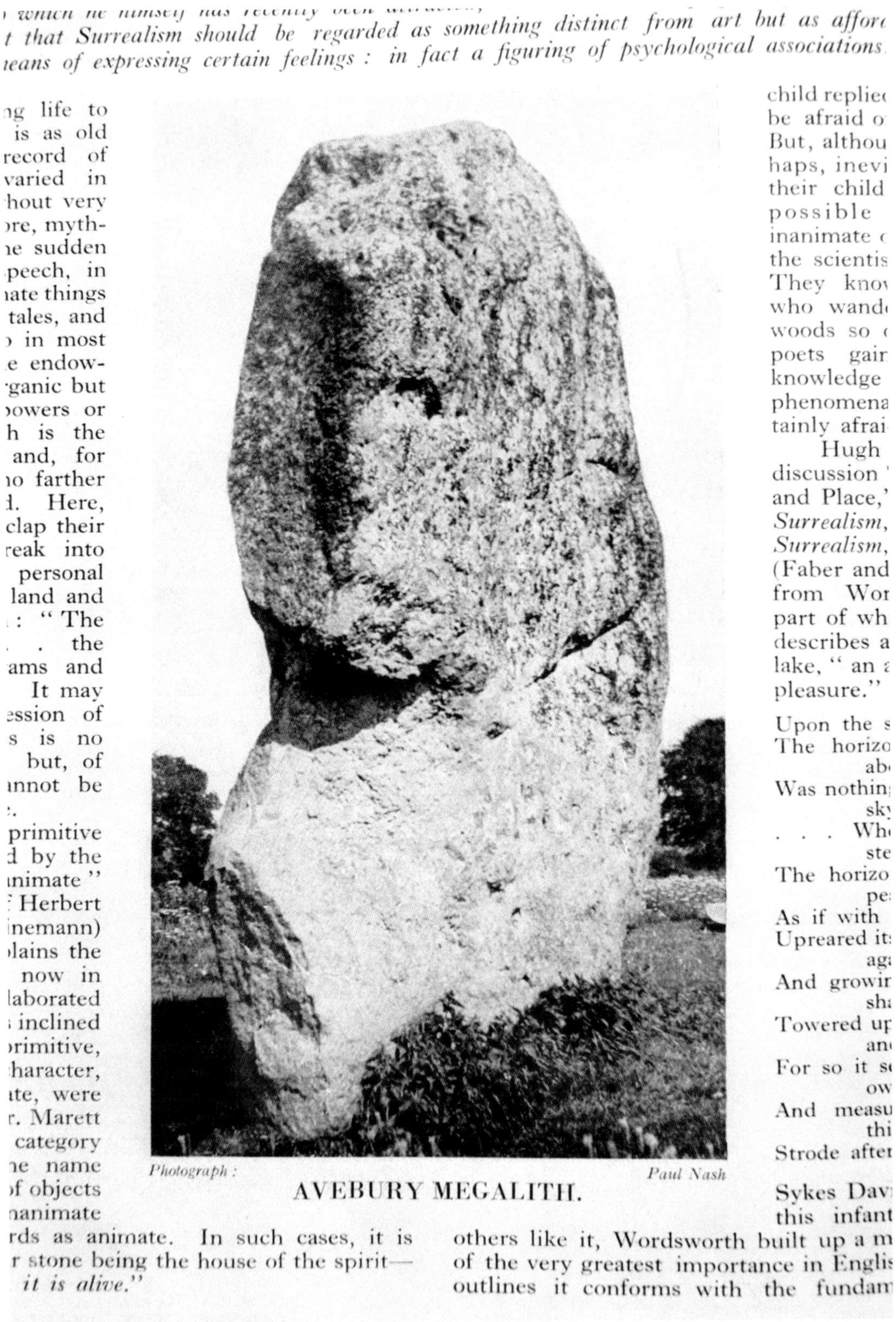

t that Surrealism should be regarded as something distinct from art but as afforc
ieans of expressing certain feelings : in fact a figuring of psychological associations

ng life to
is as old
record of
varied in
hout very
ore, myth-
ne sudden
peech, in
nate things
tales, and
in most
e endow-
ganic but
powers or
h is the
and, for
no farther
d. Here,
clap their
reak into
personal
land and
: " The
. . the
ams and
It may
ession of
s is no
but, of
nnot be
.
primitive
d by the
inimate "
Herbert
inemann)
lains the
now in
laborated
inclined
primitive,
haracter,
ite, were
r. Marett
category
ne name
of objects
nanimate
rds as animate. In such cases, it is
r stone being the house of the spirit—
it is alive."

Photograph : Paul Nash

AVEBURY MEGALITH.

child replie
be afraid o
But, althou
haps, inevi
their child
possible
inanimate
the scientis
They kno
who wand
woods so
poets gair
knowledge
phenomena
tainly afrai
Hugh
discussion
and Place,'
Surrealism,
Surrealism,
(Faber and
from Wor
part of wh
describes a
lake, " an
pleasure."

Upon the s
The horizo
ab
Was nothin
sk
. . . Wh
ste
The horizo
pe
As if with
Upreared it
ag
And growir
sh
Towered up
an
For so it s
ow
And measu
thi
Strode after

Sykes Dav
this infant
others like it, Wordsworth built up a m
of the very greatest importance in Englis
outlines it conforms with the fundam

Fig 6 Paul Nash, *Avebury Sentinel*, as reproduced in 'The Life of the Inanimate Object', *Country Life* (1 May 1937). © Tate, London 2005.

Ruth Clark recalled that, when she returned from walking to Silbury Hill, she found Nash 'sitting cross-legged in the stubble', drawing the stones. He also took a roll of photographs; there are about eight shots from that first visit to Avebury and they are a mixed bunch. There is one double-exposure (whether deliberate or accidental one cannot tell), a few unresolved images and two exceptional photographs of individual stones. When Margaret Nash published these two pictures in *Fertile Image*, she titled them 'Avebury Sentinel' (figure 4) and 'Stone Personage' (figure 7), though whether these were Nash's own titles is unclear.[37] But the titles do seem in keeping with Nash's sense of the stones, which have a formidable presence. Nash remarked that 'Avebury Sentinel' looked like a bloodhound, but it was also 'a *thing* which is an embodiment and most surely possesses power'.[38]

Nash adopted a number of photographic tactics to convey this power. He moved in close and photographed the stones from end-on, so that they fill the frame and seem to be moving towards the spectator. On the back of a print of 'Avebury Sentinel' that he gave to a friend, Nash wrote: 'A Stone Walking Over a Field'. The strong lighting on the stones also helps to give a sense of animation. Viewed from the side on a dull day, the effect that Nash achieved is completely lost (figure 5). Nash also bent down so that the stones loom up against the flat sky and with 'Avebury Sentinel', he tipped the frame to add to the sense of dynamic instability. (Curiously, when Nash later reproduced the picture with his article 'The Life of the Inanimate Object', he righted the stone through cropping (figure 6). The tipping of the camera is so pronounced that it is unlikely to have been accidental and one can only presume that, for this publication, either Nash or his editor determined on a more conservative presentation.)[39]

That stone still stands on its own in the middle of the great circle at Avebury (it is Stone 201). The 'Stone Personage', though, is at the bottom end of the West Kennet Avenue, a 15-minute walk away. (The lighting on the stones indicates that while the 'Avebury Sentinel' was photographed near midday, the picture of 'Stone Personage' was taken in the late afternoon.) At the time of Nash's visit, only two stones stood at this end of the avenue, this one and its partner; it is this situation that Nash very precisely described a year later: 'Last summer, I walked in a field near Avebury where two rough monoliths stand up, sixteen feet high, miraculously patterned with black and orange lichen.'[40] But this stone has a curious history. It had in fact been raised from a fallen position in 1912, but when Alexander Keiller excavated the West Kennet Avenue in 1934, he found it had been installed upside down. He turned it the right way up so that the majestic stone Nash photographed the year before is now half-buried in the ground (figure 8).

Over the next five years, Nash transmuted the experience of Avebury on that summer's day into a series of major paintings 'which presented Deep England at its deepest'.[41] He began this sequence the following year in Nice and the first picture he made, *Druid Landscape*, is a reworking of the 'Stone Personage'; apparently, he had brought the photo with him to the Côte d'Azur. Later, the same stone would appear in the foreground of *Landscape of the Megaliths* (and

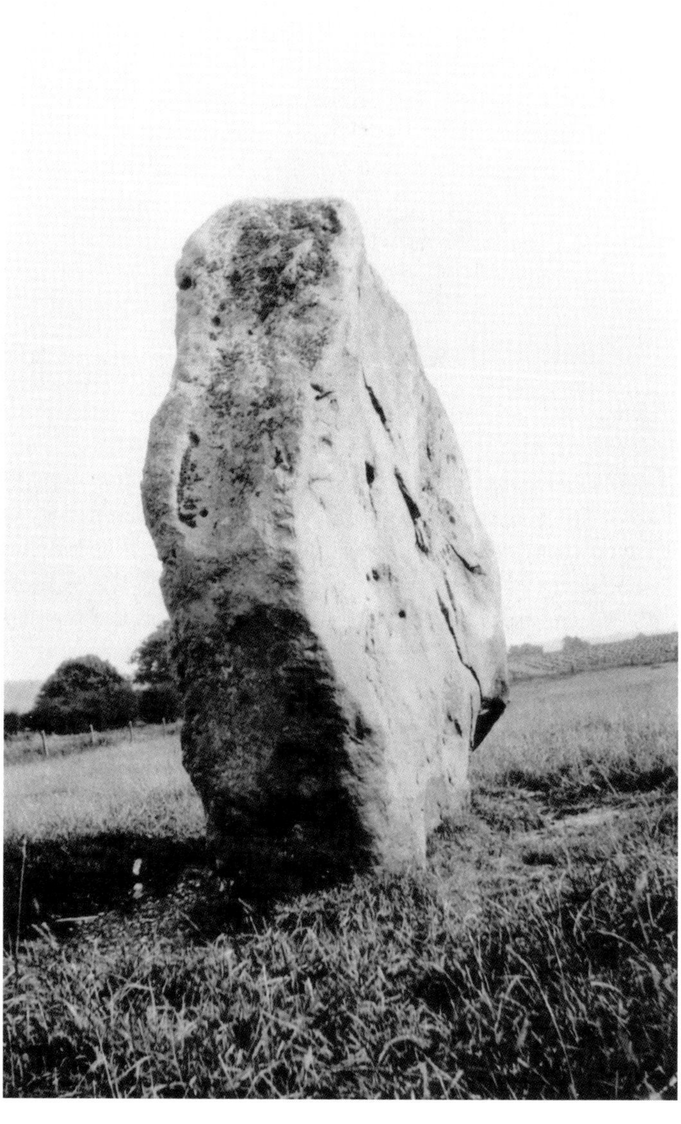

Fig 7 Paul Nash, *Stone Personage*, 1933. © Tate, London 2005.

still later in 1945, on the cover of a book on *Countrygoing*).[42] Other paintings in the series move further away from the actual experience of the stones. A second version of *Landscape of the Megaliths* of 1934 begins a process of abstraction in its flat arrangement of forms, while, in *Equivalents for the Megalith* (1935), geometric forms 'stand in' for the stones. Finally, in 1938, Nash concluded this extraordinary series of variations on the theme of Avebury with *Nocturnal Landscape* (the painting reproduced in the *London Bulletin*) and *Circle of the Monoliths*, where he brought together the twin themes of megalith and seashore

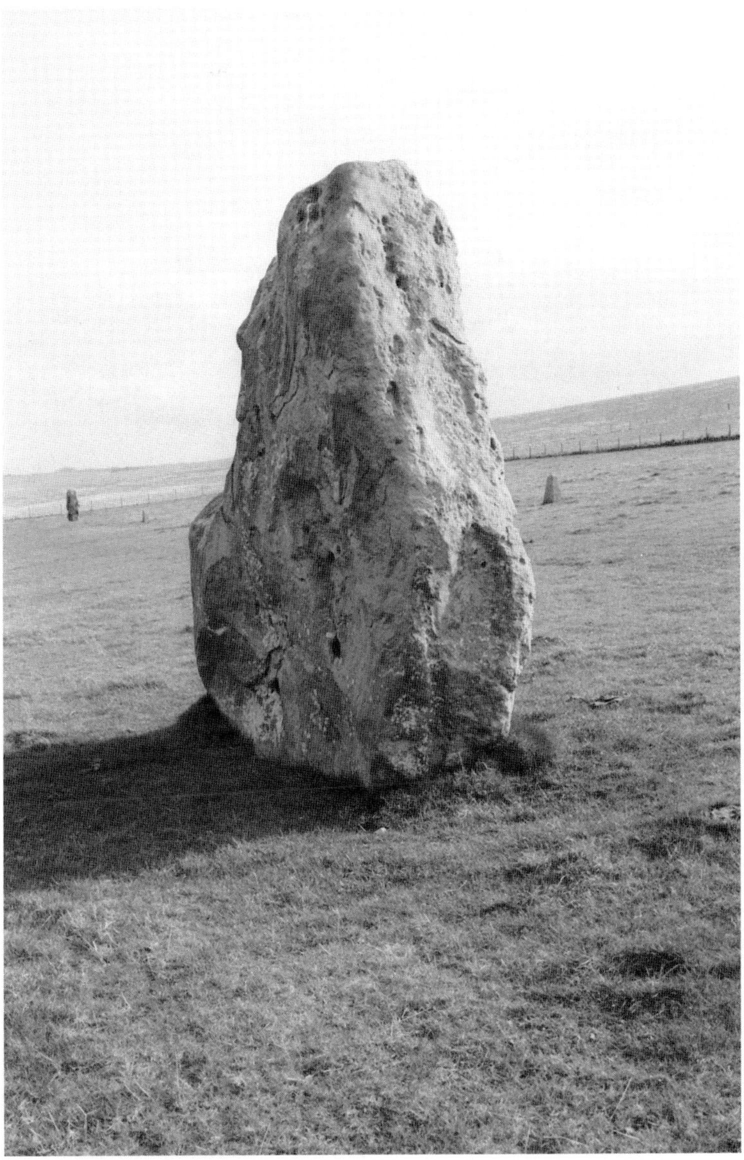

Fig 8 Ian Walker, *Stone 33a, West Kennet Avenue, Avebury*, 2006. © Ian Walker.

in 'a picture of the kind of dream that might come to a sleeper who had lately spent hours on the shore of Swanage Bay ... And not long before the dreamer had walked in a field near Avebury.'[43]

What had begun with some drawings and photographs had resulted in a rich sequence of paintings in which the historical and mythical meanings of the place, the strong sense of the stones' physical presence and their shifting place in the artist's sensibility had been explored. 'He paints three thousand years without turning a hair', wrote Myfanwy Evans in 1937. 'He has no interest in

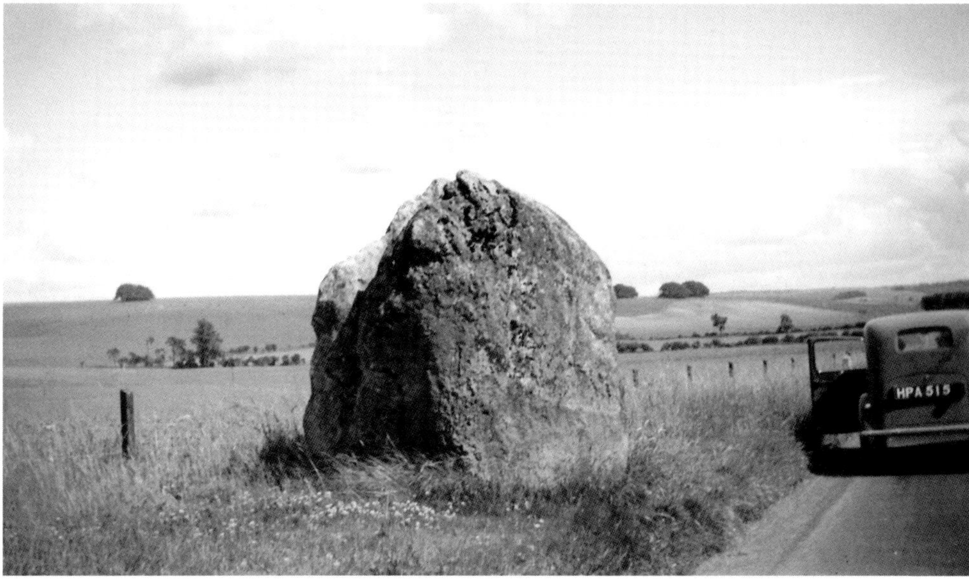

Fig 9 Paul Nash, *Avebury*, 1943. © Tate, London 2005.

the past as *past*, but the accumulated intenseness of the past as *present* is his special concern and joy.'[44] The progression from experience to photograph to memory to painting was a common movement for Nash and one which was particularly fruitful here. However, as we shall see, it was not always an inevitable or easy movement, nor did it necessarily result as here in the deepening of Nash's sense of a place.

It is uncertain when Nash made the acquaintance of Alexander Keiller. According to Keiller in 1951, Nash had visited him at Avebury once, with Clare Neilson.[45] This must have been in June 1938, when Nash was staying with Clare and her husband Charles at their home, Madams, near Newent in Gloucestershire. At that point, Keiller's restoration of the stone circle itself was in full swing. (This fits with a surviving letter from Keiller to Nash on 8 July, giving him some further information about the excavations – 'Stone 43 was re-erected today' – and saying, 'I shall be very glad to see you down here again.')[46] Keiller recalled that he 'ragged' Nash as to how, in *The Landscape of the Megaliths*, the plough had managed to leave furrows right up against the base of one of the stones and 'we laughed a good deal'. Keiller continued: 'That afternoon, we walked round the Monument ... he remained, as he always had been, fascinated by the forms of the megaliths themselves ... [but] I do not think he had any archaeological, religious ... or historical interest in the site.'

Publicly at least, Nash was respectful of Keiller's work, but he regretted the loss of Avebury's wildness, and in March 1939, published an essay in which he commented: 'Avebury may rise again under the tireless hand of Mr. Keiller, but it will be an archaeological monument, as dead as a mammoth skeleton in the Natural History Museum.'[47]

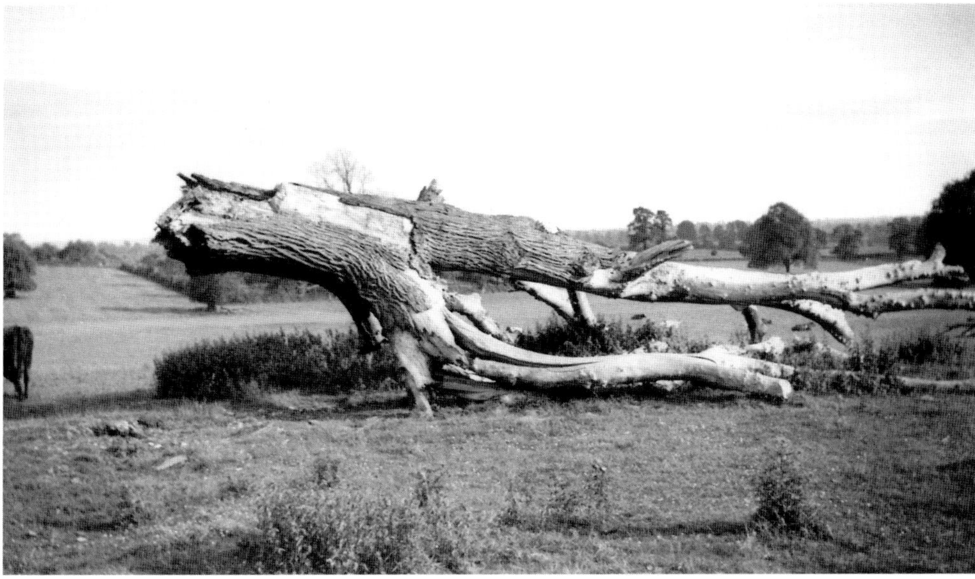

Fig 10 Paul Nash, *Monster Field*, 1939. © Tate, London 2005.

In August 1943, Nash went to Avebury one last time, 'in the course of a drive while staying at Hungerford'.[48] He admitted: 'Sometimes the effect was immensely impressive', but still felt that 'to a great extent that primal magic of the stones' appearance was lost ... I made a few rapid drawings and took a spool of photographs. Again the spell of these deeply moving monuments began to work upon me.' His photographs from 1943 differ from those of 1933, responding, it seems, to the changed circumstances. Rather than concentrating on individual stones, Nash now photographed the stones moving in a circle and their relationship to their environment. One image creates a series of rhymes between stones, white cumulous clouds and tree shadows in the foreground. Again, he tilts the camera to add to the swirling movement of the image.[49]

It was presumably on the same day, while travelling down the road alongside the West Kennet Avenue, that Nash had the car stop next to a stone perched on the grass verge. (Nash did not drive and was always dependent on friends to take him around.) Walking back a few steps, he photographed the stone next to the car with its door open (figure 9). It is an effective emblem of Nash's twin values of the ancient and the modern side by side. However, Nash's indication of how he wanted the image cropped cuts out the car to present a simpler shot of the stone on its own. The photograph could have easily been taken without the car and perhaps, this is another case where an image was subsequently reconsidered more conservatively. It has also tested editors and curators of Nash's work. Causey in 1973 reproduced the image cropped as Nash had indicated (this was his practice throughout), while in the 2003 exhibition of Nash's work at Tate Liverpool, the image was shown full-frame.[50] It is an apt reminder that there are elements in Nash's use of photography which remain ambiguous.

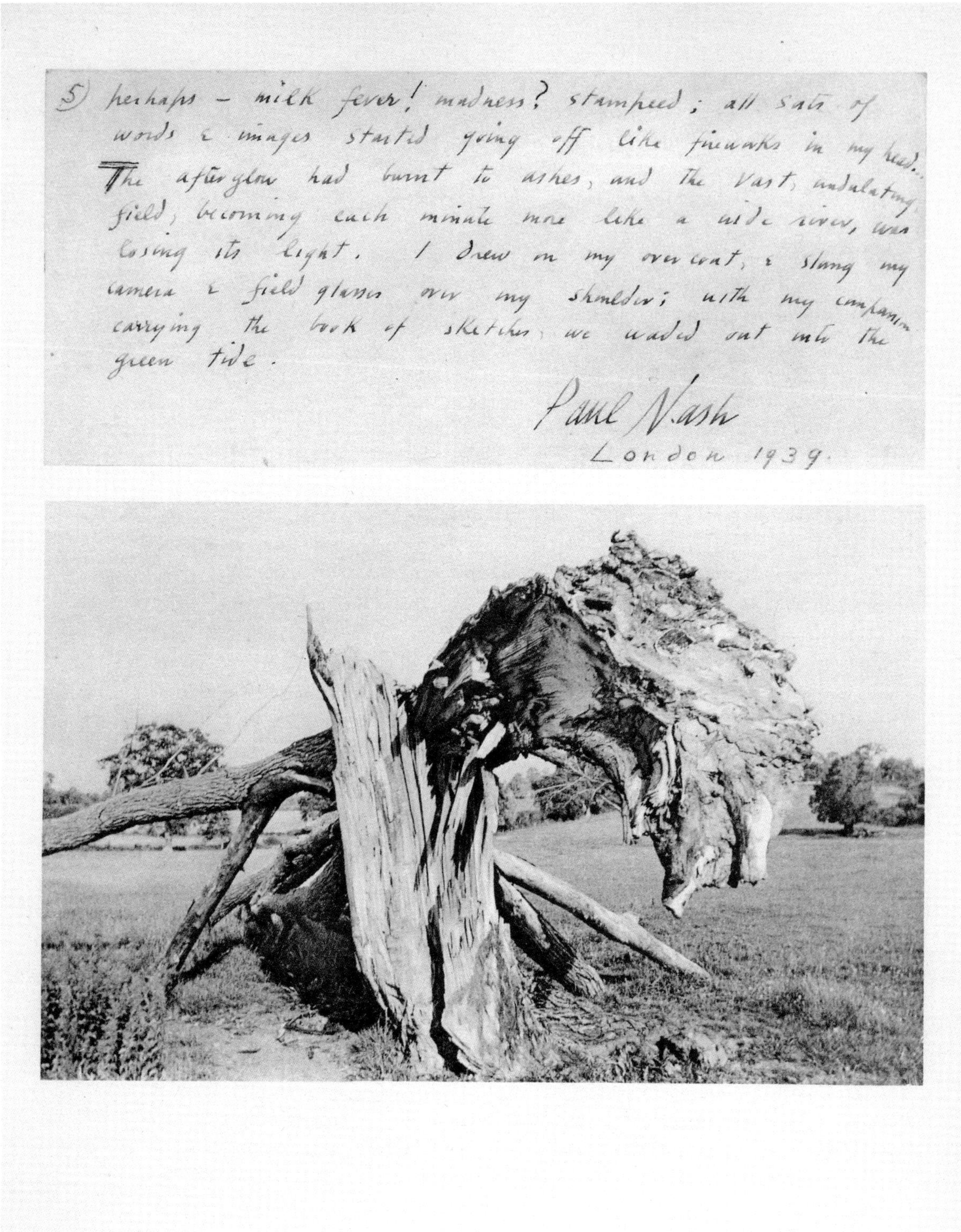

5) perhaps – milk fever! madness? stampeed; all sorts of words & images started going off like fireworks in my head... The afterglow had burnt to ashes, and the vast, undulating field, becoming each minute more like a wide river, was losing its light. I drew on my overcoat, & slung my camera & field glasses over my shoulder; with my companion carrying the book of sketches we waded out into the green tide.

Paul Nash
London 1939.

Fig 11 Paul Nash, page from *Monster Field*, 1946. © Tate, London 2005.

Nash's visit to the Neilsons' Gloucestershire home in June 1938 was also the occasion for another discovery, when, on the nearby Carswalls farm, he and Clare Neilson came across a field where two enormous elm trees had been uprooted by lightning.[51] They called it Monster Field. As early as 1912, Nash had written, 'I sincerely love and worship trees and know they *are* people.'[52] (There is an irksome whimsy here which would later give way to something more rigorous.) Nearly all of Nash's *objets trouvés* were made of wood, and on Romney Marsh, he had already photographed a dead tree and made it look alive. The trees in Monster Field extended that concern, but they also went beyond it and became something other than what they had been:

> We are not studying two fallen trees that look like animals, but two monster objects outside the plan of natural phenomena ... they have 'passed on' as people say. These now inanimate objects are alive in quite another world, but, instead of being invisible like so many of that huge community, ... they are so much with us that I was able to photograph them in full sunlight.[53]

That the monsters were both present and not-present, and that he had managed to photograph those qualities, was crucial to Nash's work in Monster Field.

In his 1937 essay 'Lost – A Valuable Object', John Piper had questioned the shift to abstraction in contemporary art and argued for a return to the object: 'it would be a good thing to get back to the tree in the field'.[54] Charles Harrison has seen this as symptomatic of a conservative shift in English art: 'it would be hard to conceive a more thoroughly English form of the *rappel à l'ordre* than this'.[55] But there was nothing inherently retrogressive in photographing or even painting trees. At the 1936 Surrealist exhibition in London, the Czech Surrealists Štyrský and Toyen had shown works based on natural forms; Štyrský's painting *Roots*, borrowed from Breton's collection, has a metamorphic quality and an edge of violence that Nash may well have remembered at Monster Field.[56]

There are other possible connections. One might see Nash's photography here as a sort of 'spirit photography', but this in fact amplifies the forcefulness of Nash's belief in a materialist approach to the subject; his pictures are clear, made in the full light of the sun, and the monsters are material ghosts appearing *en plein jour*.[57] More tentatively, one might speculate as to whether the image of another creature hovered in Nash's imagination: the Loch Ness monster, which had, in 1934, been memorably (and, as it turned out, falsely) fixed on film by the 'surgeon's photograph'. It's 'head' rearing out of the water resembles some of Nash's own monster photographs. (Nash was fascinated to discover that this Gloucestershire landscape had also once been under water and presumably populated by such creatures.)

The field itself is described by Nash as a sort of no man's land. 'Have you ever known a place which seemed to have no beginning and no end?' he asks, going on to describe how difficult it seems to find yet 'it was always the same, elusive and ubiquitous'. This idea of the *terrain vague* – a place without definition – fascinated the Parisian Surrealists and, as we will see later, can be read into sites as different as seaside Swanage, industrial Bolton and blitzed London.[58] Against the ground of such an ordinary yet somehow unnerving place, the trees themselves, at the same time 'ghosts' and 'monsters', loom up as all the more disquieting, their powerful presences standing out against the indefinability of the setting.

On site, Nash made seven photographs. He moved around one tree in a series of five shots, from one side to the other; the other tree was less extravagant and Nash only made a couple of shots of it. (In one, the back end of a cow intrudes at the edge of the frame (figure 10); it was cropped out of the published version.) Nash used two of these photos – one of each tree, seen from side on – as the basis of watercolours. Clare Colvin has noted how 'the surrounding landscape gains in significance through Nash's delicate palette, and the monsters seem to float just above the ground, hinting at their supernatural powers'.[59] The following year, he made an oil painting *Monster Field*, which uses either these watercolours or the original photographs as source. The two trees sit, one in front of the other, against a broad, open landscape, the Malverns in the distance. But as Causey remarks, the symmetry of the trees 'reduces the sense of potential movement'.[60] Nash also painted another oil titled *Monster Shore*, where the Severn Bore moves across behind two anomalous forms: a tree stump and a set of steps (actually photographed near Swanage). In the middle distance one of the monsters (also copied from a photo) seems to be dragging itself along.

It was planned that photographs, paintings and the text that Nash had written should be published together in the *London Bulletin*. The outbreak of war prevented that and, in October 1940, the text was published in the *Architectural Review*, but in a rather squashed layout, accompanied by only two photographs and none of the paintings.[61] (Nash was interested at this time in putting his paintings and photos together; he had asked Kenneth Clark to exhibit his photographs of crashed German planes alongside his watercolours of the same subject, but Clark thought this a step too far.)[62] It was not until the year of Nash's death, 1946, that *Monster Field* was satisfactorily presented in a slim book. This brought together three of the paintings, three photographs and the text.[63] It is a coherent and integrated presentation of the Monster Field 'project' and we can regard the book not merely as a gathering of the various parts, but as the work itself.

There are several felicities in the layout, which Nash presumably designed himself. The two watercolours repeat the arrangement of the first two photographs, but in reverse. The most powerful photograph – concentrating on the great mass of the monster's 'head' – is saved for the last page, which it shares with the end of the text and Nash's signature (figure 11). But most striking is the fact that the text is reproduced as a fascimile of Nash's own handwritten manuscript. Emphasis is thus placed on the work as personal testimony, for of the three sites discussed here, Monster Field was the most private – most Nash's own. The book's subtitle is 'A Discovery Recorded by Paul Nash'.

Monster Field was both an actual, physical place and a psychological site where metaphor could play freely. Nash precisely describes the play of colour across the landscape, yet subtly that shifts into a sense of hallucination. At the end of the text, he introduces the fact of foot-and-mouth disease, which he is in danger of spreading by walking across the field. Yet he goes on to wonder if the dead monsters might catch it. In a framing metaphor, the field is described as a great river, through which he and the monsters wade. And at the heart of his text, he describes the analogy he sees between the monsters and remembered images from the world of painting. One monster evokes the horse in William Blake's painting *Pity*: 'Did it then crash to earth, fusing its image with the rigid tree?' The other monster 'recalled Picasso. It was eminently bovine yet scarcely male. Surely, this must be the cow of Guernica's bull. It seemed as mystical and as dire.' As James King has noted, 'Nash's choice of Blake and Picasso as references is significant, since his career as a mature artist had been to merge the traditions of English art with European modernism.'[64] It was, in other words, another way to solve the problem he had set himself of being English and modern at the same time.

Malcolm Yorke has dismissed Nash's text as whimsy,[65] but this is to miss its deliberate irony and excess (elements that appear even more strongly in his essay on Swanage). At the same time, however, Nash is pushing his fantasy of the Monster Field so strongly precisely in order to see where it will take him, to see how far subjectivity can go before it crashes into the real. The photographs may seem to embody that 'real', yet they do not contradict Nash's play of metaphor; once stated, those meanings become embedded in the images. And these resonances operate more effectively in the apparently factual photographs than they do in the paintings.

With *Monster Field*, Nash brought together the three media of text, photography and painting. Yet oddly, given the precedent of his Avebury paintings, it is the paintings that form the weak link. Anthony Bertram in 1955 saw a natural progression from photography to what he implied was the inherently superior medium of painting: 'The painter's eye entirely superseded the camera's, but the transition is possible and easy because it was the painter's eye which set the camera to work.'[66] Alas, the paintings cannot live up to this; they seem to be trying too hard to generalise the particular experience. The photographs, however, show the very detail of the trees' physicality, a physicality upon which metaphor can be all the more convincingly grafted. They show that the trees were indeed extraordinary objects. And, in the final photograph, Nash takes that presence and, by foreshortening and using a low camera angle, amplifies it, so that the monster truly seems to loom. Actuality and metaphor are locked together as one.

By the time of his experience at Monster Field, it could be argued that Nash was no longer a Surrealist but a Neo-Romantic. Such terms, however, used as

33 H. J. Massingham, *Downland Man* (London: Jonathan Cape, 1926). As Sam Smiles pointed out, Nash later designed the cover for Massingham's 1942 autobiography *Remembrance* (see 'Ancient Country', p. 37, note 22 and fig. 10).

34 For a biography of Keiller, see Lynda J. Murray, *A Zest for Life: the Story of Alexander Keiller* (Wootton Bassett: Morven Books, 1999); for a scholarly account of his excavations at Avebury, see I. F. Smith, *Windmill Hill and Avebury* (Oxford: Oxford University Press, 1965).

35 Quoted by Anthony Bertram, *Paul Nash* (London: Faber & Faber, 1955), p. 216.

36 Paul Nash, 'Stones', manuscript *c.*1944 in Tate Archive, printed in Jemima Montagu (ed.), *Paul Nash*, p. 76.

37 Margaret Nash (ed.), *Fertile Image*, nos 22 and 24.

38 'The Life of the Inanimate Object', *Country Life* (1 May 1937), 497; reprinted in Causey (ed.), *Paul Nash: Writings on Art*, p. 139. Nash himself later claimed that 'there was no question of animism here' ('Stones', p. 76), but his other comments rather belie this assertion.

39 Nash, 'The Life of the Inanimate Object', 496. The photograph was given the neutral title 'Avebury Megalith'.

40 Read (ed.), *Unit One*, p. 81.

41 Angus Calder, *The Myth of the Blitz* (London: Jonathan Cape, 1991), p. 194.

42 *Druid Landscape* and *Landscape of the Megaliths* are reproduced in Montagu (ed.), *Paul Nash*, pp. 81 and 35. For a discussion and reproduction of the use of Nash's image on the cover of *Countrygoing*, see Smiles, 'Equivalent for the Megaliths', pp. 216–7.

43 From 'Picture History', manuscript by Nash quoted by Causey, *Paul Nash*, p. 266.

44 Myfanwy Evans, 'Paul Nash, 1937', *Axis*, 8 (early winter 1937), 13.

45 Letter from Alexander Keiller to Anthony Bertram, 18 June 1951, now in Tate Archive (7615.1.64).

46 Letter from Alexander Keiller to Paul Nash, 8 July 1938, in Tate Archive (7050.704.736).

47 Paul Nash, 'Landscape of the Megaliths', *Art and Education* (March 1939), 8.

48 Nash, 'Stones'. Some publications give this last visit as taking place in 1942 (see, for example, Causey, *Paul Nash's Photographs*, p. 17, and Montagu (ed.), *Paul Nash*, p. 118), but Nash's own dating in this manuscript clearly gives it as 'Summer 1943'.

49 See Causey, *Paul Nash's Photographs*, no. 96.

50 The cropped version is in Causey, *Paul Nash's Photographs*, no. 97, but the full frame has not been previously published.

51 It may not in fact have initially been their discovery. When Nash sent a copy of the *Monster Field* book to Clare Neilson in 1946, it was with a note: 'Wasn't it our Charles who discovered Monster Field?' (quoted by Bertram, *Paul Nash*, p. 305). But Charles's part was left out of Nash's account perhaps because some of the frisson that the site caused for him came out of it being an experience shared with Clare (this question is explored further in Chapter 2). Something of their sympathy can be felt in a set of photographs of Nash and of Monster Field which she took and which are copied on to microfiche in Tate Archives (TAM 34).

52 Letter of *c.*1 August 1912 to Gordon Bottomley, in C. C. Abbott and Anthony Bertram (eds), *Poet and Painter* (Oxford: Oxford University Press, 1955), p. 42.

53 Quotations unless otherwise indicated are from Paul Nash, *Monster Field* (Oxford:

Counterpoint, 1946); the text is reprinted in Causey (ed.), *Paul Nash: Writings on Art*, pp. 150–2.

54 John Piper, 'Lost – A Valuable Object', in Evans (ed.) *The Painter's Object*, p. 73.

55 Charles Harrison, 'England's Climate', in Brian Allen (ed.), *Towards a Modern Art World* (New Haven and London: Yale University Press, 1995), p. 215.

56 Štyrský's painting is reproduced in de la Beaumelle *et al.*, *André Breton: la beauté convulsive*, p. 320.

57 In his poem 'Les Sept Vieillards', Baudelaire wrote of the 'cité pleine de rêves, où le spectre, en plein jour, raccroche le passant'. Here, we might see Nash transposing this idea from the city to the middle of a field.

58 On the Parisian *terrain vague*, see Ian Walker, *City Gorged with Dreams* (Manchester: Manchester University Press, 2002), pp. 114–43.

59 Colvin, Clare, *Paul Nash: Places* (London: South Bank Centre, 1989), p. 62.

60 Causey, *Paul Nash*, p. 302.

61 Paul Nash, 'Monster Field', *Architectural Review* (October 1940), 120–2.

62 Clark wrote to Nash, 'Some day an art critic of authority will break down the public distinction between art and photography, but God forbid that the Ministry of Information should be the first to try and do this' (letter of 22 August 1940, quoted in Causey, *Paul Nash's Photographs*, p. 18, note 16).

63 *Monster Shore* was not reproduced in the *Monster Field* booklet.

64 James King, *Interior Landscapes* (London: Weidenfeld & Nicolson, 1987), p. 194.

65 Yorke, *The Spirit of Place*, p. 61.

66 Bertram, *Paul Nash*, p. 229.

67 Yorke, *The Spirit of Place*, p. 60.

DORSET

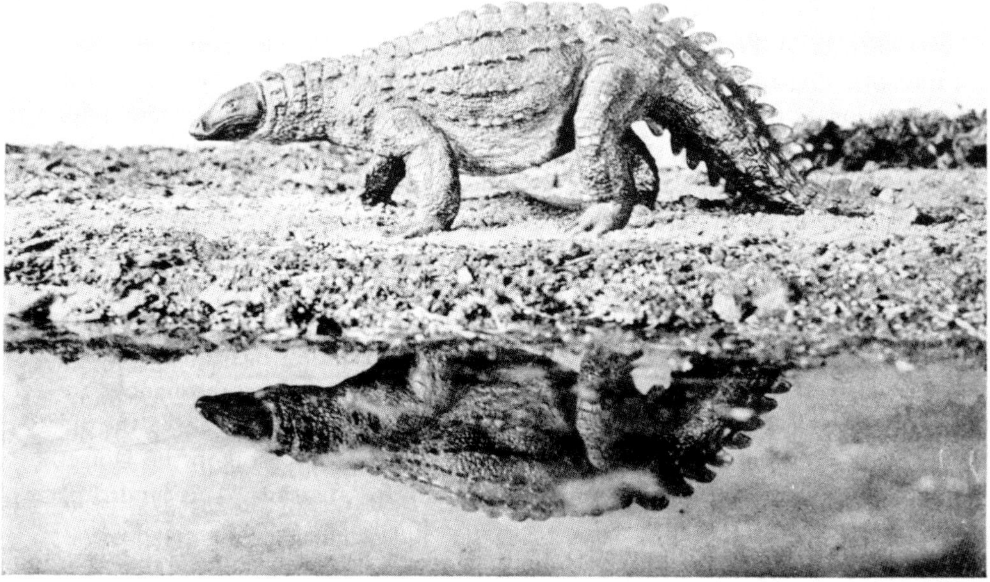

SCELIDOSAURUS HARRISONI : FORMER NATIVE

SHELL GUIDE

COMPILED
AND WRITTEN BY PAUL NASH

LONDON: ARCHITECTURAL PRESS,
9 QUEEN ANNE'S GATE, S.W.1

Fig 12 Title page of Paul Nash, *Dorset Shell Guide*, 1936.

credible'.[13] The *Shell Guides* were intended for the discerning visitor rather than the average tourist, but Nash's dedication goes further in praising 'all those courageous enemies of development to whom we owe what is left of England'. The book, then, is an odd mix of traditionalism and modernity, a duality which is also to be found in the photographs, clear and undemonstrative yet with echoes of the new photography which Nash had seen coming from Europe.

The entry for Swanage in the *Dorset Shell Guide* is brief and dismissive, and one can imagine that once the Nashs had moved from their hillside farm into the house on the seafront, the town might have seemed constricting. There one is very aware of being centrally placed 'between a finger and thumb'; 'snug' might also mean claustrophobic. Nash had lived near the sea before (at Dymchurch and later Rye) but never in such close proximity. Water always had negative connotations for him (as a child he had come close to drowning), and in his autobiography, he wrote, 'I associate them [seas] with cold and cruel waters usually in a threatening mood, pounding and rattling along the shore – a fascinating but rather fearful joy'.[14] These feelings seem to have lifted at Swanage; Nash continues, 'It is not until I think of Swanage that I recall the sea as blue and beguiling.' But here, he is describing the summer sea and there were several encounters that made the summer of 1935 particularly uplifting. With the onset of winter, it must have been very different. In Nash's notes for the unfinished continuation of *Outline*, the account of leaving Swanage includes the ambiguous phrase 'we are frightened from the sea'.[15] Whether it is the sea itself that has done the frightening is unclear.

The house where the Nashes lived on the Parade is only the width of a footpath from the sea wall. In his book *Places on the Margin*, Rob Shields examined the English seaside resort as a site of liminality – a place of indefinition and 'inbetween-ness', between land and water, the town and the sea, culture and nature. The seaside is a space where, in Shields' words, 'Liminality represents a liberation from the regimes of normative practices and performance codes of mundane life because of its interstitial nature.'[16] It is a state which is not in fact dissimilar to the Surrealist fascination with the indeterminacy of the *terrain vague* and we can see it at work in the ambiguity of Nash's response to Swanage.

The article that Nash published in the *Architectural Review* in April 1936, 'Swanage or Seaside Surrealism', is central to an understanding of his feeling for the place.[17] Emphasising that he is describing a surrealism 'with a small "s"', Nash hedges his description of the town with references to 'disquietude', 'the quality of a dream' and evocations of the work of de Chirico and Ernst. He ends by remarking that the town 'has a strange fascination like all things that combine beauty, ugliness and the power to disquiet'. His attitude had in fact changed dramatically from enchantment in the spring of 1935 to disenchantment by the autumn, when he wrote to his friend Ruth Clark, 'The people who live there, my God, the people who come there on the buses and steamers – beyond belief. Somehow they come from the North I don't know why but they somehow seep in from the more savage suburbs of our great industrial cities.'[18]

the 'Remains of early Swanage', the parish church of St Mary's surrounded by traditional houses. In the *Shell Guide*, Nash referred rather ironically to 'a few old stone houses still standing in back streets of town at time of going to press'.[20] (They are still there, though rather done up now.) The picture and comments were not, however, included merely for nostalgic reasons; rather they signal what was to follow.

Nash gives a brief account of how the town went from that rural charm to achieve its present 'surreality' (a story that suggests that the best surrealism is often achieved by those who don't know they are surrealists). Traditionally, Swanage's main trade was the quarrying and shipping of local stone, most famously the 'Purbeck marble' which had decorated many medieval cathedrals. In the mid-nineteenth century, this trade was dominated by John Mowlem (1788–1868), a local man who made his fortune in the construction business (the firm that bears his name still flourishes today). In particular, he developed the trade with London and, to ballast the ships on the way back, he would collect fragments of demolished monuments and street furniture from the capital, with which he then embellished Swanage.

His nephew George Burt (1816–94) shared Mowlem's ambition and, after his uncle's death, became (in Hardy's phrase) the 'King of Swanage'. Continuing the import of salvage from London, he built a number of extraordinary local monuments and was the leading protagonist for Swanage's growing reputation as a respectable seaside resort.[21] 'It is usual in English surrealism', wrote Nash elsewhere, 'for the place to provoke the phenomenon. But in the case of Swanage, we owe so much to those eminent mid-Victorian surrealists, Mowlem and Burt, the makers of Swanage, and the process of Pelion upon Ossa, that the significance of the original site is dubious.'[22]

Walking down the hill from the church, one comes to Purbeck House, a large mansion that George Burt built for himself in a style that has been called 'Scottish baronial', and which Nikolaus Pevsner regarded as 'High Victorian at its most rebarbative'.[23] (Nash himself described the local style as 'Purbeck-Wesleyan-Gothic'.) Behind the house lie extensive gardens lavishly but rather randomly decorated with salvage material from London buildings that Mowlem's were demolishing at the time – balustrades from Billingsgate, columns from Waterloo Bridge, an arch from Hyde Park Corner and statues from the Royal Exchange.[24] However, when Nash was in Swanage, Purbeck House was about to be converted into a convent and the gardens were probably inaccessible.[25] This may be why the only photographs of Purbeck House he took were from across the road, with the eccentric gazebo towering above the street in the foreground.

Nash made those photos from a window in the Town Hall, which he in turn photographed from the street. To enhance the rather plain Town Hall built in the early 1880s, Burt added a very elaborate and decorated façade of about 1670 that he had acquired from the front of Mercers' Hall in Cheapside. Following the opinion of the day, Nash called it 'a Wren façade of bad but genuine design', but it seems in fact to have been designed by Wren's pupil Edward Jerman. Nash

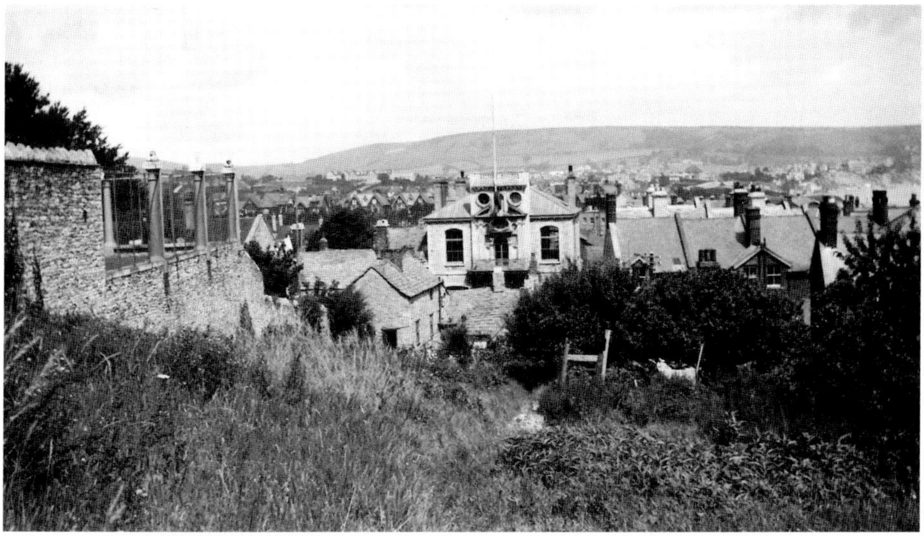

Fig 14 Paul Nash, *View above Swanage*, *c*.1935. © Tate, London 2005.

couldn't get the top of the façade in his picture from street level and found a spot up on wasteground next to the Purbeck House gardens from where he could make a picture of the top of the Town Hall with Ballard Down in the distance, setting the town against the surrounding landscape (figure 14).

Nash also took several photos of one of the most peculiar of Swanage's landmarks, the clock tower ('(clockless), a Gothic structure of stone removed about 1863 from London Bridge, where it had been a memorial to the first Duke of Wellington').[26] This stands on the headland to the east of the town and, in some of his pictures, Nash ironically again placed the tower in a natural setting, seemingly rising from the undergrowth in the foreground and set against the sweep of the bay beyond.[27] In the *Architectural Review* article, though, he used a rather more desolate image of the Tower rising above the shingle: 'grey and papery against the solid sea ... jutting out over a lonely beach'. The deliberate paradox of Nash's position is clear as he describes the 'delight' with which a visitor might view this 'repulsive' structure. Malcolm Yorke has read Nash's interest in the monuments of Swanage as prefiguring the later enthusiasm of Piper and Betjeman for Victorian architecture;[28] in 1935, that taste had not yet developed and even Betjeman was still eulogising modernism. But the surrealist filter through which Nash views them is more complex. Paralleling the Parisian Surrealists' fascination with the *démodé*, his enjoyment is heightened by uneasiness as delight and repulsion are thoroughly conjoined.

The seafront esplanade was the scene for the central drama of Nash's article: 'Let us imagine a shipwrecked stranger struggling towards the shore through angry waves on a dark night ... At last a particularly shrewd buffet from a driving wave flings the half-dead visitor clean on to the waterfront.' Here he clutches a lamp-post and as he faints away, he sees embossed on it the words 'St

George's, Hanover Square'. Waking with daybreak, 'incredulous, and fancying himself light-headed, he wanders down the deserted esplanade until a stone column surmounted by a pyramid of cannon-balls set askew looms in his path'. Nash's visitor (a sort of post-Romantic tourist) is 'convinced his reason has left him or that he is part of a dream'. But, as Nash's photographs show, what the stranger had seen was indeed there.

The old lamp-posts embossed with London street names have now unfortunately gone, but the column is still there. It was built in 1862 by John Mowlem to commemorate an alleged victory by King Alfred over a Danish fleet in AD 877. The cannon balls were actually Russian balls which had lodged themselves in the hull of a British ship returning from the Crimean War. Sir Frederick Treves noted in 1906, 'To some, these missiles may seem inappropriate, as gunpowder was not invented until more than 400 years after the assumed engagement.'[29] (There are curious copies of the column in the grounds of Purbeck House, though there the balls are meant to be tennis balls. One can see them on the left of the photograph that Nash took of the top of the Town Hall.) In 1965, when the Mowlem Institute (called by Nash 'the most dismal building in Dorset') was replaced by the equally dismal Mowlem Theatre, the column needed to be moved. A local councillor argued, 'The day of monuments has passed. This one should be demolished and sunk to the bottom of the bay.'[30] Happily, it survived.

The pictures that Nash took of these objects on the esplanade are, on the whole, quite straightforward. In the original negatives, there are often distracting elements – passers-by, benches, his own shadow – but he indicates that these are to be cropped from the final image.[31] He wants the extraordinary objects to speak for themselves. Yet this does not completely disallow some small elements of subversion, like the litter bin that sits next to the lamp-post in one picture and becomes as much an object of attention as the lamp-post itself.[32] There is also one photograph of the Alfred the Great column, where Nash stood below it looking vertiginously upwards in the manner of the 'New Objectivity' photographers whose work he knew well. But, when he came to choose a photograph

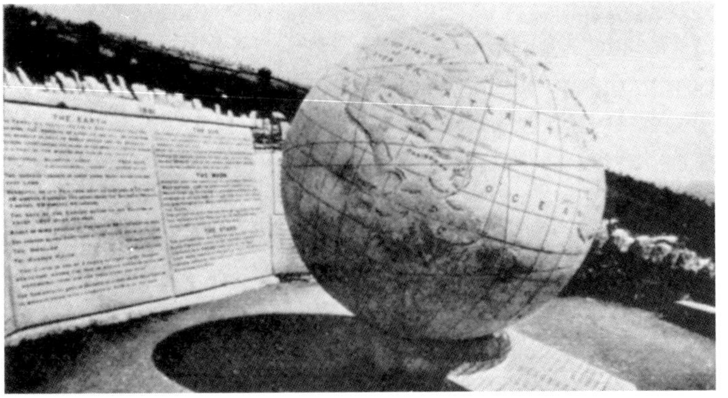

Fig 15 Photographer unknown, *The Great Globe, Swanage*, reproduced in Paul Nash, 'Swanage, or Seaside Surrealism', *Architectural Review* (April 1936).

of the column for the *Architectural Review*, he used a picture that was direct and undemonstrative, rather in the manner of the photographs of monuments in André Breton's *Nadja* (figure 13). (Though in the context of the *Architectural Review*, the column might also have looked rather modernist.)

Curiously, Nash does not seem to have photographed a couple of the more extraordinary Swanage landmarks. In his text, the shipwrecked visitor enters the grounds of a hotel and 'is not surprised to find two vast Corinthian pillars standing up in the drive without any relation to the building. A memory of Chirico starts up…' This was the Grosvenor Hotel, one of the grandest of Swanage's establishments. Though it was demolished in 1986, the columns have since been re-erected in a park near the site, where they continue to look marvellously incongrous. Nash also seems not to have taken any pictures of the monument he dubbed the 'largest of the jokes' – the Great Globe, which stands on Durlston Head, south of the town. Instead, it is illustrated in the *Architectural Review* by what appears to a commercially made photograph, perhaps a postcard (figure 15).

The complex of buildings and landscaping on Durlston Head was George Burt's largest development. Centred on the turreted Durlston Castle, a network of pathways work their way down and along a dramatic cliffside walk to the abandoned quarry workings at Tilly Whim Caves, with rocks carved with quotations and sayings along the way. One can still read carved into one rock:

LOOK ROUND
AND READ
GREAT NATURE'S
OPEN BOOK.

The Great Globe sits on the slope below the castle, carved from Purbeck stone, 10 feet in diameter and 40 tons in weight. It is the best known of Swanage's monuments; in 1932, Graham Sutherland had designed a Shell poster depicting it.[33]

In Nash's essay, a visit to this site forms the climax of the shipwrecked visitor's experience. It is late afternoon and he is attracted by the idea of Durlston Castle, 'no doubt a picturesque ruin'. But he gets lost, following a tortuous clifftop path, confused by the sound of waves and gulls, till he suddenly comes upon the Globe: 'The place at this hour has an atmosphere of doubtful enchantment, a grotesque made awe-inspiring by indefinition.' Nash's castaway starts to grow hysterical and he hurries up to the castle and in through the door: 'Before him is an immense deserted room, tenanted by what seems to be hundreds of empty tables and chairs. A long empty counter curves away into shadows. Behind the counter stands *La Femme 100 Têtes*.' This figure comes from Max Ernst's collage-novel of the same name (her name punning on *La femme sans tête*) but here she is a waitress in Durlston Castle restaurant, which, as its emptiness suggests, never seems to have been much of a going concern.

All this is ridiculous, of course, deliberately overblown for effect. But there

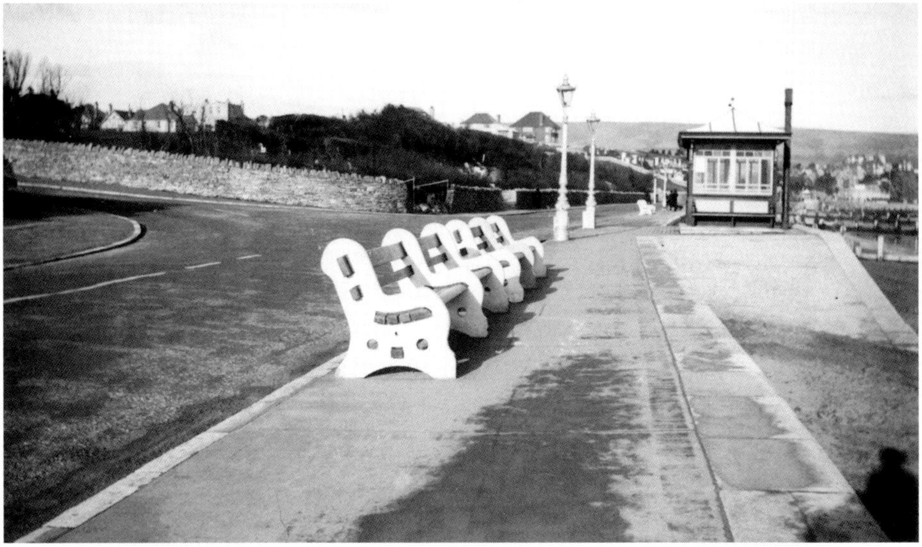

Fig 16 Paul Nash, *Seat, Swanage*, *c*.1935. © Tate, London 2005.

is also a genuine unease, which finds an echo in an experience recounted by André Breton in his book *L'Amour fou*.[34] In July 1936 (a month after he had been in London for the Surrealism exhibition), Breton and his wife Jacqueline were in Brittany. A visit to a beach near Lorient had resulted in a cache of 'those object-talismans surrealism still cares so much about', both natural (a crab skeleton) and artificial (a few small electric light bulbs). But when they return on 20 July, Breton feels a sensation of isolation, banality and strangeness intermixed. He later ascribes this sensation to the presence of a house on the shore where a murder had taken place; 'this house was the one I perceived in a fog only my own, surrounded by the worst kind of wasteland' ('flanquée du pire terrain vague').[35] But it also sounds like a parallel sensation to those he had previously experienced in the alienated cityscape of Paris and which he had described in *Nadja*.[36] The shock here lay in the fact that this natural landscape had also turned out to be 'a place especially banal and hostile'.

The parallels with Nash's position in Swanage are evident. There are evocative objects to be found here and the bay and the surrounding headlands are beautiful. But Nash feels himself estranged, disorientated by the town itself. It too is a *terrain vague*, a 'no man's land' in the battle between culture and nature, and its banality is disquieting and unnerving. The shipwrecked stranger is Nash himself, wandering the town for clues and explanations and finding only incongrous monuments. He may mock the town and even, to an extent, himself, but he is also unsure of whether the 'surrealism' of Swanage lies in the place itself or in his estrangement from it. So he bluffs detachment and wilfully seeks the ridiculous and strange wherever he turns.

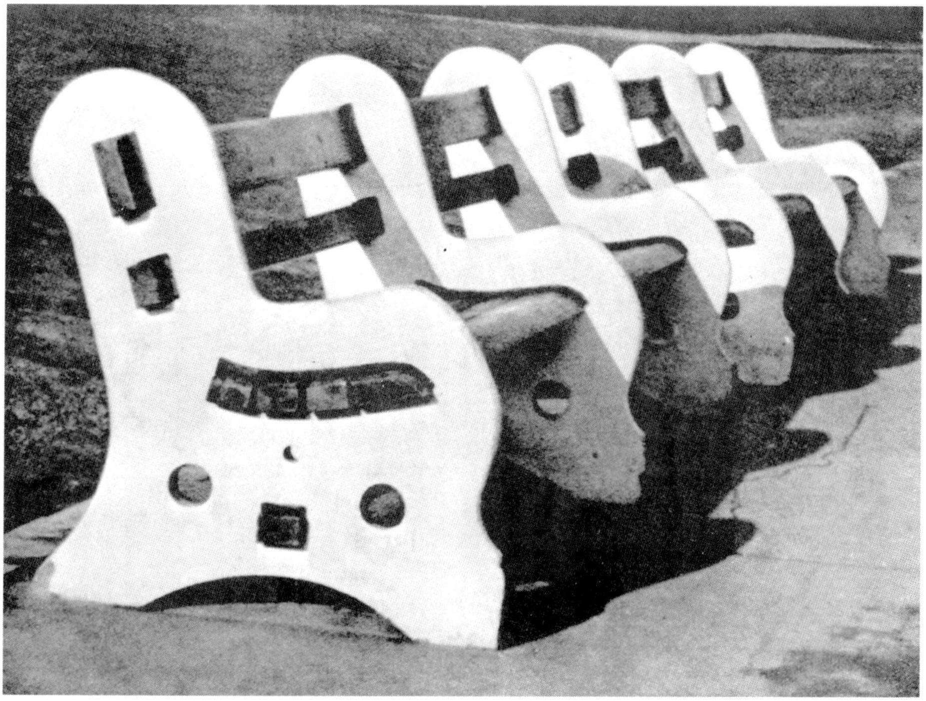

Fig 17 Paul Nash, *Seat, Swanage*, *c.*1935, as reproduced with the title 'Swanage Modernism' in 'Swanage, or Seaside Surrealism', *Architectural Review* (April 1936). © Tate, London 2005.

The most ordinary objects that Nash photographed at Swanage were the new seats placed along the Esplanade, in which Nash rather fancifully saw the symbolic form of the Swan. All of the negatives contained a great deal of ephemeral information: the town behind, houses, a bus-shelter, lamp-standards, passers-by, pavement and even his own shadow. But all of this was to be firmly cropped out and the image reproduced in *Architectural Review* was massively cut out from the centre of the image, a section 2 x 2.5 cm retained from an original negative size of 6 x 10.6 cms: about 8 per cent (figures 16 and 17). At the same time, this image as presented in *Architectural Review* acquired an importance, indeed a monumentality, deliberately out of proportion to its function. It prefaced the article, the single photograph tipped in on grey art paper. This removal of context has the effect of reinforcing the metamorphic qualities of the bench and pointing up the formal parallel with certain sorts of Modernist art (most obviously the work of Moore) which engaged in a similar exercise. Indeed, Nash referred to the benches as 'Swanage modernism'.[37]

This is again part of Nash's strategy of ironisation, but it also has other echoes. He seems to be harking back here to the 'English seaboard surrealism' of Edward Wadsworth and Tristram Hillier, which had influenced him in the early 1930s.[38] That work combines a formal reticence edging towards abstraction, a hyperrealist attention to detail and a sense of alienation derived from de Chirico. In his fastidious attention to the benches on Swanage esplanade, Nash – in the spirit of Surrealism – claims a lot for these ordinary objects, while undercutting his own pretensions with the pedantic comment that these 'Swan-like seats were designed for the esplanade by the Swanage Urban District Council'. It is, he adds, 'an instance of the peculiar formal fantasy which breaks out from time to time'.

Nash referred to 'a queer persistence in the element of the swan' that he perceived in Swanage.[39] Aside from the benches, he saw and photographed this leitmotif in the iron railing of the pier, and also in an object (part of a curved wooden chair leg) that he found in a turner's shop window. Several photos exist of this, sitting on a wall with the sea in the background. When Nash reprinted 'Swanage' in *The Painter's Object*, he included as one of the illustrations a small watercolour of this chair leg titled *Comment on Leda*. It seems that the swan came to stand for the natural beauty that was a crucial part of Nash's experience of Swanage – embedded in its very name – yet was constantly denied by the mundane nature of the town itself.[40]

Thus, one can imagine the resonance for Nash of a poignant sight that he reported in his *Architectural Review* essay: 'a single swan ... upon the choppy waters of the bay, riding uncomfortably against the incoming tide'.[41] Nash had also recorded this sight in a short sequence of photographs, some showing the swan in the open water, others in the incoming waves. One would guess that Nash was taking these pictures from his own window on the Parade, and the swan is very small but central to the otherwise rather empty images. In the context of Nash's feelings about Swanage, we can read the swan as representing the pathetic vulnerability of the purely natural in this setting. But there were also more personal resonances for Nash, both because of his enduring distrust of the sea and, more specifically, in terms of what was then happening in his private life.

Nash met Eileen Agar one afternoon in the summer of 1935 on the lawn of the Grosvenor Hotel. Agar was then 36, an independent painter, and she and her long-term partner the Hungarian writer Joseph Bard had rented Clarence Cottage in Swanage for the summer. (Agar had also been there previously as a child.) She and Nash shared a passionate interest in the use of natural forms in art. Later she recalled, 'He used to bring me curious stones that he had picked up on the beach and as he said, he felt rather like a penguin, laying them metaphorically at my feet.'[42] However, 'Joseph eyed the penguin warily', and with justification, for at some point in the next year, Agar and Nash became lovers. However, by July 1936, Agar had decided that their relationship was causing too much pain both for themselves and their partners and broke off the affair (though they would continue to meet in a more subdued way for several years yet).

On 6 July 1936, Nash sent Agar a postcard made from one of his photos of the swan in Swanage bay and wrote on the back: 'I have been going over my mementoes and came upon this – a quaint bit of reality to set against my surreality of the swan. I should have remembered, when I made that "comment" whom the disguise hid. The Gods cannot be jested with, I suppose.' The reference is cryptic and private, though one might assume that he is referring to his painting *Comment on Leda*. Agar had also made a painting called *Leda*, which Nash may have been 'commenting' on and we can read Agar as Leda and Nash as the swan (Zeus metamorphosed, of course).

A year later, in July 1937, he was more explicit. Agar had by now had another affair with Paul Eluard and Nash wrote in anguish:

> I could share you with Joseph because that was something you gave me which was not for him. But I cannot share you with Eluard because you have given him what was mine.
>
> That is why I sent you a picture of a swan facing out to sea, but it was meant only lightly – nothing pathetic you know. The swan could fly; I don't imagine he drowned. When I, somehow, drown, I shall spread my wings yet.[43]

Here, the swan is very explicitly Nash himself and the dual possibilities of drowning and flying – the one fearful, the other ecstatic – were probably there from that first sighting in September 1935, albeit not so fully articulated.

Nash used one of his photographs of the swan in the bay as the base of a photocollage reproduced with the 'Swanage' article, where a huge, unidentifiable object looms above it, its top end echoing the bird imagery but with the hooked beak of a bird of prey (figure 18). (The theme of the bird is extended in the text by a reference to 'Loplop', 'the magic bird of Max Ernst'.) This object was in fact a rusted iron anchor chain, about two feet long and covered in shells, which Eileen Agar had found buried on the beach at Lulworth Cove. This object became central to the relationship between Nash and Agar; they both photographed it, she made a watercolour of it and he used it in his collage. Agar later took the object itself to London where it was damaged in the Blitz.

In these reworkings, wrote Agar later, the anchor 'metamorphosed into a new creation, a bird snake, or as Paul Nash called it, a "seashore monster". The sea and the land sometimes play together like man and wife, and achieve astonishing results.'[44] The anchor's peculiar appeal lay in its hybrid nature, not only as bird and snake, or sea and land, but also as both natural and industrial, as both the town of Swanage and the landscape of Swanage Bay. In the context of Nash's essay, one can see its role in his collage as representing something of the threat that the town posed for the landscape. But there was a deeply personal resonance here as well and Agar's comments suggest the context of sexual and gendered meanings that she and Nash attached to the object.

In Nash's work, the connection between woman and landscape had once been overt. In the painting *Vision of Evening* (1911), for example, a woman's face hovers in the sky above a rounded landscape, which becomes her body. That overtness had long been suppressed but the resonance was never lost; 'the faces quickly disappeared from his work; in another sense, he never abandoned them'.[45] Specifically, one might wonder what latent role this played in Nash's responses to his 'elective places'. Was it only coincidence that all three of the sites

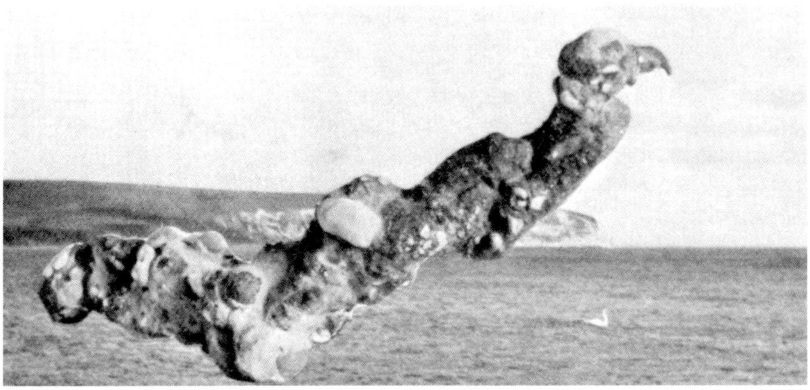

Fig 18 Paul Nash, untitled photocollage *c.*1935, reproduced in 'Swanage, or Seaside Surrealism', *Architectural Review* (April 1936). © Tate, London 2005.

discussed here were experienced in the company of close female friends – Avebury with Ruth Clark, Monster Field with Clare Neilson and, here, Swanage with Eileen Agar? Of course, only the relationship with Agar was explicitly sexual, though Nash's biographer James King does remark that, when Nash first met Clare Neilson in 1934, Margaret Nash 'had serious doubts about Clare when she sensed there was a strong attachment between her and Paul'.[46] Whatever their actual relationships with Nash, all three women had a strong empathy with his way of thinking and that in itself would have given an additional frisson to Nash's experience of these places.

The simple photocollage that Nash reproduced with the 'Swanage' article was subsequently extended to become part of a far more complex work, the photomontage *Swanage*, now in the Tate collection (figure 19). There, the earlier image forms the lower right corner, the rest being taken up with a group of Nash's *objets trouvés* which seem to loom up over Ballard Head, threatening and gigantic.[47] This is Nash's single most important Swanage work and yet it seems to have little immediately to do with the town itself. Except for the anchor, most of the objects are from other sites, and all are natural forms (again, except for the anchor, which however looks natural). But it may be that the town's very absence from an image named for it is significant. One way to read this work is as a reversal of the first photocollage, as an attack *on* Swanage, which lies behind the camera in the original photograph and towards which the 'monsters' seem to be marching, as if in some science fiction movie. It is, as it were, the 'return of the repressed', coming to wreak vengeance on the urbanity of Swanage. If this is an excessive reading, it fits the image with its almost delirious piling-up of objects and sudden shifts of scale.

It is also important that these ideas were not, as with Avebury and Monster Field, translated into the terms of painting; Nash's sense of Swanage was still most forcefully expressed through the modern, mechanical medium of photography. Nash did make many watercolours while in Swanage, but it is in his photographs, in their conjunction with the text of 'Swanage or Seaside

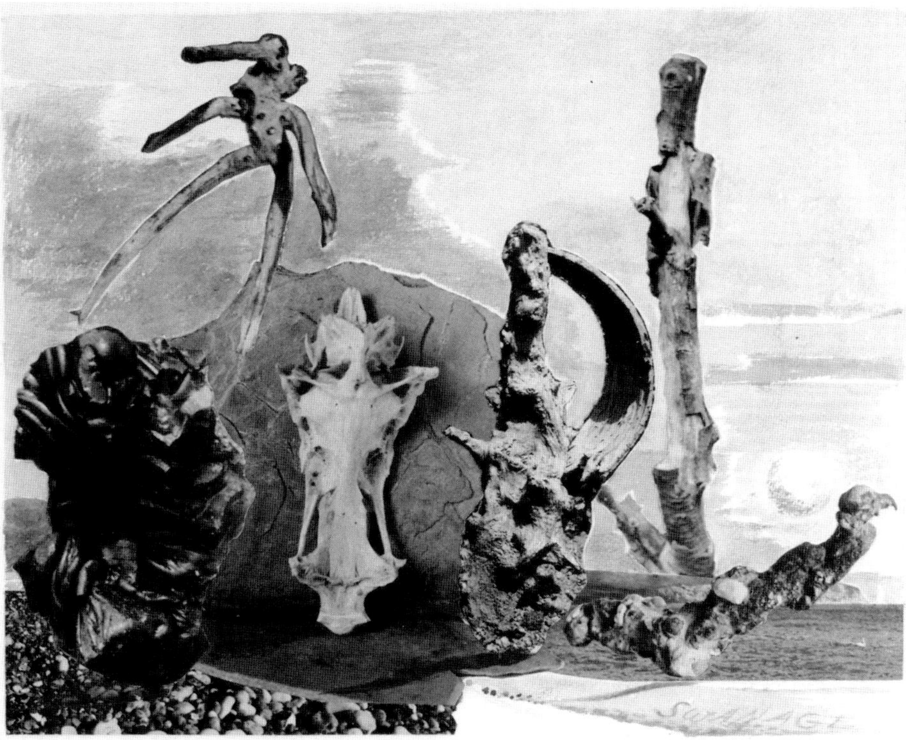

Fig 19 Paul Nash, *Swanage*, *c.*1936. © Tate, London 2005.

Surrealism', and in the final montage of *Swanage* that Nash's sense of the place most fully resides. The Swanage experience enabled Nash to break free of the too easy traditional relationship of experience followed by resolution in paint. At Swanage, he was faced with dislocation and fragmentation, which, though disorientating, proved ultimately beneficial. In particular, what was confirmed for Nash was the crucial 'disquietude' that could reside in the vernacular, the quotidian and even the mass-produced and industrial. The paintings that came from the Swanage experience – from *Event on the Downs* (1934) to *Environment for Two Objects* (1936) – exemplify this, but ultimately the attempt to thus imaginatively filter this experience was to go against its very nature. Perhaps it was best left to itself and simply – in photographs – recorded. But, as Nash knew, no photograph was that 'simple'.

In a field near Swanage, Nash found a block of three steps (figure 20). He photographed them from a three-quarters angle so that one can read the form of the block but still feel that one can approach the steps and mount them. But to what purpose did he record this most mundane of objects? The formal satisfaction one might derive from the shape and presence of the steps is weighed against one's uncertainty as to what that presence might mean. What are the steps for? By cutting out all clues, and making it look as if the steps are sitting in an empty field, Nash leaves such a question in a state of wilful suspension. It is

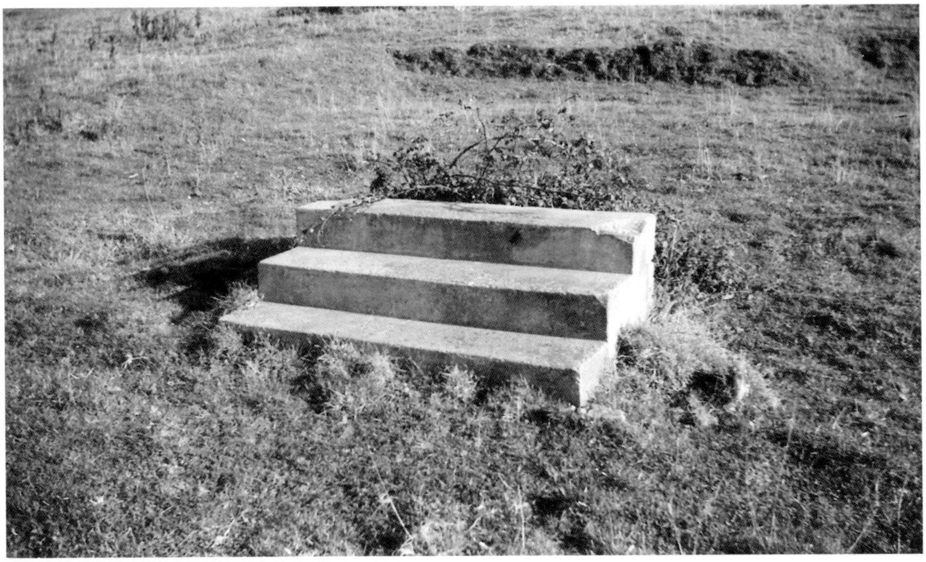

Fig 20 Paul Nash, *Steps in a field near Swanage*, *c*.1935. © Tate, London 2005.

this quality that led to the photograph becoming almost an icon of a certain sort of surrealist photograph – the ordinary rendered extraordinary. In 1982, when Simon Watney published an essay on the propensity in interwar art photography for 'making strange' (a translation of the Russian *Ostranenie*), he began with this photograph.[48]

But all this is retrospective – the photo was not reproduced by Nash himself, nor by Margaret Nash in *Fertile Image*.[49] It is perhaps a more recent taste that appreciates the steps and savours their resemblance to minimalist sculpture. (Though there is a parallel with the modernist reading that Nash himself had made of the municipal seating of Swanage.) Nash often used steps and ladders in his work to offer a sense of transcendence, but the stranded pointlessness of these steps seems to militate against that symbolic reading. Perhaps, like much else at Swanage, the steps made Nash question his established patterns of meaning.

Looking at the other photographs Nash took at this site, one can see something of the nature of the place. There are several other pieces of debris around the field – the corner of a building, another set of steps[50] – which indicate that these steps were part of a building. Moreover, the field is on more of a slope than appears evident in the first image – the steps were not purposeless or even decorative, they were a necessity. Seeing these other shots may remove some of that first photograph's aura of uncertainity, but it demonstrates why this particular image is so striking. We do not know that Nash particularly valued this image. Nevertheless, it does seem more carefully made than many others and he had to *see* the picture to take it.

Moreover, this photograph connects with an important aspect of Nash's aesthetic. Unlike Moore, Sutherland or Agar, he did not pit natural against man-made to the detriment of the latter. Rather, he was at pains to see similar concerns revolving through both and connecting. For Nash, nature and culture were not opposites, but complementary. As the Parisian Surrealists had seen the city as impregnated with nature, so Nash knew that an understanding of nature in the twentieth century had to be profoundly acculturated. But the relationship between the two is never straightforward. At Avebury, Nash had found man-made forms that were so ancient and embedded in the landscape that they seemed natural. At Monster Field, he found objects created by a force of nature, yet he had no problem in 'culturalising' their existence through his reading of them. At Swanage, most of the objects that Nash photographed were modern and man-made but they are placed within a natural setting that moved him profoundly. The disjunction proved both worrying and energising.

For Surrealist photography, Nash's use of the medium also raises a number of questions. He certainly thought of himself above all as a painter; Toni del Renzio has written that 'in a certain sense he never really understood Surrealism and consequently devalued his found objects especially by making paintings of them'.[51] One might say the same of Nash's relationship with his photographs, though that is complicated by a cultural hierarchisation of media. (It is a hierarchy that still exists – Nash's paintings hang in art galleries, the photographs must be delved for in archives.) At the same time, however, Nash was above all interested in translating place into image, and photography was another way of working with the site, another way to record his sensations, another way to make images.

Where continental artists working between media – such as Man Ray or Moholy-Nagy – continued to keep their work in different media separate, Nash sought to bring them together. The three projects discussed here – Avebury, Swanage and Monster Field – all use photography, painting and text in combination. Sometimes pulling his little camera out of his pocket was the starting point for a sequence of paintings, as it was at Avebury. At Monster Field, the photographs remained his most resolved achievement, albeit modulated by text. At Swanage, though, it was the very impossibility of resolution that was intriguing; it was the space between experience and photograph, and the subsequent juxtaposition of photograph and text, which made his work there both problematic and resonant.

Notes

1 Humphrey Jennings, 'A Determination not to Dream', *London Bulletin*, 4 (July 1938), 40, reprinted in Kevin Jackson (ed.), *The Humphrey Jennings Film Reader* (Manchester: Carcanet, 1993), p. 229.

2 For an account of Nash's time in Swanage, see Pennie Denton, *Seaside Surrealism: Paul Nash in Swanage* (Swanage: Peveril Press, 2002).

3 Paul Nash, *Outline* (London: Columbus, 1988), p. 121.

4 Letter to Richard Smart, 25 June 1946, quoted by Anthony Bertram, *Paul Nash* (London: Faber & Faber, 1955), p. 306.

5 Paul Nash, *Dorset Shell Guide* (London: Architectural Press, 1936), p. 32.

6 Thomas Hardy, *The Hand of Ethelberta* (London: Penguin, 1997), p. 233. See also David Lewer, *Hardy in Swanage: 1875 and 'The Hand of Ethelberta'* (Wincanton: Dorset Publishing Company, 1999).

7 E. M. Forster, *Howard's End* (London: Penguin, 2000), p. 170.

8 Patrick Wright deals extensively with the cultural history of Dorset in *The Village That Died for England* (London: Faber & Faber, 2002). David Matless also discusses Massingham and Gardiner in *Landscape and Englishness* (London: Reaktion, 1998); the reference to 'Wessex Regionalism' is on p. 130.

9 Peter Ackroyd, *First Light* (London: Sphere, 1991), p. 189.

10 Matless, *Landscape and Englishness*, p. 64.

11 On the formation of the Shell Guides, see Timothy Mowl, *Stylistic Cold Wars: Betjeman versus Pevsner* (London: John Murray, 2000), pp. 55–75.

12 Kate Best has made a study of the *Dorset Shell Guide* and I thank her for discussing it with me.

13 Nash, *Dorset Shell Guide*, pp. 22 and 30.

14 Nash, *Outline*, p. 41.

15 Nash, *Outline*, p. 187.

16 Rob Shields, *Places on the Margin: Alternative Geographies of Modernity* (London: Routledge, 1991), p. 84.

17 Paul Nash, 'Swanage or Seaside Surrealism', *Architectural Review* (April 1936), 151–4. The essay was reprinted with changes to both text and illustrations in Myfanwy Evans (ed.), *The Painter's Object* (London: Gerald Howe, 1937), pp. 108–15. The text in Andrew Causey (ed.), *Paul Nash: Writings on Art* (Oxford: Oxford University Press, 2000), pp. 125–9, is that from the *Architectural Review*. The text in Denton, *Seaside Surrealism*, pp. 77–82, is the version from *The Painter's Object*. Hereafter, unless otherwise indicated, references are to the original publication in the *Architectural Review*.

18 Letter to Ruth Clark, *c.*November 1935, quoted by Bertram, *Paul Nash*, p. 223.

19 Louis Aragon, *Paris Peasant* (London: Jonathan Cape, 1971), p. 135.

20 Nash, *Dorset Shell Guide*, p. 32.

21 The most detailed study of the work of Mowlem and Burt is David Lewer and J. Bernard Calkin, *Curiosities of Swanage, or Old London by the Sea* (Swanage: Purbeck Press, 1999).

22 Paul Nash, 'The Giant's Stride', *Architectural Review* (September 1939), 118, reprinted in Causey (ed.), *Paul Nash: Writings on Art*, p. 148.

23 John Newman and Nikolaus Pevsner, *The Buildings of England: Dorset* (London: Yale University Press, 1972), p. 411.

24 There are extensive details of Burt's two major building schemes in David Lambert, 'Durlston Park and Purbeck House: the Public and Private Realms of George Burt, King of Swanage', *New Arcadian Journal*, 45/6 (1998), 15–52.

25 Purbeck House is now a hotel and, with permission, the grounds are easily accessible.

26 Nash, *Dorset Shell Guide*, p. 32, where it is quoted from a local guidebook.

27 See Causey (ed.), *Paul Nash: Writings on Art*, plate 25.

28 Malcolm Yorke, *The Spirit of Place* (London: Constable, 1988), pp. 57–8.

29 Sir Frederick Treves, *Highways and Byways of Dorset* (London: Macmillan, 1906), p. 190. Treves was the Royal Surgeon and is now best remembered as the protector of the Elephant Man.

30 Quoted by Rodney Legg, *Old Swanage* (Sherborne: Dorset Publishing, 1983), p. 49.

31 See for example, the two versions of the same photograph of the Alfred the Great Column reproduced in Denton, *Seaside Surrealism*, p. 30, and in Roger Cardinal, *The Landscape Vision of Paul Nash* (London: Reaktion, 1989), p. 19. The shelter, passing motorcyclist and turning bus in the first have all been cropped out in the second.

32 Reproduced in Andrew Causey (ed.), *Paul Nash's Photographs* (London: Tate Gallery, 1973), no. 43. This picture has also been cropped to remove Nash's own shadow on the left.

33 Reproduced in John Hewitt, *The Shell Poster Book* (London: Profile, 1998), illustration 47. (Sutherland had also spent childhood holidays in Swanage and had visited it again in 1930–31.)

34 André Breton, *Mad Love* (Lincoln: University of Nebraska Press, 1987), pp. 101–4.

35 Breton, *Mad Love*, p. 104. French edition: *L'Amour fou* (Paris: Gallimard, 1976), p. 155.

36 In *Nadja*, Breton describes the Place Dauphine as 'one of the worst wastelands in Paris' ('un des pires terrains vagues qui soient à Paris') (New York, Grove Press, 1960, p. 80; French edition: Paris, Gallimard, 1973, p. 93).

37 This and the comment below about 'swan-like seats' are from the caption to the picture.

38 Andrew Causey, *Paul Nash* (Oxford: Clarendon Press, 1980), p. 206.

39 From the coda to the version of the 'Swanage' essay in Evans (ed.), *The Painter's Object*, p. 115.

40 The Saxon name of the town was 'Swanwic' and it is more likely that the name signifies a 'herdman's dairy farm' rather than any actual association with swans.

41 On 8 November 1935, Nash wrote from Swanage to his wife Margaret in London: 'A swan arrived in the Bay on Sunday & stayed two days sailing up and down. A lovely sight', and on the 12 November, it was still in his mind when in another letter, he included a drawing of what were now several swans in the bay, one saying to another, 'Don't make me laugh. I shall drown' (Tate Archives: 8313/1/240 and 242).

42 Eileen Agar, *A Look at My Life* (London: Methuen, 1988), p. 110.

43 The postcard and letter are in Tate Archives (8712–16 and 8712–31 respectively).

44 Agar, *A Look at My Life*, p. 112.

45 James King, *Interior Landscapes* (London: Weidenfeld & Nicolson, 1987), p. 29.

46 King, *Interior Landscapes*, p. 179. Curiously, writing in 1987, King does not mention Eileen Agar.

47 For an explication of all the various elements in this complex work, see its entry in *The Tate Gallery 1972–4: Biennial Report and Illustrated Catalogue of Acquisitions* (London: Tate Gallery, 1975), pp. 204–11. The anonymous text was written by Anne Seymour.

48 Simon Watney, 'Making Strange: The Shattered Mirror', in Victor Burgin (ed.), *Thinking Photography* (London: Macmillan, 1982), pp. 154–76.

49 The photograph was first reproduced in 1973 in Causey (ed.), *Paul Nash's Photographs*, no. 58.

50 These are the steps which Nash transposed to his painting *Monster Shore*.

51 Toni del Renzio and Duncan Scott (eds), *Surrealism in England: 1936 and After* (Canterbury: Herbert Read Gallery, Canterbury College of Art, 1986), p. 105.

3
The comic sublime – Eileen Agar at Ploumanac'h

On 4 July 1936, the International Surrealist Exhibition in London came to an end and, the same month, the *Architectural Review* announced a competition. In April, it had published Paul Nash's article 'Swanage or Seaside Surrealism'. Now the magazine offered a prize for readers who sent in their own surrealist holiday photographs – 'spontaneous examples of Surrealism discerned in English holiday resorts'. The judges would be Nash and Roland Penrose.[1] This might be taken by some as a demonstration of the irredeemable frivolity of Surrealism in England – it is difficult to imagine a surrealist snapshot competition in Paris judged by André Breton and Max Ernst. But in a positive light, it exemplifies the interest that English Surrealism had in popular culture and in pleasure. The freedom offered by holidays was very important for the English Surrealists and some of their most interesting work was created during them.

Eileen Agar had been one of the English stars of the Surrealism exhibition, even though she had apparently not thought of herself as a 'Surrealist' until Penrose and Herbert Read (recommended by Nash) came to her studio and declared her to be one. But in her case, there was a good deal of justification for the label. Agar was, of course, primarily a painter and object-maker and that is where any larger examination of her work would have to centre.[2] But here I want to leave that in the background to examine the photographs she made just after the Surrealist exhibition in July 1936, when she and her partner Joseph Bard went to Brittany on holiday and 'landed up at Ploumanach', a small village on the north coast, famous for its extraordinary rock formations.[3]

In her autobiography, published in 1988, Agar wrote: 'We chose this stopping place by looking out of the train and trusting to chance, like all good Surrealists.'[4] This is a splendid image, suggesting a spontaneous discovery of the site. But even in the 1930s, the rocks of Ploumanac'h were well known, and the *côte de granit rose* of which they formed part was popular with holidaymakers, as well as being of cultural significance (having been the first coastal site in France to be protected by law in 1901). Ploumanac'h featured in British guides to Brittany alongside Perros-Guirec, the larger resort two kilometres to the east. In one, a large fold-out advert announced: 'Intending visitors to Brittany should note that the hotels and pensions of Perros-Guirec cater especially for British visitors throughout the season.'[5]

Perhaps Agar and Bard had deliberately travelled without a guidebook. The second problem, though, is more particular. Agar makes it sound as if they just leaned out the train window and, 'Before us were the most fantastic rocks.'[6] Unfortunately, it could not have happened quite that way since the railway line didn't actually go to Ploumanac'h, but stopped at Perros-Guirec (a far less rocky scene). It would have been difficult to go to Ploumanac'h unintentionally, and without knowing that one would find a magnificent rocky coastline when one got there.[7]

Anyway, there they were and Agar was stunned by the extraordinary landscape; 'a camera became a necessity' so a day or two after their arrival, Agar and Bard went to Brest where she bought the Rolleiflex 6 x 6 cm. camera that was to be 'my constant companion for many years'.[8] It is the photographs that Eileen Agar took at Ploumanac'h that now provide one of the most coherent group of images to exemplify the Surrealist fascination with the fantastic in nature. However, because of their 'documentary', even 'amateur' status, they have been consistently undervalued – not least by Agar herself.

At her death in 1991, Eileen Agar donated her photographs to the Tate Archives, some in the form of prints, many only as negatives. There are in all about seventy images made at Ploumanac'h – six films' worth – and their aesthetic and technical success is variable. Agar and Bard photographed each other as well as some of the significant local buildings, but the vast majority of Agar's photographs concentrate on the rocks and, even working with a new camera and sometimes getting her exposures wrong, her visual instincts enabled her to make a clutch of remarkable images.[9] But one might ask why Agar in fact felt the need for a camera. Why did she not do what any other painter would do and start *sketching* the rocks? The probable answer is twofold – first, she was overwhelmed by the physical actuality of the rocks and initially impelled to record them rather than transmute them into art. That might come later. Also, she knew of other artists (the most immediate example being Paul Nash) who had used a camera alongside the pencil and paintbrush, which made the idea of shifting between mediums both more possible and more attractive.

The second question, though, is – why that camera? After all, Nash had never moved beyond a little Kodak. The Rolleiflex square format camera was generally the choice of professional photographers – Bill Brandt used one as did Brassaï. According to Agar, she went into a camera shop in Brest and said, 'I've never done any photography but I'd like to do some, and I want the best camera you have.'[10] And they sold her a Rolleiflex. It was a very good choice, since the camera had a number of qualities which would help her to achieve her aim. The larger negative gives a sharpness and density, the square format gives a formality and centrality, while the fact that one makes the pictures looking down at a screen rather than through a viewfinder distances the photographer from the scene itself and renders it already into a composition.

If the direct experience of Ploumanac'h was the major impulse for these pictures, there was also an artistic context to which they can be related. Looking

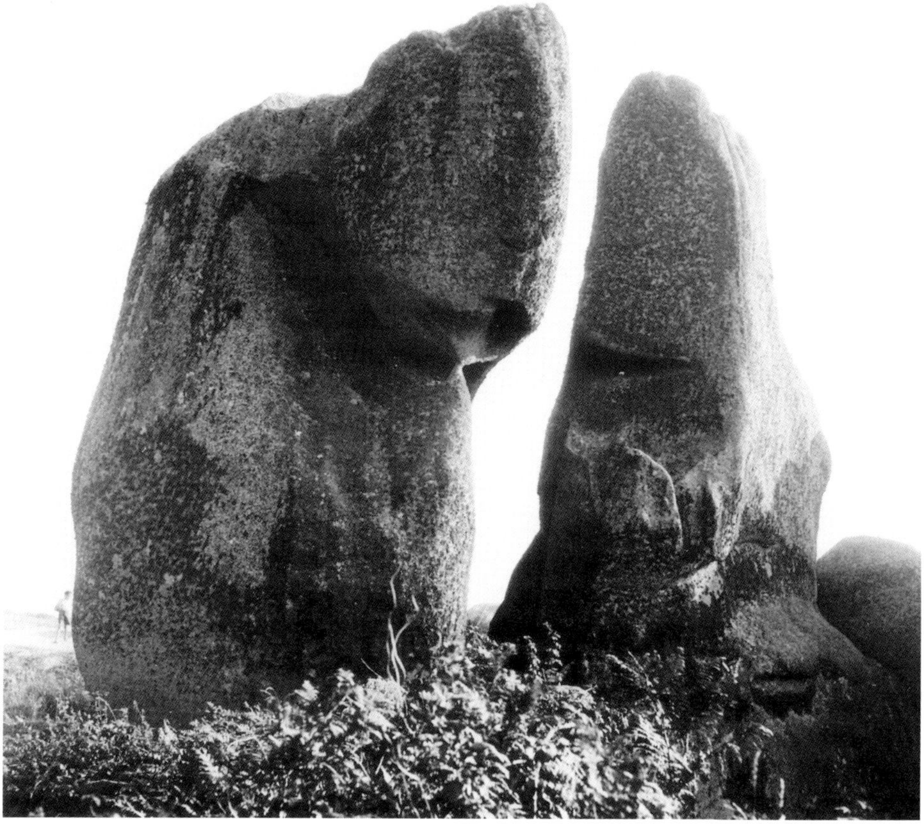

Fig 21 Eileen Agar, *Rocks, Ploumanach*, 1936. © Tate, London 2005.

for parallels to Agar's photographs, one most obviously turns back to the interest in natural forms so central to English Surrealism, nowhere more so than in the work of Paul Nash. There are important differences – Nash's art has little of the humour and love of excess one finds in Agar's work – but certainly Agar's sense of the *objet trouvé* in nature had been extended by her relationship with Nash. One might, for example, recall Nash's habit of collecting stones, such as the 'Nest of Wild Stones' which he found that same year.[11] But those rocks were tiny, hand-sized; part of the effect of Ploumanac'h was its scale. In terms of size and animistic presence, the closest parallel we might find is in the stones of Avebury which Nash had photographed in 1933. (Agar herself went there later in 1938.)[12] Agar described one rock at Ploumanac'h as 'a foot rearing up like a dolmen',[13] and there are several rocks which remind one of standing stones (figure 21). However, as we shall see, it was crucial for Agar that these forms were not man-made but natural, 'sculpted by the sea, that master-worker of all time'.[14]

Looking elsewhere in English Surrealism, the examples of Henry Moore and Graham Sutherland also serve to remind us of just how diverse the 'Surrealism of nature' was in the late 1930s. It is not only that the natural forms evoked by Moore and Sutherland are so different – rounded on the one hand, spiky on the other – it is also that the meanings the two artists read into nature were opposite: harmony and wholeness as opposed to struggle and antagonism. Agar found herself between these two poles.

Throughout the late 1930s, Henry Moore continued to identify himself as a Surrealist and, in June 1940, his large *Reclining Figure* held centre stage in the *Surrealism Today* exhibition at the Zwemmer Galleries.[15] Yet, even in his work of that period which still had a Surrealist edge, one can now see the extent to which it was already informed by what Geoffrey Grigson, in 1948, would refer to as the quality of a 'wide sea embracing unity and humanity'.[16] Moore's work had a direct influence on the photographer John Havinden who, in 1935, made some Dufaycolour images of seaside rock forms, emphasising this harmony of natural forms.[17] But for Agar, while Moore's example would have encouraged the sculptural and the monumental, his forms lacked the strangeness and excess of the rocks at Ploumanac'h – and indeed the humour.

In comparison, Graham Sutherland's metamorphoses were animistic, disquieting and indeed threatening, albeit that they were largely vegetable. In the late 1930s, Sutherland was only on the fringes of Surrealism; he had two untypical works in the 1936 exhibition and thereafter severed formal ties altogether. But he later acknowledged the role that Surrealism played in forming his aesthetic: 'Surrealism helped me to realize that forms which interested me existed already in nature, and were waiting for me to find them.'[18] It was the same revelation that had struck Agar and Nash. Perhaps the closest equivalent in Britain to the Ploumanac'h landscape is Brimham Rocks in Yorkshire, which Sutherland had visited in 1935. In 1937, he would produce an image of Brimham for a Shell poster and, the same year, he published his essay, 'An English Stone Landmark' in the anthology *The Painter's Object* (figure 22).[19] This short text has much in common with Agar's response to Ploumanac'h, especially when Sutherland

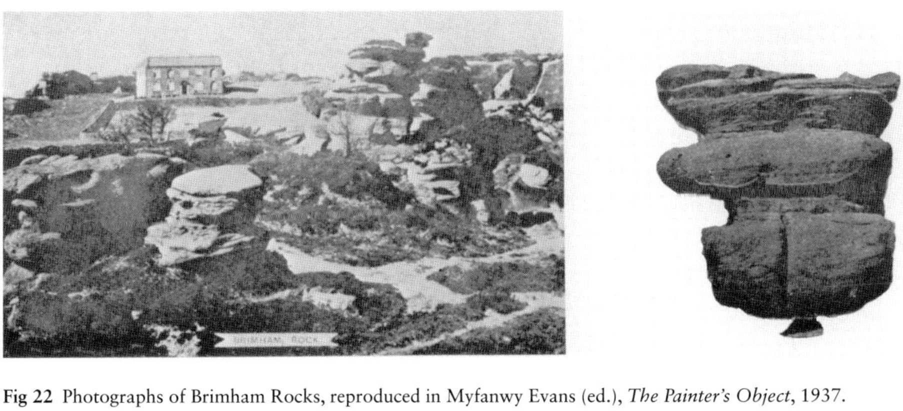

Fig 22 Photographs of Brimham Rocks, reproduced in Myfanwy Evans (ed.), *The Painter's Object*, 1937.

compares a particularly dramatic stone to 'a growth which one sometimes sees attached to the nose of a peasant'.

It is not only to English art that we should look for parallels and possible influences for Agar's Ploumanac'h photographs. For Agar was quite different from Moore, Sutherland and especially Nash in that she showed no concern at all for the 'Englishness' of her response to nature. She had spent her first twelve years in Argentina, and in the *London Bulletin*, was described as having 'a foreign eye but an English finger and is Irish'.[20] Her work is far less attached, if at all, to any particular sense of place and it is not insignificant that she found her rocks in Brittany rather than Dorset or Yorkshire. Of the English Surrealists, only Penrose would be closer to the French group.

In the summer of 1936, Agar's mind must have been full of images from the International Exhibition. Her own later account of the discovery of Ploumanac'h emphasised the sense in which it was an extension of the Surrealist summer of 1936: 'Our surprise and delight at the discovery came as a bonus after the excitement of the exhibition in London. It was as if nature had arranged a show of sculpture in the open air, just to prove that she too was keeping her hand in.'[21] (It is characteristic of Agar here to elide the workings of nature and art.)

One tends to think of Parisian Surrealism as essentially urban – as indeed it was – but looking at photographs of the London exhibition, it is striking how much imagery of nature there actually is – in paintings by Miró, Ernst, Tanguy and Dalí, sculptures by Arp and Brancusi as well as Moore. It is, therefore, as valid to suggest continental parallels as much as British ones for Agar's Ploumanac'h images and Edouard Jaguer proposed three. One is in a particular photograph where an individual rock resembles the Easter Island heads as depicted by Ernst in his collage-novel *Une semaine de bonté*. But more generally, he also cites resemblances to the rock-like forms in the paintings of Tanguy and of Dalí.[22]

As we have seen, the paintings of Yves Tanguy have their roots in the Breton landscape and it is also particularly apt that Agar made her photographs there, where both natural rock formations and prehistoric monuments are integral to the terrain.[23] André Breton also made regular visits to Brittany and, at the same time that Agar and Bard were in the north, he and his wife Jacqueline were on the south coast, where on 20 July, they walked along a beach near Lorient and had the disquieting experience that Breton later recalled in *L'Amour fou*.[24]

But probably the most direct connection with Agar's images was with the way that Salvador Dalí derived many of the forms in his paintings from the Catalan coastline near his birthplace Cadaqués.[25] His description of the 'grandiose geological delirium' of these rocks is similar to Agar's comments about Ploumanac'h.[26] However, Dalí hardly used the rocks themselves directly in his work (except for their appearance at the start of the film *L'Age d'or*). As Oriana Baddeley argued, Dalí transmuted the forms of the rocks through memory and desire while Agar's work 'reveals not her personal fantasies but her recognition of the magical and comic power of nature itself'.[27] (Though the distinction between fantasy and reality is not quite that clear-cut in Agar's work either.)

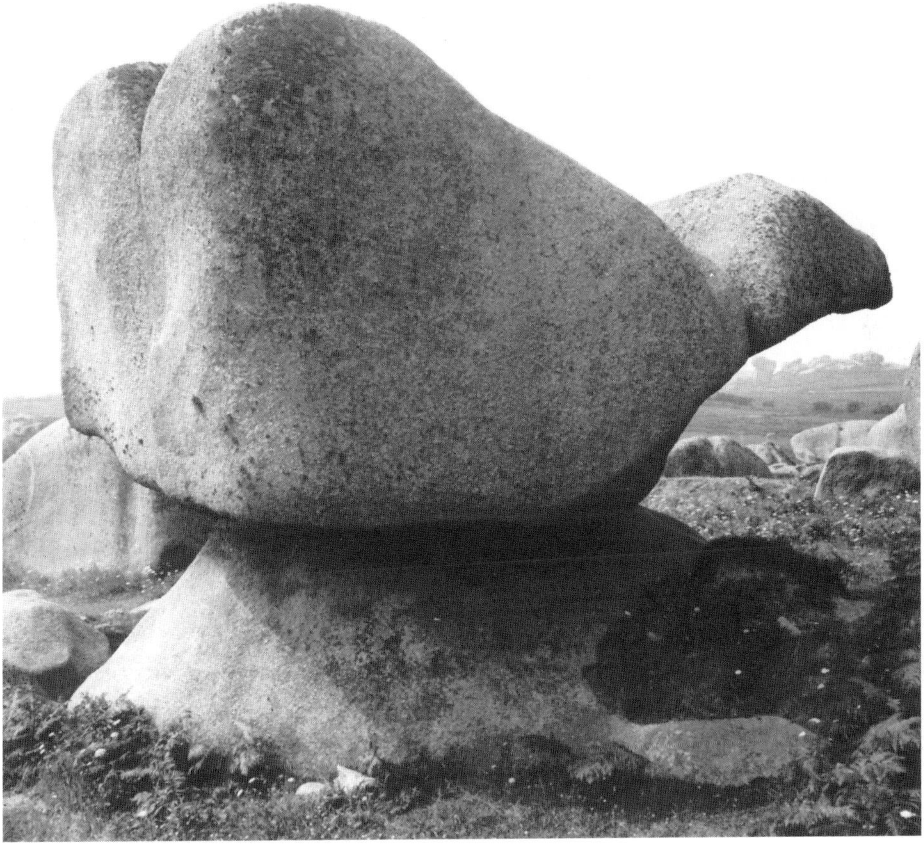

Fig 23 Eileen Agar, *Bum and Thumb Rock, Ploumanach*, 1936. © Tate, London 2005.

There is, finally, one other continental parallel – this time a photographic one. In 1933, Raoul Ubac had photographed the rock formations on the island of Hvar off the Dalmation coast.[28] Of this experience, Ubac later said, 'It was there that was born my love of stone',[29] an attraction which would manifest itself indirectly in the better known solarisations and 'bas-relief' fossil photographs that he made for *Minotaure* in the late 1930s. However, it seems that none of his Dalmatian photographs were reproduced until 1938, when one of them appeared in the *Dictionnaire abrégé du surréalisme*, along with two strange 'objets naturels'.[30]

There was, then, a plethora of parallels for Agar's Ploumanac'h photographs, but whether any of them related specifically to her images, one cannot say. When asked about this in 1985, she cannily replied that she wasn't aware of influences from these other artists, but that didn't mean they weren't there.[31] Nevertheless, the primary revelation of Ploumanac'h for Agar was to experience for herself something akin to the understanding evoked by Sutherland – that the surreal pre-exists any attempt by the artist to make images of it. But the second phase, the documentation of that experience through photographs, was equally important. It was a necessary concretisation of the experience, and the photographs were to stay with her for many years as a sort of 'proof' of that reality.

In her account of the rocks, as in the photographs she took of them, Agar stressed their animistic qualities: 'They lay like enormous prehistoric monsters sleeping on the turf above the sea.'[32] Both her description of the rocks and the titles she later gave some of them – 'Rockface', 'Bum and Thumb Rock' (figure 23) – transposed them into so many bodily parts. Nevertheless, it was crucial for Agar that these forms were created by the forces of water, wind and chance. Much later, she was to say, 'I am very much a nature-worshipper and I always try to bring nature into my work ... On the whole I feel that nature is something free. Nature can produce the most astonishing shapes that you could never dream of', and continued by referring to the 'wild frenzy that Nature can show'.[33]

In this, perhaps, lay the very particular appeal of the Ploumanac'h rocks. They are the frozen relics of this natural frenzy, held in a perpetual tension. A tension that is increased by the gap between our knowledge that the rocks are freak, meaningless objects created by accident and the fact that the human mind can so easily, it seems irresistibly, make such a close anthropomorphic reading of them. As Nash also knew, Nature is both something determinedly other and something that we are part of and are drawn to reconceive in human terms.

But was this relationship different for Agar as a woman than it was for Nash as a man? Whitney Chadwick reproduced one of the Ploumanac'h photographs alongside paintings by Toyen and Frida Kahlo and a photograph by Lee Miller under the rubric 'The Female Earth'.[34] Unlike some other female Surrealists, Agar *did* consider her gender important for her work, arguing that women, through what she called their 'womb-magic' had a more direct line to a natural and unconscious creativity.[35] Agar always claimed that her art was incompatible with motherhood and one might perhaps see Lee Miller's photograph of Agar 'pregnant with her camera' (the phrase was apparently Picasso's) not only as a good joke but also as an apt insight into the nature of Agar's creativity (see figure 31 p. 74).[36]

However, Agar herself never suggested that she thought of the Ploumanac'h photographs as particularly feminine images, and perhaps she did not consider the mechanical medium of photography in the same terms as the rest of her art. But one element in the Ploumanac'h images lay in their parallel fusion of a natural ('feminine') subject with a mechanical ('male') medium. One could also take a clue from Agar's discussion of the important role that the 'Seashore Monster' had played in her relationship with Paul Nash, where she describes the object as a sort of hermaphrodite – male and female fused. She significantly sees it – as she did the rocks – as created by a fusion of land and sea which 'often play together like man and wife, and achieve astonishing results'.[37]

The relationship between Nash and Agar had reached a crisis point immediately before she and Bard went on holiday. On 15 July, just before they left, Nash wrote her an impassioned and agonised letter: 'Eileen forgive my last desperate attempt to see you again. It was foolish & selfish but I had faced the idea of parting and we had said goodbye and then the knowledge of your being here still for several days was too difficult to ignore – that damned gnawing began again – I couldn't resist.' He went on to state that they should end their affair, for the sake of their partners as well as themselves. But the letter concludes by ecstatically celebrating the relationship: 'If we break now it is not because we are tired, we break at the peak of our flight where we have climbed dizzily like birds who make love in mid-air heedless of where they soar. We have not yet fallen down our bright sky, we only could not face the threat of the storm – O my bird my dear love.'[38]

It is impossible to know what effect this created for Agar once she was in Brittany. But one might wonder whether her choice of rocks to photograph was not affected by Nash's rhetoric, whether she chose a subject so deliberately solid and earthbound in contrast to his evocation of weightless flight. And to go further, whether the rocks did not represent in some way her relationship with the reliable Bard – a man of considerable bulk – whose sexual vigour she constantly extolled in contrast to the asthmatic and ailing Nash.

In considering the sexual connotations of the Ploumanac'h pictures, it's interesting to put them next to the slightly later painting *Scylla* by another female English Surrealist, Ithell Colquhoun. Painted in 1938, it was, according to the artist, based upon 'what I could see of myself in a bath – this, with a change of scale due to "alienation of sensation" became rocks and seaweed'.[39] But at the same time, the two knees are transformed into phallic rocks which converge to form a vagina-like slit through which a small but sharp pointed boat is about to slip. As Dawn Ades has noted, this painting poses 'a challenge, so explicit as to verge on parody, of a specific form of sexual imagery exploited by the Surrealists, that which treats landscape metaphorically as a woman ... [it is] an almost mocking response to the prevailing imagery of eroticism with Surrealism'.[40] What is male and what is female becomes thoroughly confused, the distinction between them undermined by a sharp and darkly Surrealist wit.

Agar's photos are also often rather funny, full of what Tacita Dean has called 'levity, mirth and re-imagination',[41] qualities that separate Agar from the other English nature-artists and might signal her female undermining of their male pomposity. As the 'bum' ends in a 'thumb', as rocks seem to whisper to each other, as a smaller rock balances on a larger like some fashionable hat (see figure 29 p. 66), one senses that Agar delights in the ridiculousness of her images, a ridiculousness created in the space between the sense of the rocks as simply rocks and her readings of them as heads and faces, bodies and monsters. Agar takes the 'pathetic fallacy' that can be so dangerously sentimental and plays with it to make images that are truly sublime and, at the same time, carnivalesque – a 'comic sublime'.

But that quality of humour is in turn held in place by Agar's rigorous picture-making. (Though she was a novice photographically, she was not so pictorially.)

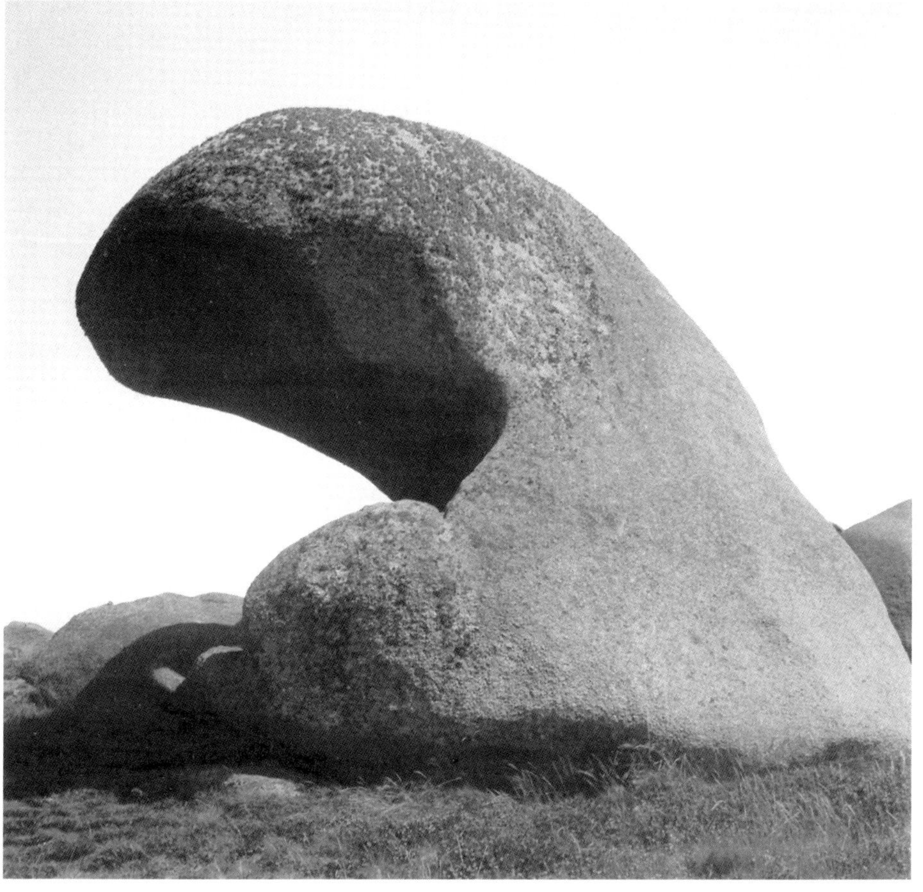

Fig 24 Eileen Agar, *Rocks, Ploumanach*, 1936. © Tate, London 2005.

The square format gives a balance and stability to the pictures, while the large negatives have an intensity of detail altogether unavailable to Nash with his little Kodak. The rocks are also usually photographed so that they fill the frame and dominate the space with no apparent context (figure 24). The intensely black shadows thrown by the summer sun dramatise and animate the rocks, while their consistent placement against a flat, empty sky emphasises the crisp delineation of their outlines. So while the rocks may often be comic, they are also dramatic characters, standing alone and eloquent.

Because she subsequently cut the negative strips into single images, it is now difficult to reconstruct Agar's working process as she photographed. (Moreover, the film lacks frame numbers indicating the chronology of the shots.) However, on a couple of occasions, she photographed the same rock from different points of view and, since the negatives are cut rather roughly with a pair of scissors, one can fit them together to confirm that for most of the best shots, Agar actually took just one image and got the picture. We might see this either as a indication

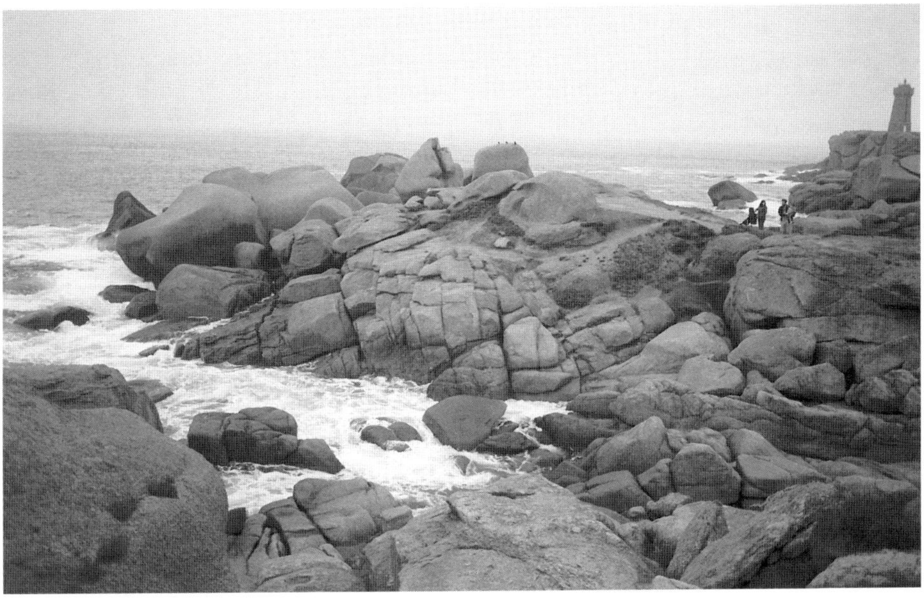

Fig 25 Ian Walker, *Rocks, Ploumanac'h*, 2004. © Ian Walker.

of her certainty or her naivety (or indeed that she had only bought a limited amount of film), but she rarely shot from a number of angles as a more experienced photographer might have done.

A visit to Ploumanac'h itself helps to emphasise just how very particular Agar was in making her pictures. Arriving there, two things hit one straight away, primarily because both are absent from Agar's photographs. One is the sheer scale of the site, the excessive piling up of rock on rock, which makes one realise that Agar had been very disciplined in restricting herself to the 'portraiture' of individual rocks (figure 25). The other element is the colour of the rock, which can shift through the day from a pale beige to a rich, deep red at sunset.[42] Eileen Agar was an enthusiastic colourist in her paintings and would surely have been so in her photographs had it been technically possible. But perhaps she was lucky that at the time she made the photographs, colour was not yet the norm for the aspiring amateur. Certainly, she would have lost much of the dramatic physicality that black and white gave her.[43]

Finding the individual rocks that Agar photographed also demonstrates something of her tactics. In several cases she photographed them from very low down against the sky, eliminating the background and emphasising their scale. Eileen Agar was quite short and she had the camera at waist level, but often, she must have crouched or knelt down even further. This suggests a process of careful observation before she actually made the picture (a process which may also have affected her decision to make just one shot of each rock). In the final pictures, the size of the rocks is quite deceptive, since features that might give scale are often missing. A rock that is perhaps 15 feet high (figure 24) and one that is 5 or 6 feet (figure 26) seem equally grand.

The other thing that is striking at Ploumanac'h is the fact that nearly all the major rocks have acquired names – 'le champignon', 'la tête de mort', 'la palette du peintre' and so on. On one level, this provides an enjoyably folkloric element to the viewer's experience of them. In another sense, though, it actually restricts the play of meaning, assigning just one identity to each rock, and Agar was wise, on the whole, to avoid such overt (if tempting) naming of the rocks. In only one case – 'Le Lapin' – did she use the name already given to the rock and that was part of her own play with the rock's metamorphosis (figure 26). With a couple of other images, she gave the rocks names that emphasise the metamorphic qualities that she herself had found in them and which are at odds with their common naming. The 'Bum and Thumb Rock' is actually known as 'The Tablets of the Law' because, when seen from end on, the 'bum' flattens out to resemble the double shape of the Ten Commandments (figure 27). (One can imagine Agar's quiet delight that she had managed to turn the tablets of the law into a bum.)

A few of the Ploumanac'h photographs differ from the majority in that they show things other than the rocks themselves. In several pictures, Agar's fellow

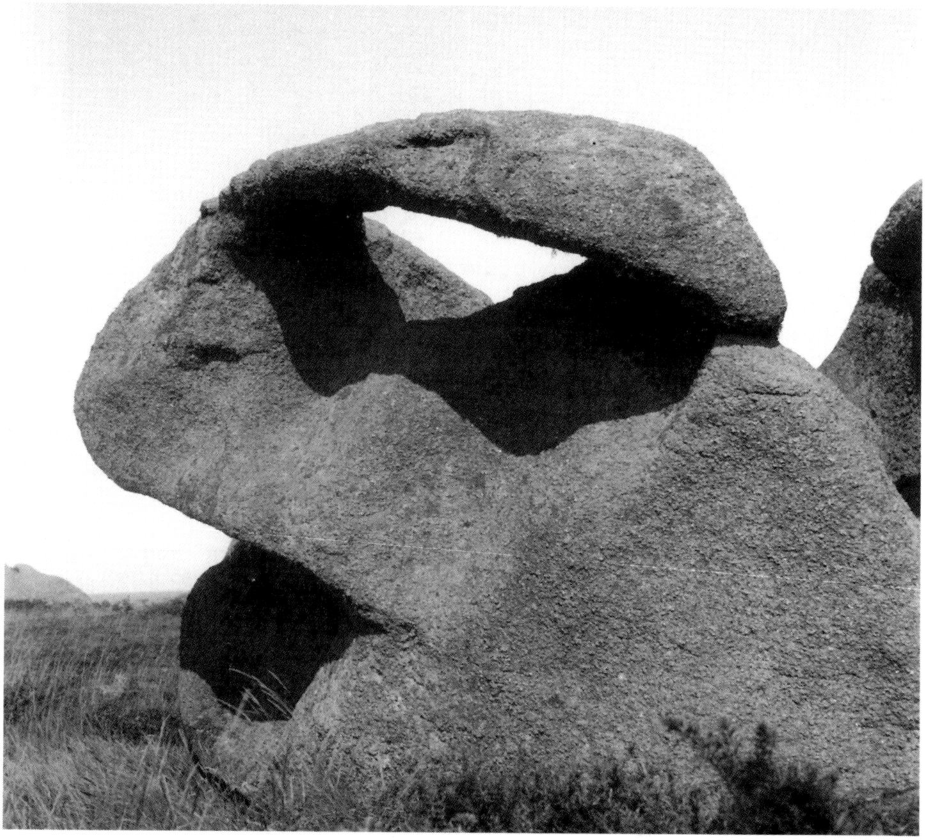

Fig 26 Eileen Agar, *'Le Lapin'*, *Ploumanach*, 1936. © Tate, London 2005.

holidaymakers are included in the image, in one case pushing a pram (figure 28); in the words of Edouard Jaguer, they act as 'a humorous and absurd counterpoint to the majestic mineral mass'.[44] The placement of these figures at the bottom of the frame, small beneath the rocks yet apparently unheeding of their power, suggests the fragility of human activity in this context. However, there is a more problematic way of reading these images with the holidaymakers – that Agar, in her primary desire to record the rocks themselves, was actually uninterested in what else was in the picture and able to ignore the presence of the people. The implication of this reading is that Agar was also uninterested in the photographs themselves as images and that her photos operated simply as a sort of indexical sketchbook, a process leading to something else of more substance and value.

She herself was later to deny her photographs any serious place within her art (as opposed to the informational, inspirational role they certainly did play). But the best of the photographs are too well made, too compositionally exact and too precisely framed to be thought of as mere notetaking. It would seem that, in making these pictures, Agar was able to be both playful and serious, casual and rigorous, so that we can never be quite certain as to their status,

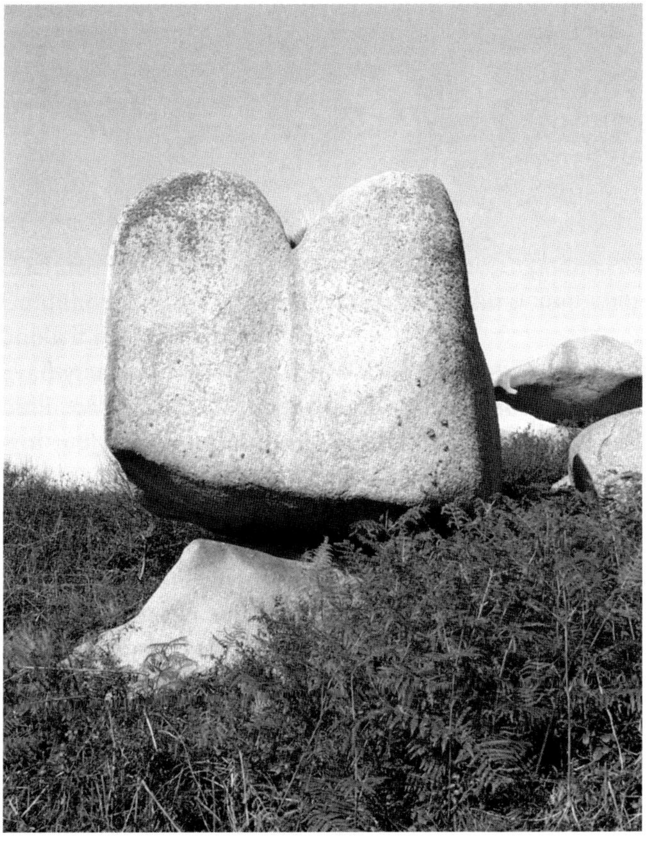

Fig 27 Ian Walker, *'Les Tables de la Loi', Ploumanac'h*, 2004. © Ian Walker.

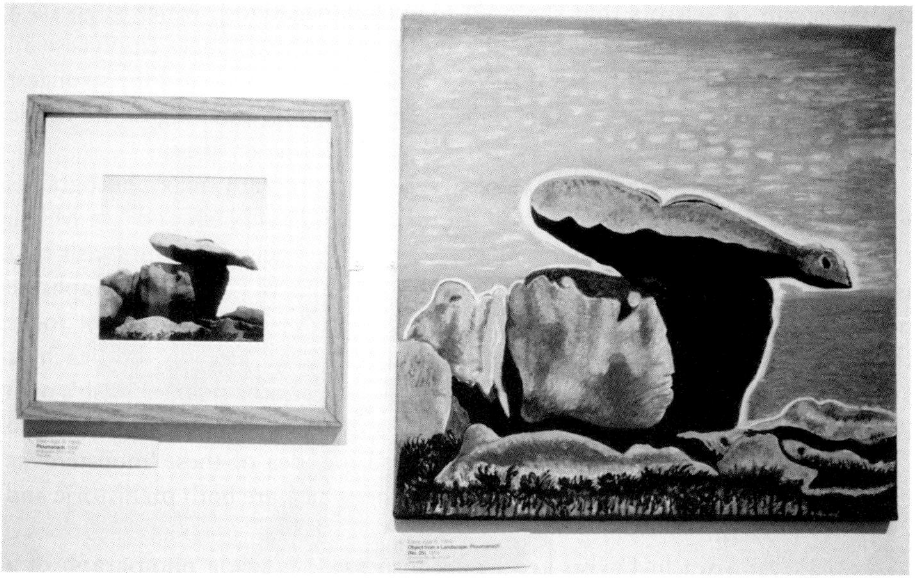

Fig 29 Eileen Agar, *Rocks, Ploumanach*, 1936, and *Object from a Landscape: Ploumanach (no. 25)*, 1984, as exhibited in *Contrariwise*, Glynn Vivian Art Gallery, Swansea, 1986. © Tate, London 2005.

a group of twenty-one photographs, two of which were of the Ploumanac'h rocks.[52] Roland Penrose wrote the catalogue introduction, remarking: 'The whole of nature began to open up treasures for her and speak to her in a new way. Stones became her children, the sky and the sea her intimate friends.' It was his interest that led to two of the photographs being included in the mammoth 1978 exhibition *Dada and Surrealism Reviewed* at the Hayward Gallery.[53] They were, however, not hung in the main gallery space, but rather placed in a vitrine with a selection of 'chosen objects'. It seems that it was the rocks themselves that were of interest, not the photographs. By implication, they acted as a sort of stand-in for the actual rocks (which were obviously too solid to ship to London and too large to fit in the vitrine). The two images were intriguingly and evocatively titled *Magnetic Memories I and II*, titles which, though suggestive of the continuing power of the rocks, were not used again.

Thereafter, the photographs were included in a number of exhibitions and books on Surrealist photography. What was probably the first exhibition of Surrealist photography was curated in 1979 by Nancy Hall-Duncan for the New Gallery of Contemporary Art in Cleveland, Ohio; in the catalogue, one of Agar's Ploumanac'h pictures was placed across from Paul Nash's photograph of a beached boat at Toulon.[54] In 1982, when Edouard Jaguer published the first full study of Surrealist photography *Les Mystères de la chambre noire*, he included three of Agar's pictures.[55] (It is interesting to note that both these early publications featured the images that Agar had made of holidaymakers with the rocks, suggesting that these were not unintentional juxtapositions.)

By the mid-1980s, it would seem that Agar had established a small corpus of

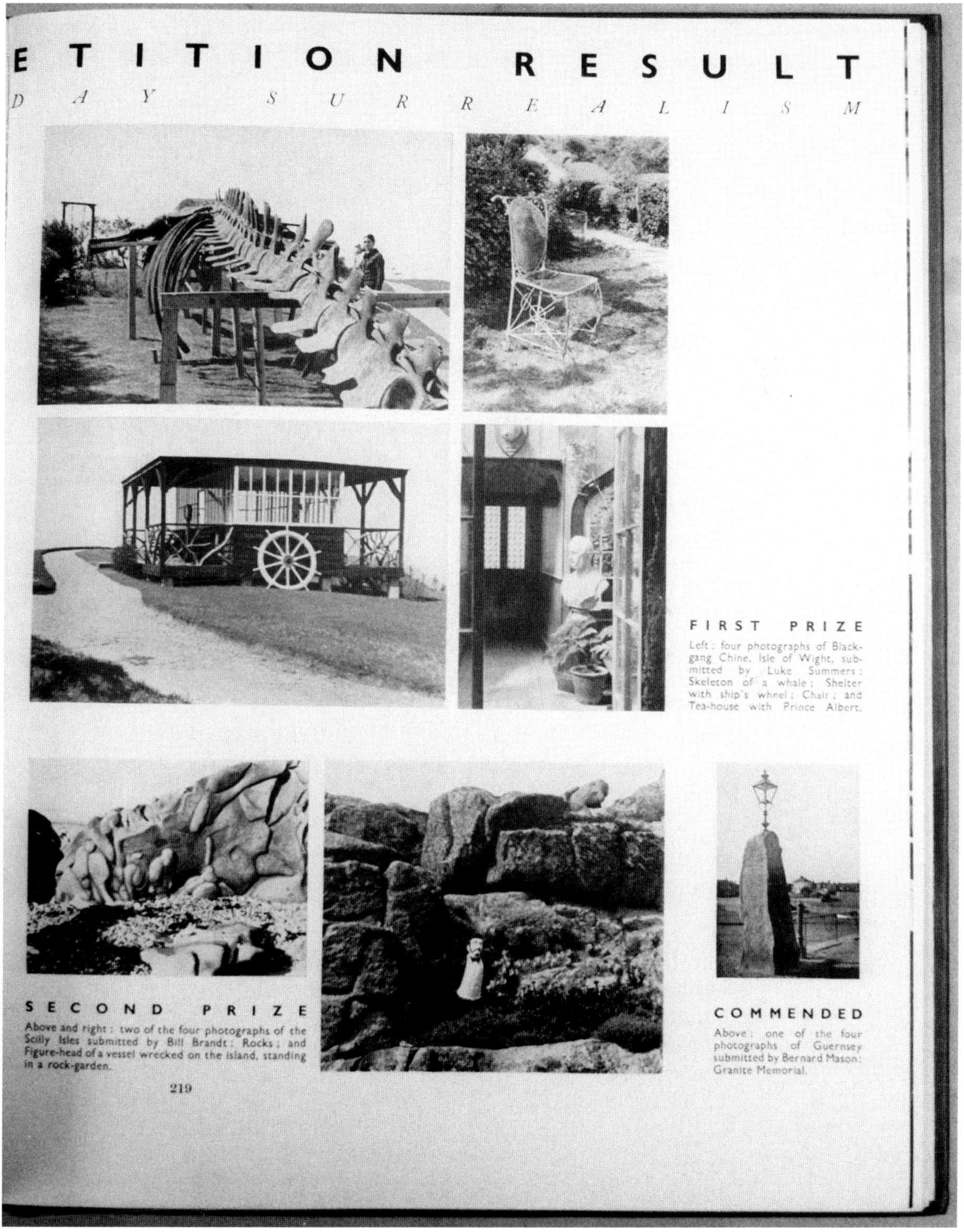

ETITION RESULT

DAY SURREALISM

FIRST PRIZE

Left: four photographs of Black-gang Chine, Isle of Wight, submitted by Luke Summers: Skeleton of a whale; Shelter with ship's wheel; Chair; and Tea-house with Prince Albert.

SECOND PRIZE

Above and right: two of the four photographs of the Scilly Isles submitted by Bill Brandt: Rocks; and Figure-head of a vessel wrecked on the island, standing in a rock-garden.

COMMENDED

Above: one of the four photographs of Guernsey submitted by Bernard Mason: Granite Memorial.

219

Fig 30 'Competition Result: Holiday Surrealism', *Architectural Review* (November 1936).

the Ploumanac'h photographs with which she was satisfied. It was this re-evaluation that probably led her, in 1985, to make a series of paintings from the photos under the title *Objects from a Landscape*.[56] Agar's own comment was that 'the photographs I took in Brittany have now come to fruition'.[57] (She herself did not show photographs and paintings together and it seems that the only time that happened was in the exhibition *Contrariwise*, curated by the author in 1986 (figure 29).)[58] But surely, decorative and striking as the paintings are, they are also crude when seen next to the photographs. In particular, as with the paintings that Paul Nash made from his 'Monster Field' photographs, the humanoid features are too emphasised, too literally represented, closing down rather than opening up the viewer's imaginative space. With the original photographs, it is the fact that one has to read the rocks and is thus drawn into projecting meanings upon them which is an important part of their effect. Above all, what is lost in the paintings is the essential knowledge that the rocks do indeed look as extraordinary as that.

Eileen Agar's Ploumanac'h photographs are few in number and do not form part of any larger project. As we re-read them now, we must remember that they were largely undervalued by their author. Nevertheless, the best of the images are very successful, representing an intriguing nodal point – a meeting of Surrealism and documentary, nature and art, England and France, male and female, subjective and objective. And also work and pleasure. For Eileen Agar's activity as an artist was inseparable from her belief in pleasure as a life-fulfilling principle and her sense of play as an essential yet underrated Surrealist activity. That she took the extraordinary Ploumanac'h photographs on holiday – able to indulge her pleasure in the comedy of their forms to the full – may not be the least reason for their success. And perhaps it is just as well that Agar never really thought of these pictures as part of her oeuvre. Made as a sublime and heightened sort of snapshot, the Ploumanac'h photographs have a directness and a freshness which otherwise might have been fatally compromised.

There is one final parallel which is worth remarking. In November 1936, the *Architectural Review* announced the result of their Surrealist holiday competition (figure 30); the first prize went to one Luke Summers, but more intriguing today is the winner of the second prize: Bill Brandt.[59] Earlier that year, Brandt had published his book *The English at Home*, now considered one of the major works of social documentary photography, so it is instructive to see his pictures here, in a situation that emphasised the popular over the artistic and the surreal over the documentary.

The accompanying commentary (which reads as if it were written by Paul Nash) sounds a slightly superior note: 'In photographic technique this entry was probably the best sent in, but the perception of Surrealism was more stereotyped than the winner's'. Whether the writer knew it or not, Brandt's connections with Surrealism were well established. He had acted briefly as Man Ray's assistant in Paris and published work in *Minotaure* on two occasions, one of them a page of photographs of ships' figureheads taken in the Scilly Isles in August 1934.[60] (Brandt also had some connections with the London Surrealists; he visited the 1936 exhibition to photograph it and knew Penrose slightly, Mesens better.[61] He would later have pictures reproduced in the *London Bulletin*.[62])

Brandt's entry for the 'Holiday Surrealism' competition recycled some of the pictures he had taken in the Scilly Isles and, in relation to Eileen Agar's photographs from Ploumanac'h, the picture that is most intriguing shows a rock face on the sea shore in which the shapes in the rocks look like melting figures. Nash (if it were he) commented that the picture was 'almost the best example we have seen of natural objects photographed to show their disturbing Surrealist content'. This emphasises once more the importance of this subject in English Surrealism, while also pointing forward to Brandt's own later work, particularly *Perspectives of Nudes*, which he would publish in 1960. There, Brandt would use a wide-angle camera to create disturbing rhymes between the nude female bodies and the chalk cliffs and pebble beaches against which they were posed. In one sense, these pictures are quite opposite to the photographs Agar had made in Brittany – he made bodies look like rocks, she made rocks look like bodies. But they also parallel each other in depicting a landscape that is full of echoes and suggestions at the same time that it is altogether strange. Again, we find ourselves caught between the familiar and the alien.

Notes

1 'The Architectural Review Competition: Holiday Surrealism', *Architectural Review* (July 1936), 42. This formed part of a theme issue on the seaside, designed with photographs by Laszlo Moholy-Nagy.

2 See Ann Simpson, *Eileen Agar 1899–1991* (Edinburgh: Scottish National Gallery of Modern Art, 1999).

3 Eileen Agar, *A Look at My Life* (London: Methuen, 1988), p. 124. The Breton name of the village has an apostrophe in it – Ploumanac'h – but Agar, like other writers in English, omits it.

4 Agar, *A Look at My Life*, p. 124.

5 *Normandy and Brittany: Guide to the Seaside Resorts* (London: Southern Railway Company of England, eighth edition, 1934).

6 Agar, *A Look at My Life*, p. 124.

7 In an interview in 1990, Agar gave a less romantic account, suggesting that they actually stayed in Perros-Guirec and took the bus to Ploumanac'h, adding, 'I'd heard about these fantastic stones' (Interview with Cathy Courtney, 8 August 1990, for the National Sound Archive; there is a copy of the tape in Tate Archives, TAV 976 AB).

8 Agar, *A Look at My Life*, p. 124. In the 1990 interview, Agar mentions that they were told there were superior camera shops in Brest used by the French Navy.

9 Agar had taken photographs before, at the age of 16 or 17, but her subject had mostly been 'holiday pictures and family gatherings' (Agar, *A Look at my Life*, p. 30).

10 Interview with Cathy Courtney, 1990.

11 See Chapter 1, note 28.

55 Jaguer, *Les Mystères de la chambre noire*, pp. 105–6.

56 Exhibited at the New Art Centre, London, November 1985–January 1986.

57 Agar, *A Look at My Life*, p. 124. However, later in the book she comments that she is 'not so sure that the idea was particularly successful' (p. 229). In the 1990 interview with Cathy Courtney, she also remarked of the paintings, 'I don't think they're very serious art, because they're not invented.'

58 Ian Walker (ed.), *Contrariwise* (Swansea: Glynn Vivian Art Gallery, 1986), nos. 1 and 6.

59 'Competition Result: Holiday Surrealism', *Architectural Review* (November 1936), 218–9.

60 Bill Brandt, 'Au cimetière des anciennes galères', *Minotaure*, 6 (Winter 1934–5), 4.

61 Interview with the author, 6 April 1979.

62 Two photographs of graves from England and Spain titled 'A Chacun son Tombeau', *London Bulletin*, 12 (12 March 1939), 6.

4
The road is wider – Penrose and Miller in the Balkans

A year after their visit to Brittany, Eileen Agar and Joseph Bard were on holiday again. Towards the end of June 1937, Roland Penrose took over his brother's house at Lambe Creek in Cornwall and invited Surrealist friends to join him. As well as Agar and Bard, the visitors included Paul and Nusch Eluard, Man Ray and his girlfriend Ady Fidelin, Max Ernst and Leonora Carrington, E. L. T. Mesens and Henry and Irina Moore.[1] Penrose had indeed proved himself to be as André Breton had described him: 'surréaliste dans l'amitié'.[2] But the most important guest was more than a friend, for, at a party in Paris on 21 June, Penrose had met the new love of his life – Lee Miller. It was, he later wrote, a *coup de foudre*.[3] When she came to Cornwall a couple of weeks later, it cemented the relationship.

Lee Miller had first come to Paris from her native USA in 1929, after establishing a career as a model for *Vogue*. In Paris, though, she started to work on the other side of the camera and became Man Ray's assistant, muse and lover. In 1931, she met the wealthy Egyptian Aziz Eloui Bey and there had been a traumatic split with Man Ray. Lee and Aziz married and moved to Cairo in 1934, where she continued to photograph in a more fragmented way, concentrating on the Egyptian landscape. But social life in Cairo bored her and the trip to Paris in 1937 had been intended as a temporary escape. It was to turn into much more.

When Penrose and his visitors left Cornwall, they agreed to meet in a few weeks' time in the south of France where Picasso was spending the summer. It must have been between their return from Cornwall and leaving for the continent that Penrose, Miller, Agar and Bard visited Brighton where Miller made her best-known portrait of Agar (figure 31). The afternoon sun is coming in low, throwing Agar's shadow onto one of the voluptuous, bulbous forms around the base of the Pavilion. It looks gigantic in the photograph; in reality, it is no more than about three feet high. The spatial geography is quite hard to work out. There is the softer shadow of another figure to the right; since there exists a 35mm photo by Penrose taken at the same moment, one would guess it is he, hunched up with his camera to his eye.[4] The picture primarily operates as a good joke, of course, Agar's pointed pixie hat balancing the camera that protrudes

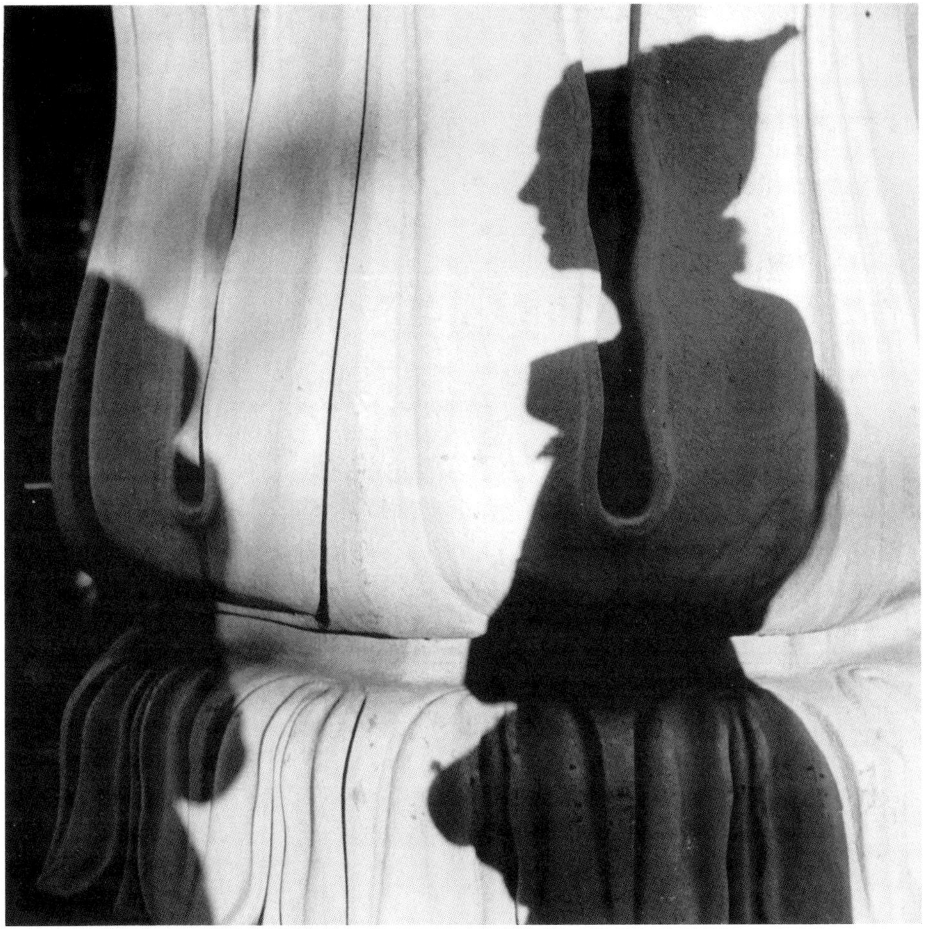

Fig 31 Lee Miller, *Eileen Agar, Brighton*, 1937. © Lee Miller Archives, England 2007.

from her stomach. Agar herself wrote that when Picasso saw the picture a few weeks later, he demanded a print, delighted with the image of her 'pregnant with a camera, transformed by Rolleiflex'.[5] It is a playful picture, contrived between friends. But it is also formally satisfying, the curving shapes of the Pavilion exaggerating Agar's own curves, the solid white stone overlaid with the transitory black shadow.

In early August, Penrose and Miller made their way to Mougins in the south of France via Brussels, where Mesens introduced them to the Belgian Surrealist group. Arriving on the Côte d'Azur, they met up with Picasso and his lover Dora Maar, the Eluards, Man Ray and Ady. A few days later, Agar and Bard joined them. The pleasures of that summer are evident in the photographs made by the three women – Maar, Agar and Miller, and by Penrose. No image is more resonant than one that Miller took at a picnic, where the men (Penrose, Man Ray and Eluard) are dressed in jaunty leisure wear and the women are naked to the waist (as indeed was the photographer herself).[6] As Antony Penrose has written,

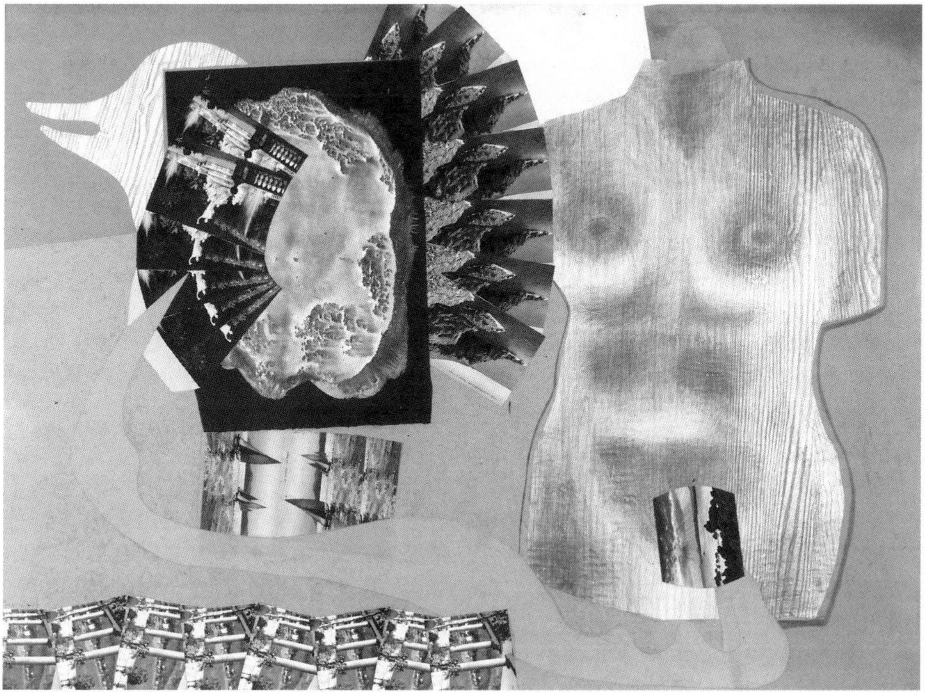

Fig 32 Roland Penrose, *The Real Woman*, 1937. © Roland Penrose Estate, England 2007.

'Roland has the look of complete ecstasy on his face ... This is the appearance of a liberated Englishman freed from the burdens of his puritan past'.[7] (Penrose had been raised a Quaker.)

This heightened pleasure led to a heightened creativity and, back in their room, Penrose started to work on collages, made with highly coloured postcards bought in local shops. Antony Penrose has also remarked that 'Roland's creativity was inextricably linked to his romantic life... It was Lee who was the catalyst for his invention of the postcard collage.'[8] And indeed, there is an eroticism embedded in the images, most particularly *The Real Woman*, where a frottage version of Lee's torso has a flaming sunset laid over its sex (figure 32). In these collages, Penrose plays with repetition, rhythm and pattern, piling allusion on allusion in playful excess, and it was appropriate that he used picture postcards in these works, expanding their connotations of pleasure and a release from everyday normality.

It seems likely it was during this time that Miller also made her best-known collage using the photograph she had taken in Brighton of Eileen Agar. Since Picasso saw the picture, she must have brought prints with her and she used two of them in this collage, one reversed to become a white silhouette, with the back of the head forming the profile of Dora Maar.[9] Other ingredients include a postcard of the Côte d'Azur and a bit of decalcomania, which suggest that she was taking over elements from Penrose. But then, perhaps, the work made by the pair was already collaborative.

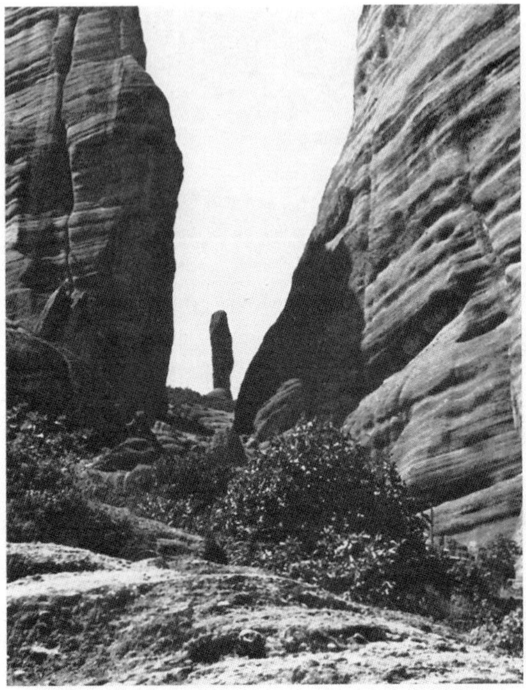

to a world of dead music
blown across drained swamps
and mountains caught in a net

Magic lived in this rock

With the end of the summer, Penrose and Miller went in different directions, he returning to London, she to Egypt. The following summer, Miller went to Athens to visit friends; she shipped her giant American Packard car over with the intention of touring the country. (One might imagine it a little like the Packard being hoisted aboard ship at the start of Evelyn Waugh's *Vile Bodies*, 'bearing the dust of three continents'.)[10] She begged Penrose to join her, but it wasn't until the end of June that he was able to do so, bringing with him his camera to document their journey.

From Athens, they first visited the islands of Delos and Mykonos and travelled to the Peloponnese to visit the theatre at Epidaurus. Then they drove north-west to the sanctuary at Delphi and via the mythic pass of Thermopylae to the monasteries at Meteora, poised atop rocky outcrops. Next they travelled

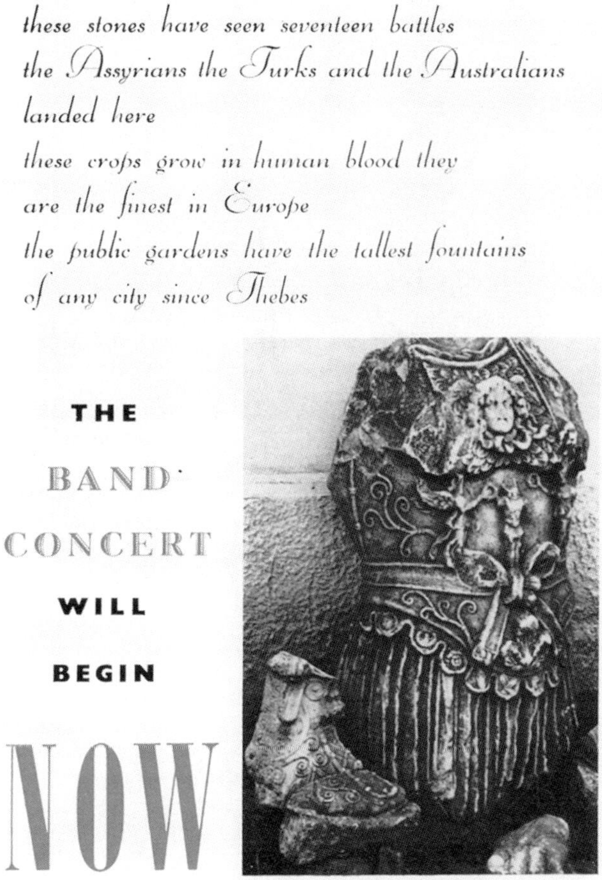

Fig 33 Roland Penrose, spread from *The Road is Wider than Long*, 1938. © Roland Penrose Estate, England 2007.

to northern Greece for an idyllic visit to the island of Thassos. From there, they drove north through Bulgaria to the Romanian capital of Bucharest, where they had arranged to meet Harry Brauner, the brother of the Surrealist painter Victor Brauner. An expert on gypsy and folk music, he conducted them around the countryside, and in particular into the Carpathian mountains, where they encountered the local gypsies.

Miller and Penrose said goodbye again in Bucharest, he heading west, she east. Penrose arrived at Munich station on 9 September, where 'a sudden reminder of political reality awaited me ... The vault of the main station was decorated along its entire length with thousands of Nazi flags in honour of Chamberlain's appeasement visit to Hitler'.[11] He continued on to London and arrived back like the other summer travellers described by Louis MacNeice in his epic poem *Autumn Journal*: 'the people / Back from Holiday are tanned / With blistered thumbs and a wallet of snaps and a little / *Joie de vivre* which is contraband.'[12] Except that Penrose's 'snaps' were rather more exotic than most and his memories more ecstatic.

Throughout that autumn, Penrose worked on a book that would combine his Balkan photographs with an extended poem evoking the journey: *The Road is Wider than Long* (figure 33). It must have been an intensive period of work, for by the end of the year, Penrose was able to publish two lengthy sections of the poem in the *London Bulletin* in a form that would change only slightly in the final book.[13] At the same time he was preparing the book for publication, he was also working on a private version. Penrose was able to go out to Egypt in January 1939, and he took with him two presents for Lee, one of which was a handmade copy of the book. (The other was a pair of golden handcuffs so that they could engage in Roland's favourite fetish.) That summer two years after their first meeting was marked both by the publication of *The Road is Wider than Long* in book form and by Lee's arrival in London, to stay.[14]

The Road is Wider than Long, then, is a book that had its beginnings in the heightened personal relationship between Penrose and Miller. Perhaps this is one reason why it has been little discussed, because it has been regarded as a sort of vanity publication. Yet it is in fact rather interesting and, indeed, unique. Perhaps another reason for the silence that surrounds it is because it sits in no particular genre and partakes of several. This is precisely what makes it intriguing – it looks like a different book regarded from different angles.

It is, however, inevitable that we must start with biography, for interest in Lee Miller's remarkable life story has fitted alongside and indeed sometimes dominated the understanding of her work. We cannot now go back to 1939, when an uninformed reader might have picked up the published book, seen its brief inscription 'For Lee' and wondered who he or she was – male or female? The circumstance of the book's making is indeed one of the several ways that we can understand its nature, but it is not the only one, and I want to cast the net wide here to conjure up comparisons with a range of other publications.

First, though, it is necessary to outline the book's history, for the way it has shifted between private and public suggests something of its complexity. The earliest extant version is a draft in the Penrose Collection in Edinburgh, which must have been made when the work was already well under way.[15] It is an almost complete version of the text, written out in longhand on foolscap sheets, often in prose with indications where the line breaks might come. The photographs are represented either by little stuck-on contact prints or else by rectangles with 'gypsies', 'funeral' or 'tree' written inside them to indicate which pictures go where. This suggests that the text was finished before the choice of photographs was finalised, though the existence of the pictures surely helped to propel the writing of the text.

The individual frames stuck on the draft had been cut out of contact strips, which were then placed in envelopes labelled by subject and place. They are also in Edinburgh, and there is something moving and poignant about these fragmentary remnants – three or four frames long – slipped into their envelopes and forgotten.[16] Sometimes they can be connected with pictures that made it into the final book, but equally they often represent other elements of the trip that Penrose deliberately excluded – photos of the car parked on the roadside, of a picnic with friends or of Lee sunbathing. The photographs made by most holidaymakers are of two sorts – images of places and people encountered and of themselves experiencing their holiday. While compiling the book, Penrose edited out the latter for either personal or artistic reasons.

The single handmade copy that Penrose gave to Lee when he arrived in Cairo at the end of January 1939 is an exquisite and carefully made object. (It is still in the family collection.) It is bound in soft brown leather, with the title and author's name tooled in gold on the spine, so that it might comfortably sit on the shelves of a gentlemen's club. Yet that traditional exterior belies its contents, where the text is handwritten in a range of different coloured inks and each of the photographic prints pasted in.[17] This, of course, gives the book a more personal and immediate quality; the pictures are much more striking since they are hand-printed and larger than the reduced images in the later printed versions. On some pages, additional pieces of paper have been stuck in, such as, at one point, graph paper laid down at an angle. Probably the most delightful feature is actually on the title page where Penrose wrote 'An image-dairy from the Balkans'. (This is probably due to an unguarded moment of dyslexia, but it does add a surrealist edge to the rich confection of material that follows it.)[18]

Following this title page and the dedication 'For Lee', Penrose laid out a list of the place names they had visited and a photo of Lee being led on horseback (a photograph taken on their ascent of the Meteora rocks) before the first page of the poem proper. In preparing the book for publication, those factual references were removed, part of a process whereby some of the more personal elements were excised. There is, for example, a place in the manuscript where the line 'old dust new car a bridge' is followed by 'daily we make love under that bridge / But we don't understand a word', which had gone when the book was published. (It is a shame, because the line interestingly brings together their erotic attraction with a sense of being out of place. *The Road is Wider than Long* is both a love poem and a travel poem and merges two states, both of which can be disorientating.)

Antony Penrose is undoubtedly right to suggest that it was not prudery but decency that made Penrose excise these more personal references.[19] Miller was, after all, still married and the affair with Penrose secret. But the effect is also to make the book stranger, with its genesis and much that is in it left deliberately unresolved. Where we are when and what is going on is precisely not explained and this must have given the first public edition an estranged purity (at least for those readers who didn't know who Lee was). For example, at that point where the reference to lovemaking has been excised, we are left with a picture of a rocky landscape with a chequered cloth on the ground. It acts as an indication of some activity – a picnic presumably – but we cannot know for sure.

The circulation of *The Road is Wider than Long* would have been limited in 1939: 500 copies were printed using the new and inexpensive process of offset lithography. Ten copies were also made using handmade paper, but apparently the photos did not print well, so Penrose laboriously pasted them in. As with much else in English Surrealism, the book's fate was caught up in the advent of war just a couple of months after its publication. It did not re-emerge until 1980, when a second edition was produced to coincide with an exhibition of Roland Penrose's work, shown in London at the ICA, which, of course, he had been instrumental in founding.[20]

The 1980 edition was, on the whole, a faithful reproduction of the first published edition of 1939, but, perhaps, most important was what was added at the end. For here Penrose included the list of names and the photograph of Lee Miller on horseback which had been in the private version, as well as adding an informative text about the making of the book. This restored the book's history while making it again more personal. A year later, in his autobiographical *Scrapbook*, Penrose revisited his photographs to select a couple showing Lee talking with gypsy women.[21] When Antony Penrose published his biography of his mother in 1985, it became impossible to read *The Road is Wider than Long* except through the screen of biography.

The latest edition of *The Road is Wider than Long* appeared in 2003, when the J. Paul Getty Museum in Los Angeles published another facsimile edition.[22] This is different yet again, since the photographs were reproduced from the handmade edition, while painted decorations have been added from copy number 1 of the limited edition which Penrose had given to Miller. These additions shift the book still more towards the personal, particularly with the erotically charged dedication on the title page: 'Lee who caught me in her cup of gold'.

The Road is Wider than Long, then, is a book whose form has changed subtly over the years, with at least four versions being produced, each the same yet each different. But, fundamentally, what sort of book is this? Penrose's subtitle 'An Image Diary from the Balkans July–August 1938' is ambiguous. Does he mean that it is a diary accompanied by images or, more intriguingly, a diary made up of images? In other words, how important are the photographs? At the start of the book, it states 'The photographs are by the author'. This seems clearly to place the text first (that is where the authorship lies) and the photographs second. But of course, this is merely a statement of convention or rather a contradiction of the convention whereby the author – the writer – would *not* provide their own photographs. The innovation that Penrose initiates with *The Road is Wider than Long* is precisely as author of both words *and* pictures.

If rare in a literary or artistic context, this situation would not, however, have been as surprising in another genre – that of travel writing. It might initially seem odd to think of *The Road is Wider than Long* as a sort of travel book. But, for our hypothetical early reader in the late 1930s, the idea of a journey round an exotic part of Europe, told in the form of a diary and illustrated with the author's own photographs, would have been altogether familiar.

As Paul Fussell has eloquently demonstrated, the years between the two wars were a high point in English travel writing, as exemplified both by the work of authors who specialised in the genre such as Robert Byron and Norman Douglas and in forays by writers better known for other sorts of work, like Graham Greene, Evelyn Waugh and W. H. Auden.[23] *The Road is Wider than Long* intersects with these writings in various ways, the simplest of which is the criss-crossing of actual physical space. Robert Byron had visited Greece on several occasions and felt particularly at home there (his surname helped). On a visit in 1931, he had gone to the monasteries of Meteora, and written about them (and photographed them) for *Country Life*.[24] In 1933, the 18-year-old Patrick Leigh Fermor decided to walk across Europe to Constantinople; it is quite possible that the gypsies he encountered in the Carpathians were related to the ones that Penrose and Miller met and photographed later in the decade.[25]

This is not to suggest any direct influence (though Penrose would surely have known Byron's writing), but rather the ways in which *The Road is Wider than Long* connects with, extends and in some ways challenges the conventions of that genre of travel writing. As Fussell has remarked, the mythic presence of the Mediterranean was a crucial element in the genre: 'To sketch the history of the British imaginative discourse with the Mediterranean is virtually to present a survey of modern British literature. It was a magical place, like the island in *The Tempest*, capable of generating God knows what lubriciousness and of virtually unmanning the intellect.'[26] It was, in other words, the very opposite of England with its changeable weather, its stodgy food and its puritan traditions. For Penrose, it put a smile on his face.

The first part of their journey took Penrose and Miller through Greece, a country with a huge literary and artistic weight within Western culture. But there were no comparable cultural associations for them as they travelled north. What would the average Englishman have known of Romania, other than vague associations with Transylvania and Ruritania? Their journey became a voyage into a more innocent, almost primitive world. It was travel rather than tourism, a distinction which still was tenable in the 1930s, though more recent writers than Fussell have been rather sceptical as to whether there is actually any fundamental difference between the two.

Perhaps it is more useful to think of this journey in other terms. In his book *Travelling Light*, Peter D. Osborne usefully analysed the category he called 'Romantic travel', which demanded an openness to 'the Other in which terror or love might represent a means to a transformatory end'.[27] And he references the argument of Dean MacCannell that, in modern society, 'reality and authenticity are thought to be elsewhere: in other historical periods and other cultures, in purer, simpler lifestyles'.[28] Penrose and Miller were travellers and lovers both, and their trip divided into two parts, each connecting with a different sort of 'authentic' otherness: the classical ruins of Greece and the peasant culture of Romania. But it was the unfamiliarity of the latter with which they most thoroughly engaged.

Osborne also extends his discussion to what he calls 'the Surrealist tour guide', his main example being the work that Henri Cartier-Bresson made in the 1930s. But his analysis might also apply to Penrose: 'For the Surrealist travel was a method, a means of smoking out the unconscious ... more than simply pleasuring its subjects, the surrealist journey conveyed them towards an encounter with some kind of otherness which might also destabilize and transform them.'[29] The journey undertaken by Penrose and Miller was not only through the Balkans, it was also inside themselves, and its aim was not understanding (though that might occur) but revelation.

But this is not all there is to 'Surrealist tourism' and Penrose's book is far from being a merely escapist celebration of otherness. There is also a sceptical irony which breaks through at certain moments and Penrose seems to be fully aware of the dubious politics of the region. And, of course, he and Miller must have been very conscious that they couldn't really 'go native'. Driving a big American car through the mountains is not truly the way to experience authentic peasant life. Yet their position as outsiders is important to the slightly estranged feel of both Penrose's text and photographs. The line between romantic exoticisation and a positive recognition of 'otherness' is thin, but Penrose negotiated it through a constant shifting of tone, switching between elevated rhetoric and conversational familiarity. He was at once both there and here – experiencing the events in Carpathia and recollecting them in Hampstead.

In the mid-1930s, a self-consciousness seems to have come over the travel book – a sort of critique from within – which manifested itself in two otherwise quite

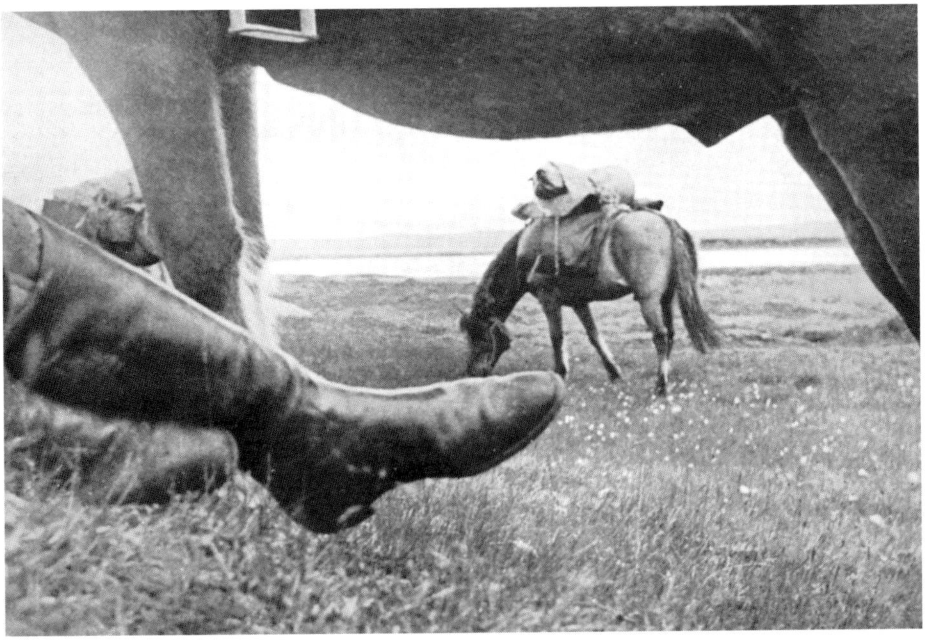

Fig 34 W. H. Auden, 'Stella's boot', photograph from *Letters from Iceland*, 1937.

different books, both published in 1937: Robert Byron's *The Road to Oxiana* and *Letters from Iceland* by W. H. Auden and Louis MacNeice.[30] Paul Fussell wrote of Byron's book: 'perhaps it may not be going too far to say that what *Ulysses* is to the novel between the wars and what *The Waste Land* is to poetry, *The Road to Oxiana* is to the travel book ... It is an artfully constructed quest myth in the form of an apparently spontaneous travel diary.'[31] He is less generous to *Letters from Iceland*, which he perceives as marking a decadence: 'the narrative is disturbingly discontinuous, interrupted by jokiness ... and self-consciousness about the *travel book* genre itself'.[32]

But postmodernism enables us to read these parodic disjunctions more positively. Marsha Bryant, in her study of Auden and documentary, calls *Letters from Iceland* 'a fragmented text that appropriates the discourses of poetry, rhetorical documentary, travelogue, and high modernism' and 'suggests strategies for breaking out of conventional documentary framings'.[33] In fact, both *The Road to Oxiana* and *Letters from Iceland* use the tactics of collage and Fussell's description of Byron's book – 'as if obsessed with frontiers and fragmentations, it juxtaposes into a sort of collage the widest variety of rhetorical materials'[34] – is perhaps not so far from Auden's own description of *Letters from Iceland*:

> 'Every exciting letter has enclosures,
> And so shall this – a bunch of photographs,
> Some out of focus, some with wrong exposures,
> Press cuttings, gossip, maps, statistics, graphs;
> I don't intend to do things by halves
> I'm going to be very up to date indeed,
> It is a collage that you're going to read.'[35]

Photography was a key ingredient in the construction of these books – as it was of many travel books – but it operates rather differently in each case. The pictures taken by Byron have a doubled effect of validation – they validate the scene and they validate the presence of the author within it. To do that, they need to be as straightforward and undemonstrative as possible. Auden's photographs, on the other hand, undercut that authority with a knowing and deliberate excess. Sometimes the picture itself is just plain ridiculous and sometimes it is the caption that dismantles its meaning (figure 34). It is interesting to think of this in relation to Penrose's photos. Certainly, in their directness, they are more like Byron's pictures; in themselves, they are mostly very unsurrealist. But, as they interlock with the text that floats around them, the factuality they seem to offer becomes increasingly unstable. A conventional touristic photograph of a sunset has above it the phrase 'Vapours escape from the rocks' (a reference to Delphi) and below it 'writing tomorrow's news in the sky', so that the rays of the setting sun become both the vapours and the news.

'Perhaps it is when we cannot satisfactorily designate a kind of work with a single word', wrote Fussell, 'that we sense we're entering complicated territory,

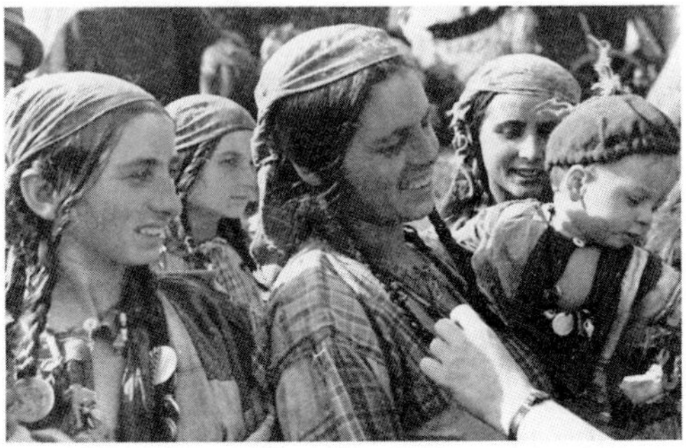

She tore her dress
a dress covered with a dress
and covered with a dress
she tore her dress to mend it
joined by her fingers
torn by her breasts
her dress tears from within.

whose description, let alone definition, is hazardous, an act closer to exploration than to travel.'[36] If 'travel book' is one such complex double-barrelled genre, then 'image-diary' is another. And if travel books could – and often did – include both images and diaries, they were never brought together as they were in *The Road is Wider than Long*. For what is important in the book is not only what it shares with travel books, but the ways in which it is quite different.

One can see this clearly if one imagines trying to retrace the journey through Greece and the Balkans using only *The Road is Wider than Long* as a guide. It is fundamentally non-narrative and non-sequential whereas it is the journey, the quest which drives any good travel book forward. Only in a few places, can we tell where we are and even then the sites are out of order. The theatre at Epidaurus, for example, visited early in the journey, does not appear until two-thirds of the way through the book, while the rocks of Meteora are pictured both at the beginning and near the end. We are constantly thrown around in space and time, with broken fragments of texts placed next to ambiguous images, so that what we end up with is not a guide, but an evocation, a reverie, even. As the title *The*

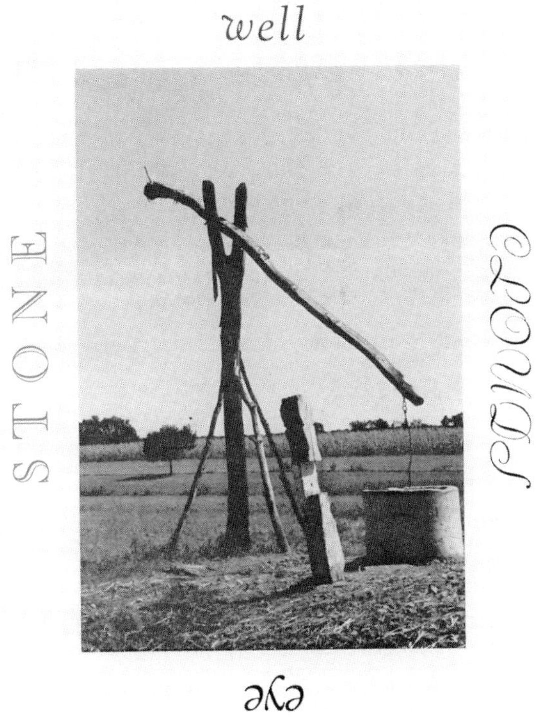

Fig 35 Roland Penrose, spread from *The Road is Wider than Long*, 1938. © Roland Penrose Estate, England 2007.

Road is Wider than Long emphasises, where most travel books are concerned with the story of a journey, Penrose is more interested in how the meaning of the experience spreads, shifts and connects with other experiences.

There are also some deliberate omissions. For example, Penrose took some photographs of the large phallic sculptures on Delos, but they were not included in the book. Perhaps their eroticism was too obvious and too public. And looking down the list of places visited in Romania, one name jumps out for any student of modern art: Tirgu-Jiu. In 1938, Constantin Brancusi had recently completed his extensive series of large public sculptures there and it is surely incredible that Penrose would not have wanted to see them. But if he did, he does not seem to have photographed them and they would in any case have intruded on his image of Romania as peopled by peasants and gypsies.

So, while the travel book of the 1930s can provide one context for *The Road is Wider than Long,* it is in fact a very different sort of book and we must turn back to Surrealism to find parallels for its poetic and formal qualities. There are many sites where one can find the Surrealists exploring the conjunction between image and text, but the publications where poetry is poised against photograph are rather fewer.[37] There were two main ways of doing this – juxtaposition and integration. In the first, the poem and the photograph are placed across from each other and the resonance operates in the space between them; the best example here is the later book *On the Needles of these Days*, produced in Prague in 1941 by Jindřich Štyrský and Jindřich Heisler.[38]

But it was not this restrained and formal opposition of picture and text that interested Penrose. Rather, he was concerned with the integration of the two and there were examples more immediately to hand and which he would have known. These were *Facile* with poems by Paul Eluard and photographs by Man Ray, published in 1935, and *La Septième face du dé* by Georges Hugnet of 1936.[39] Both were produced in Paris in the years immediately preceding the flowering of Surrealism in England, and both have elements that would have been important for Penrose as he worked on *The Road is Wider than Long*.

But the three volumes are also different. *La Septième face du dé* is one of the most spirited marriages of image and text within Surrealism – indeed in its dynamic layout and excessive piling up of fragments, it seems almost closer to the earlier experimentations of Dada.[40] One can imagine that Penrose might have been inspired by it to make his own typographic experiments in *The Road is Wider than Long*, but he retained a greater restraint – his text never flies across the page as does Hugnet's. And, although *La Septième face du dé* is full of erotic imagery, this has all been clipped from magazines and is emotionally disengaged. The grounding of Penrose's book in personal experience gives it an altogether different quality.

Facile, on the other hand, does embody a personal engagement. Made soon after Eluard's marriage to Nusch, it combines his lyrical poems written for her and Man Ray's sensuous photographs of her nude body. In the words of Renée Riese Hubert, 'the poem is made up of images, and the images coalesce into a poem';[41] the two elements move around each other so that one seems to flow into the other. This intense sense of integration led Nicole Boulestreanu to coin the term 'photopoème' to describe *Facile*, though it is a term that could in different ways describe all these books.[42] In particular, the term emphasises that, with both *Facile* and *La Septième face du dé*, one cannot say which came first – poem or image. *The Road is Wider than Long* is also more than the sum of its parts; when either the poetry or the photographs have been published separately, they have seemed diminished.[43]

Facile looks very different from *The Road is Wider than Long* – its images are exquisitely lit and framed studios shots, where Penrose's are made out in the real world. And the poetry does not intersect the photography as Penrose's does. But there is another intriguing point of connection, for both books have a female presence at their heart. Both books were written for a woman, as an expression of the male author's love. But this presence can seem more like an absence. Nusch is only a body in these photographs – we never see her face. And Lee is a name in a dedication.

In fact, Lee Miller does appear twice in *The Road is Wider than Long*, but in ways that are coded and would not have been apparent to an uninitiated viewer. One is below the line 'The Prefect has no time to waste', where a uniformed man leans towards a car in which a woman in a straw hat is sitting, her face in shadow. She is Lee, the car is her Packard and the picture is one in a sequence where she seems to be both charming and mocking the 'Prefect'.[44] Her other appearance is over the page where a group of gypsy women are smiling at someone out of frame on the right. All we see of that person – Lee – is her hand coming into the shot (figure 35).

The next shot on the contact strip is the image of Lee talking with the women which Penrose reproduced in *Scrapbook*. Often, in the photographs that Penrose took but didn't use, it is Miller who is engaging with the people they encounter as Penrose steps back to make the picture. The process of photography starts to look more collaborative and the question of the book's authorship slides around a little. In one sense, it is quite straightforward – Penrose made the book on his own, in London, in the autumn of 1938. Yet in other senses, its authorship is more complex. First, there is the question of the photographs themselves.

Antony Penrose, in his biography of Lee Miller, attributed one photograph in *The Road is Wider than Long* to her – an image of a dead child laid out at home before her funeral.[45] Though this is an image made on Roland's 35mm camera, Antony Penrose attributes it on stylistic grounds to Miller and argues that this is a situation in which the lighter more manoeuverable camera may have been handed round and pictures taken by either of them.[46] This specific question cannot of course be resolved, but in a more general sense, the influence of Miller is present throughout *The Road is Wider than Long*. It is easy to imagine that Penrose, an amateur, somewhat novice photographer, was both encouraged and cowed by the example of Miller, with her experience of the medium, her keen photographic eye and her heavy camera. The Leica was lighter; perhaps this could make his pictures seem less weighty also.

Attribution has always been an interesting issue with Miller, who had previously seemed happy to let Man Ray take the credit for the pictures on which they had worked together: 'I do not know if it was I who made them', she apparently told Penrose. 'But that's of no importance … we were nearly the same person at work.'[47] In particular, it would seem that it was she who accidentally rediscovered the potential of solarisation, when something crawling across her foot in the darkroom made her switch on the light hurriedly.[48] Jane Livingston has described Miller as 'almost egoless' and, in a feminist reading, Miller's submergence under the reputations of her male partners might be yet another telling parable that, while Surrealism may have been revolt against many things, patriarchy was not one of them.[49] But it is also worth remembering that collaboration, commonality and indeed anonymity were important values in Surrealist creativity, even if the major artists and writers of the group did not always act accordingly.

In fact, on their trip through the Balkans, Lee Miller was taking her own pictures with her Rolleiflex as Penrose was using his Leica.[50] She does not seem

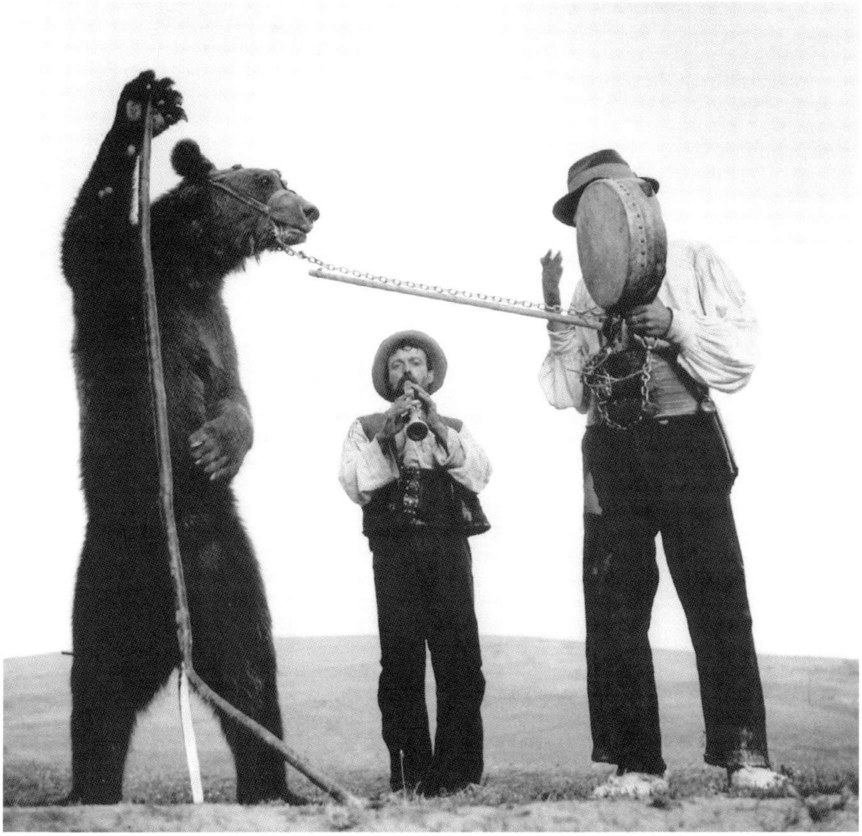

Fig 36 Lee Miller, *Gypsy musicians with bear, Romania*, 1938. © Lee Miller Archives, England 2007.

to have made many pictures in Greece, but in Romania, she shot a prodigious amount of images – about 500 negatives survive. While she does photograph buildings and objects, it is the people she seems to engage with. (This is unusual in her work from the 1930s and looks forward to her later wartime photography.) Opinions differ about these images, few of which have ever been published. Antony Penrose has written: 'She photographed with care and sensitivity, as if the talisman of the captured image could somehow protect these innocent people from disaster.'[51] Certainly, the peasant women look into Miller's camera with a mixture of shyness and self-confidence. Livingston, though, felt that 'the work on the whole lacks either the emotional intensity or the compositional distinction of which she was so patently capable'.[52]

It is true that, often, the heavy, square format camera is not very handy for capturing swiftly changing situations. She shot a film of gypsy children dressed in leaves dancing to produce rain, but the images are rather static compared to the photograph Penrose included in *The Road is Wider than Long*. But there are other occasions when one can see her working her way round a subject to produce a resolved image. In photographing a performing bear and its handlers,

Miller shot a whole film – 12 frames – moving from the front to the side, in close and further away, directing some shots and letting others be more free. The most successful shot has an almost uncanny precision of placement and composition, the bear's paw raised, the musician's hand poised above the tambourine obscuring his face, the low viewpoint giving the ensemble an almost epic grandeur (figure 36). Penrose's image of the bear troupe in his book is, by comparison, rather diffuse and distant.

But Penrose was not an absolute amateur and he also made some fine pictures. When I first saw his contact strips, I was surprised to realise that he was using a 35mm Leica camera, having assumed from the book that he was working with a Kodak, like the one that Nash used. Certainly, Penrose had started off as a snapshooter – there are pictures of his from the late 1920s shot on a different camera that are less distinct. But it looks as if he had bought the Leica the previous year – his Cornwall photographs are made on it – and this suggests a greater seriousness to his photographic purpose. At the Greek theatre of Epidaurus, he moved around and made a series of 18 shots from different angles. The one he chose – symmetrical and focused – was the best. The picture with which he concluded the book – a view up to a wrapped statue – was also the result of concentration (it looks from the contacts as if he returned to get the shot when the sky was more expressive) and it takes its place in a surrealist iconography of wrapped objects that goes back to Man Ray's *Enigma of Isidore Ducasse*.[53]

It is evident, however, looking at the whole range of images that Penrose took on this trip, that photography for its own sake was not his aim. It is very noticeable that while he took many pictures of Miller, she took none of him. Her photographic concentration was on her subject and their experience of each other was something separate. For Penrose, the two were elided, and only in retrospect, back in autumnal London, did he extract the pictures for his book. To revisit those images alongside all the others he took – to see, for instance, a romantic shot of a group of gypsies against the sky followed by those same gypsies eyeing the Packard parked on a dusty road – is to understand both something of the context of the trip and the process of editing which Penrose undertook in London.

When, some twenty-seven years ago, I asked Roland Penrose about *The Road is Wider than Long*, he commented, 'So you found my little book.'[54] (The second edition had not yet been published and I had looked at a copy of the 1939 edition in the British Library.) The photographs he called 'just snapshots'. This modesty was apparently typical of Penrose's comments on his own work and we should not take them at face value. *The Road is Wider than Long* is a little book and the photographs unassuming, but it is far more than just a holiday album.

Roland Penrose preserved two written responses to his book, which now sit together in a file in Edinburgh alongside his first draft version. One is a cutting from the *New Statesman* of 30 September 1939, a brief review by Stephen Spender: '*The Road is Wider than Long* is a ninny book ... A great deal of credit goes to the printers and binders, but none at all to Mr. Penrose, whose poems and photographs are pretentious and dull.' The other is a letter from Irène Hamoir and Louis Scutenaire, members of the Belgian Surrealist group to whom Penrose must have sent a copy (their letter is dated 28 June):

> Your book, which catches hold of the very heart of the world, is impressively lucid. Leaving behind a land where faith turns into doubt and severity into resignation, you lead us into a truly marvellous region where what really counts once more raises its standard. ... We admire your self-possession, which is all discretion and confidence, the resolve you show as you approach the walls of desire and the modesty of your reserve once the walls have fallen.[55]

A balanced assessment lies somewhere between these two extremes. Of course, Penrose's photographs are not as good as those that, say, Cartier-Bresson might have taken, nor is his poetry as fine as Eluard's. But that is rather besides the point, for it is the juxtaposition of the text and images and the imaginative space opened between them that makes *The Road is Wider than Long* a rather extraordinary and particular achievement. As well as its formal qualities, it also represents something important for English Surrealism – the furthest point of removal from the deadening hand of 'Deep England'. Nash had moved to the coast, Agar jumped across the Channel and Penrose went to the other side of Europe. And it is appropriate that it should be the English Surrealist from the most repressed background but with the greatest sense of connection to continental culture who made that leap. It was, in some ways, an escape, but it was also a discovery. Meanwhile, there were still parts of England itself which to many seemed alien, and it was to that England that other participants in Surrealism turned their attention.

Notes

1 See Antony Penrose, *The Surrealists in Cornwall* (Falmouth: Falmouth Art Gallery, 2004).

2 Quoted by Roland Penrose, *Scrapbook 1900–1981* (London: Thames & Hudson, 1981), p. 60.

3 Penrose, *Scrapbook*, p. 104.

4 A contact print of this image is in the Scottish National Gallery of Modern Art: Penrose collection, File 813.

5 Eileen Agar, *A Look at My Life* (London: Methuen, 1988), p. 139.

6 Miller's picture has been widely reproduced; see for example Antony Penrose *The Lives of Lee Miller* (London: Thames & Hudson, 1985), p. 76. Penrose's picture with Miller in it is reproduced in Mary Ann Caws, *Dora Maar: With and without Picasso* (London: Thames & Hudson, 2000), pp. 134–5.

7 Antony Penrose, *Roland Penrose: the Friendly Surrealist* (Munich: Prestel, 2001), p. 80.

8 Antony Penrose, *The Home of the Surrealists: Lee Miller, Roland Penrose and Their Circle at Farley Farm* (London: Frances Lincoln, 2001), p. 38.

9 This last element also points to the fact that they must have had access to processing facilities in Mougins. (My thanks to Antony Penrose for pointing this out, letter to the author, 19 June 2006.)

10 Evelyn Waugh, *Vile Bodies* (London: Penguin, 2000), p. 7.

11 Roland Penrose, 'The Road *was* wider than long', postscript to the 1980 edition of *The Road is Wider than Long.*

12 Louis MacNeice, *Autumn Journal* (London: Faber & Faber, 1998), p. 8.

13 The two extracts are published in *London Bulletin*, 7 (December 1938/January 1939), 17–22, and 8–9 (January/February, 1939), 51–6.

14 The first edition was published by the London Gallery Editions.

15 Penrose Collection, File 0465.

16 The original negatives are in the Lee Miller Archive in Sussex.

17 Pages from this handmade copy are reproduced in Penrose, *Roland Penrose: The Friendly Surrealist*, p. 55, and Penrose, *The Home of the Surrealists*, p. 43.

18 Antony Penrose (*The Friendly Surrealist*, p. 149) mentions his suspicion that his father was 'acutely dyslexic'. If so, there are no other signs in this handwritten version. Perhaps the title – the simplest bit to write – was where he momentarily let down his guard.

19 Letter to the author, 30 September 1986.

20 *Roland Penrose* (London: Arts Council of Great Britain, 1980), text by Norbert Lynton.

21 Penrose, *Scrapbook*, p. 116.

22 This was to coincide with the exhibition *Surrealist Muse: Lee Miller, Roland Penrose and Man Ray* held at the Museum.

23 Paul Fussell, *Abroad: British Literary Traveling Between the Wars* (Oxford: Oxford University Press, 1980). See also Valentine Cunningham, *British Writers of the Thirties* (Oxford: Oxford University Press, 1988), Chapter 11: 'Seedy Margins', pp. 341–76.

24 Robert Byron, 'The Monasteries of the Meteora', *Country Life* (21 May 1932), 561–4. See also James Knox, *Robert Byron: A Biography* (London: John Murray, 2003).

25 Patrick Leigh Fermor, *Between the Woods and the Water* (London: John Murray, 1986).

26 Fussell, *Abroad*, p. 130.

27 Peter D. Osborne, *Travelling Light: Photography, Travel and Culture* (Manchester: Manchester University Press, 2000), p. 30.

28 Dean MacCannell, *The Tourist: A New Theory of the Leisure Class* (London: Macmillan, 1976), p. 3.

29 Osborne, *Travelling Light*, p. 166.

30 Robert Byron, *The Road to Oxiana* (London: Macmillan, 1937; republished London: Pimlico, 2004); W. H. Auden and Louis MacNeice, *Letters from Iceland* (London: Faber & Faber, 1937). Later editions of *Letters from Iceland* do not contain Auden's photographs.

31 Fussell, *Abroad*, pp. 95–6.

32 Fussell, *Abroad*, pp. 219–20.

33 Marsha Bryant, *Auden and Documentary in the 1930s* (Charlottesville: University Press of Virginia, 1997), p. 62.

34 Fussell, *Abroad*, p. 108.

35 Auden and MacNeice, *Letters from Iceland*, p. 21.

36 Fussell, *Abroad*, p. 202.

37 For broader studies of Surrealist image-text work, see Renée Riese Hubert, *Surrealism and the Book* (Berkeley: University of California Press, 1988) and Judi Freeman, *The Dada and Surrealist Word-Image* (Los Angeles: County Museum/Cambridge, Mass: MIT Press, 1989).

38 Jindřich Štyrský and Jindřich Heisler, *Na jehlách těchto dní* (Prague: Borovy, 1945). See Ian Walker, 'Between photograph and poem: a study of Štyrský and Heisler's *On the Needles of these Days*', *Papers of Surrealism*, 3 (spring 2005).

39 Paul Eluard and Man Ray, *Facile* (Paris: GLM, 1935); Georges Hugnet, *La Septième face du dé* (Paris: Editions Jeanne Bucher, 1936).

40 For a detailed analysis, see Robert Sobieszek, 'Erotic Photomontages: Georges Hugnet's *La Septième face du dé*', *Dada/Surrealism*, 9 (1979), 66–82. Hugnet was writing about Dada at the time he produced *La Septième face du dé*, in essays published in *Cahiers d'Art* between 1932 and 1936.

41 Hubert, *Surrealism and the Book*, p. 76.

42 Nicole Boulestreanu, '*Facile*: un nouveau livre dans les années 1930', *Melusine*, 4 (1982), 163–8.

43 Extracts from the poem were published in Edward Germain (ed.), *English and American Surrealist Poetry* (Harmondsworth: Penguin, 1978), pp. 142–8, and in Alexander Robertson (ed.), *Surrealism in Britain in the Thirties* (Leeds: Leeds City Art Gallery, 1986), pp. 78–80. Penrose's photographs are in Rosalind Krauss and Jane Livingston (eds), *L'Amour Fou* (Washington: Corcoran Gallery/New York: Abbeville Press, 1985), pp. 227–8.

44 On the envelope containing the contact prints, he is referred to as the 'Colonel'.

45 Penrose, *The Lives of Lee Miller*, p. 87.

46 Interview with the author, 20 July 2005.

47 From an interview in French with Roland Penrose in Philippe Sers (ed.), *Atelier Man Ray* (Paris: Centre Pompidou, 1982), p. 56.

48 Miller tells this story in her interview with Mario Amaya, 'My Man Ray', *Art in America* (May–June 1975), 54–60. On the relationship between Man Ray and Lee Miller, see Renée Riese Hubert, *Magnifying Mirrors: Women, Surrealism and Partnership* (Lincoln: University of Nebraska Press, 1994), chapter 8, pp. 199–229.

49 Jane Livingston, *Lee Miller: Photographer* (London: Thames & Hudson, 1989), p. 35.

50 A shot by Penrose of Miller with her camera, surrounded by gypsies, is in *The Surrealist and the Photographer* (Edinburgh: Scottish National Gallery of Modern Art, 2001), p. 77.

51 Penrose, *The Home of the Surrealists*, p. 43.

52 Livingston, *Lee Miller: Photographer*, p. 54.

53 This is the statue of Mehmet Ali, Pasha of Egypt, in Kavála. Penrose used the image in a painting *Enemy the Sun* that he must also have made in the autumn of 1938 (see *The Friendly Surrealist*, p. 55). In the 1930s, wrapped statues can also be found in the work of photographers such as Herbert List, Berenice Abbott, Cartier-Bresson and Lee Miller herself.

54 Interview with the author, 2 August 1979.

55 My thanks to Yves Abrioux for this translation. (It sounds even better in French: 'Votre ouvrage, qui s'attache au coeur du monde, s'impose dans sa lucidité. On laisse à vous suivre un pays où la foi vire ou doute, où la dureté à la resignation, pour gagner une contrée merveilleuse où le principal retrouve son pavois. ... Nous aimons bien votre flegme fait de pudeur et d'assurance, votre résolution au pied de la muraille des désirs, et votre réserve modeste une fois la muraille abattue.')

5
'Subjective Cameras' – Humphrey Jennings and Mass-Observation

There is a photograph of Humphrey Jennings taken by Lee Miller in 1943, which shows him spotlit from behind, gazing past a cloud of smoke, which he has just exhaled. This is Jennings at the high point of his creative life, in the middle of making the series of wartime documentaries that have ensured his reputation as one of Britain's greatest film-makers. But those films were what they were because of the streams that fed into them from his earlier work in the 1930s, when he operated in many areas – as poet, critic, editor, painter and photographer, as well as film-maker. But his work was fragmentary and often left incomplete, almost as elusive as that cloud of smoke.

It is particularly difficult to come to any conclusions about Jennings' photography. Unlike Nash, Agar, Penrose or Miller, there is no archive where one can go to substantiate an assessment of his work. All that seems to exist is a handful of individual photographs which have survived as prints or reproductions and are disparate in subject and approach. Moreover, one cannot consider Jennings' photos in isolation, for they relate closely to ideas that he was developing through his involvement first with Surrealism and then Mass-Observation. Read in these contexts, Jennings' photographs are intriguing and suggestive. Before considering the pictures in detail, therefore, it is necessary to review how Jennings and some of his Surrealist colleagues made the shift to Mass-Observation in the months after the International Surrealist Exhibition in the summer of 1936.

In the autumn, a group of friends began to meet at the home of Charles Madge and his wife Kathleen Raine in Blackheath to develop issues raised by Surrealism in a more public direction. They included Madge and Raine, Humphrey and Cicely Jennings, Stuart Legg and David Gascoyne. Some of them had been centrally involved in the development of Surrealism in England; Jennings was on the organising committee for the 1936 exhibition and showed six works, while Gascoyne had at the age of eighteen written *A Short Survey of Surrealism*.[1] Madge and Raine were poets with an interest in Surrealism (though Madge was then a journalist on the *Daily Mirror*) while Legg was Jennings' colleague in the GPO Film Unit. As Gascoyne later described it, they were interested in 'a sounding of the English collective unconscious together with a particular atten-

me as English. I spent the summer of 1934 in the Soviet Union after an absence of 17 years. I can assure your readers that protection of the family in the Soviet Union is something totally different from the "protection of the family" in Victorian England.

In this connection, it may have escaped Mr. Woolf's notice that the families protected in the Soviet Union (by such trifles as economic equality for men and women, maternity allowances, abolition of unemployment, etc.) are the families of the whole people, Tartar and Uzbek no less than Russian. Victorian England gave limited protection to the families of the rich at the expense of thousands of workers' families—and relative protection to British families at the expense of millions of families in the colonies.

20 rue Sturm, Geneva. EDITH LUNN (Rothstein)

BROADTAIL AND ERMINE

SIR,—Major Van der Byl describes revolting cruelty to Karakul sheep in certain parts of Russia and Asia in his letter to you published December 12th.

In 1934 I visited some of the research institutes of animal husbandry in Russia, and also saw several flocks of Karakul sheep, although I did not actually visit the chief breeding centres.

I was much impressed by the high standard of skill in animal husbandry and the humane treatment of farm animals generally, although conditions were often primitive. In some respects the handling of stock was better than in this country.

This favourable impression alone would make me doubt the accuracy of Major Van der Byl's informant, but I was also specifically told by one of the research staff that stories of maltreatment of Karakul sheep had been deliberately fostered by trade rivals and were in fact baseless. He gave several reasons, other than humanitarian, to support his claim. Since the information was given me two years ago my memory may be faulty, but I believe the following to be correct. Artificial abortion is not practised because the difference in price between the foetal and newly born lamb is not sufficient to compensate for the injury and risk of death of the mother. Secondly, a large number of females and a small number of males are required annually to carry on the flock.

In order to improve or even maintain the standard of the flock, these must be carefully selected. If lambs are killed before birth, this selection cannot be made. A lamb with a really valuable skin is worth much more for breeding purposes than for slaughter.

Lastly, from internal evidence, the information supplied to Major Van der Byl savours more of "manufactured atrocity" than fact. Although I have some knowledge of the causes of abortion, I am not aware that beating sheep will produce it at will. I think it unlikely. Why should iron rods be specified if not just to "make our flesh creep"? And finally, if a lamb were produced by this treatment, it is extremely likely that it would be dead. How, then, could it be skinned alive?

School of Agriculture, ARTHUR WALTON
Cambridge University.

SIR,—In reply to your correspondent, it seems hardly necessary for me to say that I always make the fullest possible inquiries before giving publicity to any particular acts of cruelty. The Anti-Steel-Trap League of America, with whom I am co-operating, have now removed Broadtail from their White List of humane furs, after making their own inquiries. I also understand that our own R.S.P.C.A. are not recommending any lamb skins from India.

As regards Ermine, this is undoubtedly one of the cruellest of the trapped furs. I find that my distribution of Fur Crusade leaflets with White List of humane furs now averages 1,500 each week.

C. VAN DER BYL (MAJOR),
Wappenham, The Fur Crusade and Humane
Towcester, Northants. Trapping Campaign.

"JAMAICA"

SIR,—I am sorry that the heat of Lord Olivier's displeasure should make him displace quotation marks. Of the words, at least one of which he misquotes, in the second paragraph of his letter I attributed to him only two: on p. 81 of his book he concedes that "painstaking students" might extract something from stipendiary magistrates' reports and other unpublished official files—adding a footnote, "Parliamentary papers, C.O. papers in the Record office." This vagueness is unfortunately characteristic of his references to such important sources. Had I understood that the book claimed to cover the whole field of social and economic history I should have felt it my duty as a reviewer to be more severely critical. As it is, to deal fully with other points in his letter can only divert attention from what is of value and importance in his study of a special aspect of Jamaican social history

Elmhurst, Penn, W. M. MACMILLAN
High Wycombe.

ANTHROPOLOGY AT HOME

SIR,—Mr. Geoffrey Pyke suggested in your columns the other week that the constitutional crisis had begun to produce material for an anthropology of our own people.

Some days before the precipitation of the crisis, a group was formed for precisely this purpose. English anthropology, however, hitherto identified with "folk-lore," has to deal with elements so repressed that only what is admitted to be a first-class upheaval brings them to the surface. Such was the threatened marriage of the new "Father-of-the-people" to Mrs. Ernest Simpson. Fieldwork, i.e., the collection of evidence of mass wish-situations, has otherwise to proceed in a far more roundabout way than the anthropologist has been accustomed to in Africa or Australia. Clues to these situations may turn up in the popular phenomenon of the "coincidence." In fact it is probable that in the ultra-repressed condition of our society they can only materialise in this form, so mysterious in appearance. But the "mystery" is part of the mechanism of repression. It can be reduced scientifically into the constituent terms of the hidden wish, and referred back to the accepted principles of anthropology. These principles and those of psycho-analysis, and the sciences dealing with the behaviour of man, have been applied by the group to the Crystal Palace-Abdication symbolic situation.

The real observers in this case were the millions of people who were, for once, irretrievably involved in the public events. Only mass observations can create mass science. The group for whom I write is engaged in establishing observation points on as widely extended a front as can at present be organised. We invite the co-operation of voluntary observers, and will provide detailed information to anyone who wants to take part. CHARLES MADGE

6 Grotes Buildings, Blackheath, S.E.3.

Miscellany

COCONUT MOON

A PHILOSOPHY OF CANNIBALISM, IN THE NEW HEBRIDES

WHERE is Hog Harbour? The blackboard to my hand
slide on. For I have a brother, a black hard brother,
away in the jungles where no white bibbler ever goes.

Stamping, stamping it, stamp, oh lift now
the shapely charger of your two black feet
hand down and up, hurt spear, now stamp,
Stamp
and in the last thick *stacat* remember how
small rushes warm black blood,
(rushes that cut the hand). The small spear
gathers its way.
Oh gather together the terrible relic of our hate of our Heren
enemies.

Lift
Lift curled head for your fury
For the longing to kill, for the quivering shudder of death in
a chief
Circle the fire. Men hurling to rush,
Men stamp, retreat again.
Drum drumming drums drumming drunken
As the women shuffle and stomp; lift, one two, small feet,
slither in slots.
While the darkness wides the firelight swells

Fig 37 *New Statesman and Nation (*2 January 1937), page 12.

tion to what was implied by Lautréamont's expression "Poetry ought to made by all, not one"'.[2]

When the abdication of Edward VIII was announced on 10 December, the group imagined that, like themselves, the whole population 'marvelled at the open emergence of forces so powerful, and realized as never before the sway of superstition in the midst of science'.[3] As it happened, they were not the only ones engaged by such ideas and, on the 12 December, the *New Statesman and Nation* published a letter from the educationalist Geoffrey Pyke, proposing an analysis of the public reaction to the Abdication as 'an anthropological study of our own situation'.[4] This provoked Madge to write a letter to the *New Statesman*, published on 2 January, stating, 'Some days before the precipitation of the crisis, a group was formed for precisely this purpose' and inviting 'the co-operation of voluntary observers'.[5] Pyke did not reply, but for one man reading the magazine in the public library in Bolton, Lancashire, it caused great excitement. He was Tom Harrisson, who had gone there to look for his own poem 'Coconut Moon', which had in fact been printed immediately after Madge's letter (figure 37). It was this coincidental juxtaposition that would lead to the formation of Mass-Observation.

Harrisson's background was very different.[6] In his teens, he had been an accomplished ornithologist, which established early on his interest in the collection of visual 'facts'; he later said that the best instrument for anthropological fieldwork was a pair of earplugs. In 1932, at the age of 21, Harrisson led an anthropological expedition to Borneo, from where, in 1933, he went on to the island of Malekula in the New Hebrides. While there, he wrote the book *Savage Civilization*, which now seems almost to prefigure the postmodernist anthropology of fifty years later.[7] 'When the expedition was over,' wrote Harrisson in 1970, 'I determined to return to study the cannibals of Britain.'[8] In the New Hebrides, he had noticed the omnipresence of one western commodity – Sunlight soap made by Unilever. 'Unilever stemmed directly from William Lever. He was born and started business in Bolton. So I followed there.'[9] Harrisson arrived in Bolton in October 1936, where he later found himself reading Madge's letter.

Harrisson travelled to London to meet the Blackheath group and on 30 January, Madge, Jennings and he became the co-signatories of another letter in the *New Statesman*, announcing the formation of Mass-Observation to instigate an 'anthropology at home'.[10] 'Already', they wrote, 'we have fifty observers at work on two sample problems. We are further working out a complete plan of campaign, which will be possible when we have not fifty but 5,000 observers.' For the moment, Madge and Jennings worked from Blackheath collecting monthly reports from observers across the country, while Harrisson in Bolton gathered together a group to observe that one town in detail.

Kathleen Raine once succinctly described Mass-Observation as 'that strange half-poetic half-sociological expression of the pre-war years'.[11] Such double-barrelled attempts to conjure up the hybrid nature of Mass-Observation have been common. 'It was at once literary and scientific, realist and surrealist,

and Hugh Sykes Davies as just a more modern form of Romanticism and related back to a specifically English Romantic tradition of Wordsworth, Coleridge and Blake. (Of course, Paul Nash was of that mind as well.) Jennings' irritation boiled over in the review he wrote of the volume *Surrealism* edited by Read:

> To the real poet the front of the Bank of England may be as excellent a site for the appearance of poetry as the depths of the sea ... [Breton says] that Surrealism has replaced the 'coincidence' for the 'apparition' and that we must 'allow ourselves to be guided towards the unknown by this newest *promise*'. Now that is talking; and to settle Surrealism down as Romanticism only is to deny this promise. It is to cling to the apparition with its special 'haunt'. It is to look for ghosts only on battlements, and on battlements only for ghosts. 'Coincidences' have the infinite freedom of appearing anywhere, anytime, to anyone: in broad daylight to those whom we most despise in places we have most loathed: not even to *us* at all.[22]

At the same time, there was another factor operating on Jennings from another direction, for he was also profoundly uncomfortable with the dominant ideology of the GPO Film Unit, as articulated by its leader, John Grierson. In 1934, Grierson had written: 'I look on cinema as a pulpit and use it as a propagandist.'[23] Even for Grierson, this was an excessive statement and hardly matched the actual practice of the unit, where figures like W. H. Auden, Benjamin Britten and even Len Lye found a creative place to work. Still, while Grierson was in charge, education and social reform were the main aims of the unit and realism was the essential documentary tactic. Jennings as a Surrealist would have been profoundly sceptical both of a simplistic socialism and of a belief in an unreflexive realism. (Grierson, in his turn, was to be rather disparaging of Jennings: 'He was a minor poet ... stilted, I think, a little literary ... he was safely, safely sorry for the working class.')[24]

So, working with Madge, Jennings sought in Mass-Observation to make of Surrealism something other than romanticised escapism, and of documentary something other than realist usefulness. And that involved not compromise, but dialectic. As Nowell-Smith wrote, Jennings saw in Mass-Observation 'an opportunity of democratizing the discoveries of Surrealism and of representing popular subjectivity dialectically and in unromanticised form'.[25] This in turn engaged another set of dialectical opposites which, for Mass-Observation more generally, were immensely problematic: fact and fiction, science and art, the objective and the subjective.

'Our first concern is to collect data, not to interpret it', wrote Madge and Harrisson in their first publication in Spring 1937.[26] And in the essay 'Poetic Description and Mass-Observation', Madge remarked of one piece of observation: 'the observer has simply been a recording instrument of the facts'.[27] However, he continued by complicating that simple statement, 'The interest of the ... passage is (i) scientific, (ii) human, and therefore by implication (iii) poetic.' This seems to be a way to reinsert subjectivity alongside the objective statement of 'the facts'. Madge further commented that observations 'though subjective, became objective because the subjectivity of the observer is one of the facts under observation'.[28] In all its early publications, Mass-Observation veered between statements of a belief in objectivity and statements which suggest that is impossible (or at least improbable).

In their *First Year's Work*, produced early in 1938, Harrisson and Madge utilised a photographic metaphor to try to deal with this paradox:

> The Observers are the cameras with which we are trying to photograph contemporary life. The trained observer is ideally a camera with no distortion. Mass-Observation has always assumed that its untrained Observers would be *subjective* cameras, each with his or her own individual distortion. They tell us not what society is like, but what it looks like to them.[29]

As Ben Highmore remarked, 'in this Mass-Observation can be seen as generating a radically democratic project ... the potential for everyone ... to become "natives".'[30]

In order to channel the inescapable subjectivity of the viewer viewing, Madge conceived the idea of the 'dominant image', considered by the observer to have threaded its way most persistently through their mind during any one day: 'the image might present itself in the form of a photograph in a newspaper, then an incident in a film, thirdly perhaps an encounter in the street; in other words, the image was expected at least to verify itself through the medium of coincidence'.[31] One can see the relationship of this idea to 'objective chance' in the way that the Surrealist Robert Melville, then based in Birmingham, responded to it. On 26 April 1937,

> on the way to work, I noticed that the flagpoles on the roof of Lewis's multiple-store had just had a fresh coat of paint. It reminded me immediately of a scene in a film that had particularly interested me when I was a child ... A man was blundering through a tropical forest. A tall silver tree was lighting his path. He fell against it – it was a huge snake. On the same day, I saw a news item in the *Daily Herald*: '6-Foot Typist Dead in River' ... She was found in the Thames near Tower Bridge still in her pink dance dress. In some way, it made me think of one of Giacometti's surrealist sculptures ... It was a long, thin, headless figure in white marble and I called the dominant image of the day 'Long Pale Objects'.[32]

Melville mixes the interior and the exterior, the social and the personal, the popular and the avant-garde, in a way that would surely have entranced Humphrey Jennings.

Throughout the time he was involved with Mass-Observation, Jennings was taking photographs. According to his friend Allen Hutt (writing a profile of Jennings under the pseudonym 'George Pitman' in 1944), Jennings had taken up photography in 1934, when he joined the GPO Film Unit: 'Jennings quickly realized that to master the cinema meant among other things, mastering photography.'[33] (Like Penrose, he bought himself a 35mm Leica.) He worked with photography between 1935 and 1938 – the period when he actually moved away from film-making and engaged with Surrealism and then Mass-Observation. The devotion of his energies to film-making during the war meant there was no time for photography, but, according to his biographer Kevin Jackson, he later made about 200 photographs on a trip to Burma in 1947.[34]

One of the first projects of Mass-Observation in 1937 was to have their observers make out day reports for the twelfth day of each month. On 12 April, Jennings himself wrote a report; he was 'Day Survey Respondent no. 360, Male, Married, Film Director, Blackheath, London SE'.[35] He got up, had a bath, chatted with his wife and children over breakfast. The Jennings and the Madges lived near each other in Blackheath, and Jennings walked to Madge's house:

> Went round to back to let myself in. Crossing loggia noticed contrast of bicycles, old boxes and rubbish with sunny garden seen through round-headed arches. Nearly photographed one arch as I have experienced that in photographing from shadow through an arch into sunlight a curious optical effect is produced.

Inside, he did some tidying and typing while he and Madge talked. 'Then I sat on sofa under the window with sun streaming in and read Ch's new material which was difficult for me: too abstract. I looked through window at landscape through new yellow filter. Compared reality with what it would look like in a photo.'

Jennings went home for lunch and then returned to Madge's:

> Wandered into churchyard to take photo of tombs: as I was using filter I had to wait a long time for really good sun. Shot no good in the end because while waiting for sun I was afraid someone would come and complain of my photographing in churchyard. Walked again. Arrived about 2.30. As I rang bell I thought 'I suppose photography has to get more and more realistic as one gets older'.

Later, he went out with Madge: 'We walked across grass to Greenwich park. Ch. good on Lenin and table: I connected what he said about contemporary psychology with Nelson I suppose from looking down on Royal Naval Hospital.' In the evening, Jennings went into town to see the new film of *Romeo and Juliet* starring John Barrymore. 'Caught a tram home. Walking to house remembered the loggia arches and photographing tombs: both images reappearing in *Romeo and Juliet*. Decided to write up today. Wrote in pencil till 12.33.'

On this one day, then, in between conversations with friends and family, Jennings returns again and again to photography, musing on a number of issues. How does a photograph relate to the reality it records? Does it change our perception of that reality? What's its relationship to memory? And how do the impulses of the practitioner intersect with the ethical issues engaged by the medium? Evidently, he saw photography not only as recordative, but also transformative. (Indeed, the photo he took in that graveyard was eventually printed in negative.)[36]

It is instructive to place these personal reflections next to one of the few theoretical texts that Jennings wrote: the short essay 'Who Does That Remind You Of?', published in the *London Bulletin* in 1938.[37] On a basic level, says Jennings, the appeal of photography lies in its simplicity, democracy, reproducibility and apparent realism. But it goes deeper and, alongside his understanding of the ontological status of photography and its ethical demands, he places the complex psychology of the medium: 'Intellectually, the importance of the camera lies clearly in the way that it deals with problems of choice – choice and avoidance of choice.' Citing Freud's view that *déjà vu* 'corresponds to the memory of an unconscious fantasy', Jennings calls the camera 'an instrument for recording the object or image that prompted that memory. Hence the rush to see "how they come out".' It is also typical of Jennings that he should relate his subtle theoretical reading to an experience of photography which everyone in an industrialised society senses and yet hardly thinks about.

David Mellor has related Jennings' ideas here to Walter Benjamin's concept of the 'optical unconscious' – the seeming ability of photography to get beneath the surface of reality.[38] In the introduction to his unfinished work *Pandaemonium* (an opus which has also been compared with Benjamin's *Arcades* project),[39] Jennings wrote of what he called 'Images' (which in this case were not pictures but quotations from a wide range of writers): 'they contain in little a whole world – they are the knots in a great net of tangled time and space – the moments at which the situation of humanity is clear – even if only for the flash time of the photographer or the lightning'.[40] One can imagine that Jennings had a similar ambition for his actual photographs as he did for these metaphorical ones. In 1944, Jennings would say to his friend Allen Hutt, 'It's the whole question of imagination in an industrial society.'[41]

After Jennings' untimely death in 1950, an exhibition of his work was organised at the ICA. Writing in the *New Statesman*, a reviewer identified only as 'J. B.' (possibly the French Surrealist Jacques Brunius, domiciled in London?) wrote of Jennings:

> His sensitivity and imagination led him into, not away from the ordinary, effective world ... He looked for and often found, an urgent sense of purpose and meaning in the confusion of familiar appearances. In his excellent photographs ... he found it either by focusing attention on common, often ignored details – a child's scribble on a wall, the texture of wet bricks in a back street – or

> by examining the usual with a strange initiative – a gasometer seen from its top, the leaves of a tree lit up white at night, a vegetable marrow juxtaposed with an electric light-bulb.[42]

Some of these photographs are recognisable, others not, for only a rather disparate group of prints have survived. (Some images seem to exist now only as reproductions.) One cannot know how much is missing, but there is enough left to intrigue.[43] His experimental work with photomontage, printing in negative and studio set-ups does not centrally concern us here, important as they were for Jennings' own enquiries into the medium. However, concentrating on the small group of 'documentary' photographs with a connection to Mass-Observation, one can start to build up a suggestive sense of Jennings' photographic tactics.

The day of the Coronation, 12 May 1937, was the occasion for Mass-Observation's first attempt at 'mass' reportage. Jennings was again an observer roving round central London and his report would be incorporated in the book he subsequently edited of the event: *May 12: Mass-Observation Day Survey*.[44] He was also taking photographs and, in one picture, wittily brought together the resonance of English history and the inescapability of the industrial present (figure 38). It is taken looking up at the statue of Charles I, which stands at the head of Whitehall; this is the oldest surviving outdoor statue in London, occupying the site of the final Eleanor Cross, destroyed during the Commonwealth, and it was also the spot where the regicides were executed. We can be sure that Jennings would have known all this.[45] Here, however, the King is surrounded by loudspeakers which proclaim: FILM INDUSTRIES LTD, and perched on the

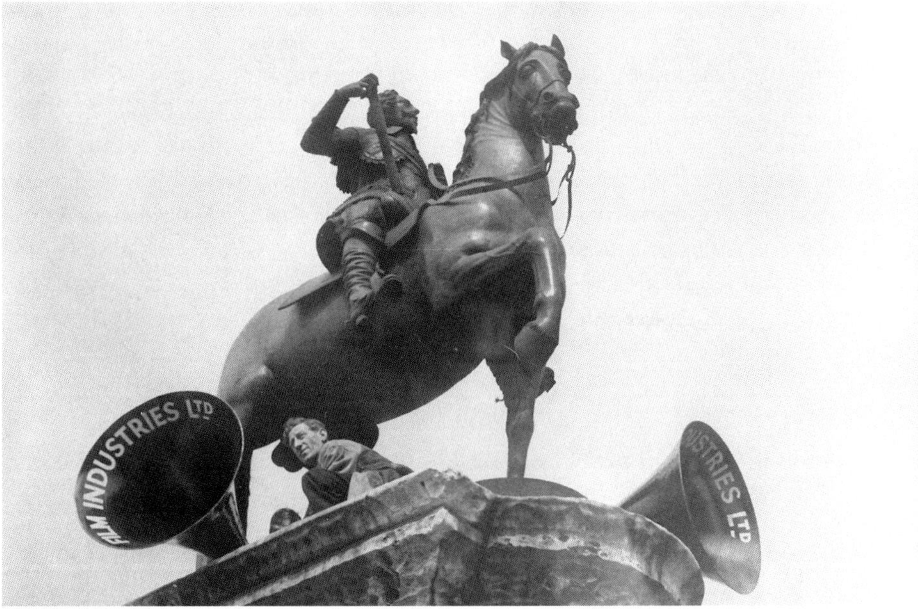

Fig 38 Humphrey Jennings, *Statue of Charles I, Whitehall*, 1937. © Mary-Louise Jennings.

base below him an anonymous man looks out in the opposite direction. (Is he a film technician or just a member of the public who has clambered up there for a better view?) The picture not only evokes the growing role of the media in public culture, and the ironies of its relationship with traditional values; for Jennings himself, it must also have been a comment on his own role in that process.

That photo does not feature in a montage that Jennings made of his own photographs from 12 May (figure 39). Perhaps it was too individually dramatic, for the montage is notably reticent. Jennings has placed twelve images together in a block, with the high culture of the statue of Achilles at top left and a gutter filled with rubbish at bottom centre. Jennings' tactics of looking away from the main event of the day parallel those of Henri Cartier-Bresson, who that day was also photographing the crowds on the Mall. The people are largely seen from behind – as a mass – and the photos form an overall and densely detailed pattern, packed with cultural information.

Jennings' montage can be seen as a microcosmic partner to the *May 12* book, which also borrowed the model of montage or film editing. Working with a vast amount of material, Jennings managed to cut it down into a book that is merely

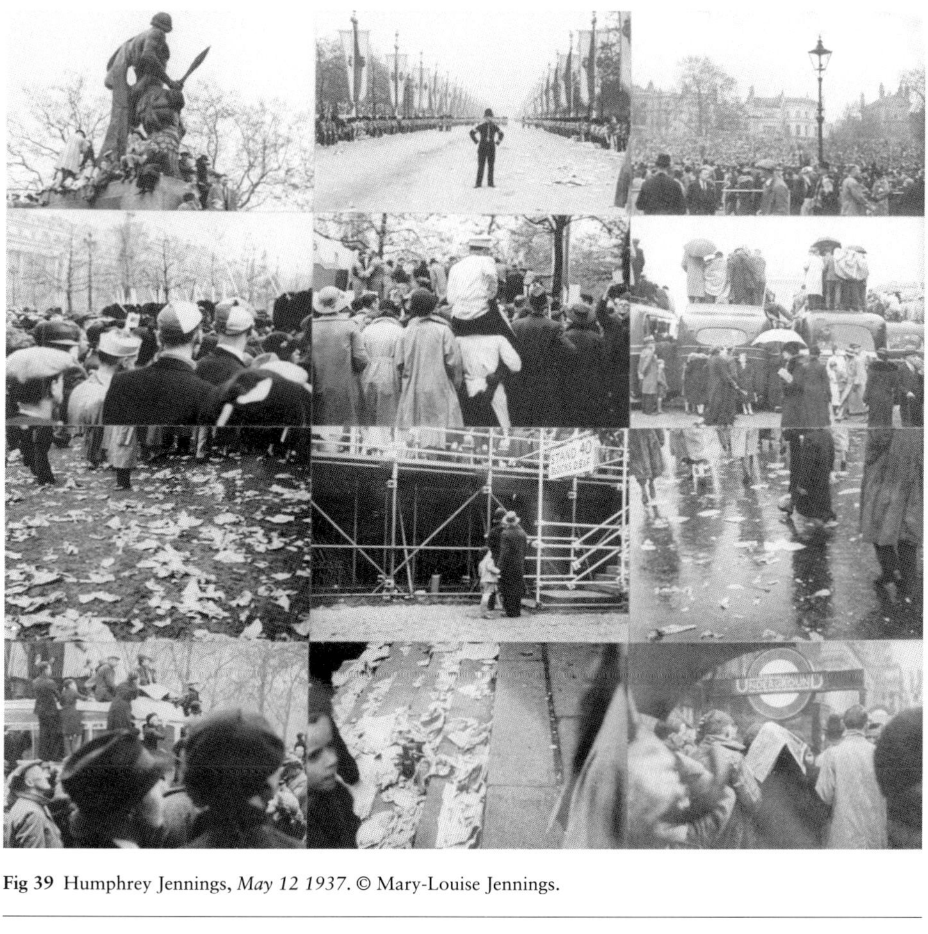

Fig 39 Humphrey Jennings, *May 12 1937*. © Mary-Louise Jennings.

sprawling. Sociologists have since been critical of its apparently random massing of material, as indeed was Tom Harrisson.[46] But that, in a way, is the point. It needs to be as large as it is and as unformed as it is to convey the sheer excess of the day, to pile up detail upon detail until one feels that there is at once far too much *and* never enough.

It is thus not a documentary in the Griersonian sense, which involves the cutting and shaping of raw material to make a narrative. Rather it is reminiscent of the modernist documentary form that had been developed in Russia by Dziga Vertov or, to take a literary example, a book such as John Dos Passos' *USA*.[47] (It is unclear whether Jennings knew of Dos Passos' work at this time, but in a letter to his wife in 1944, he says he is reading *Manhattan Transfer*.)[48] Carol Shloss has connected Dos Passos and the Russian cinema, saying 'Their raw material, like his own, was the cultural fragment: their aim, as his own came to be, was to weld "into a sentient whole the rigid honeycomb of our pigeonholed lives".'[49] As much could also be said for Jennings' ambitions with *May 12*. If it was a failure, it was on the grand scale. It was also, according to Madge, 'the first and last time Humphrey contributed to a Mass-Observation publication'.[50]

One does not usually associate Jennings with Bolton – that was Harrisson's territory – but he did go there in 1937 and the experience was pivotal for him. When his friend Allen Hutt published his profile of Jennings in 1944, he began with comments which obviously drew upon Jennings' own recollections:

> At 5 a.m. one summer day in the middle nineteen-thirties, a young man, with a Leica slung over his shoulder, stepped out of the station at Bolton and took his first look at that typical Lancashire manufacturing town. He saw more than Bolton; the vision of mill-stacks and operatives' dwelling-boxes introduced him to an England he had not known before – the land of industry, of the factory and of the working-class.
>
> That was perhaps the most important turning-point in the life of Humphrey Jennings ... Bolton, and the months he spent there working with Mass-Observation, living in an unemployed spinner's house, and avidly attacking the classics like Engels' *Condition of the Working Class in England*, brought Jennings (as he himself says) from medievalism into modern times.[51]

Some of this is, of course, pure exaggeration. One could hardly describe Jennings' activities with Surrealism as 'medievalism' and he certainly did not spend 'months' living in 'an unemployed spinner's house'. Rather, his visits to Bolton seem to have been brief and sporadic. (Humphrey Spender recalled being in the same room with Jennings but they had no interchange.[52]) But there is no reason to doubt the importance of this first experience of industrialisation for Jennings, who, like most men of his class and education, had no first-hand experience of its actuality.

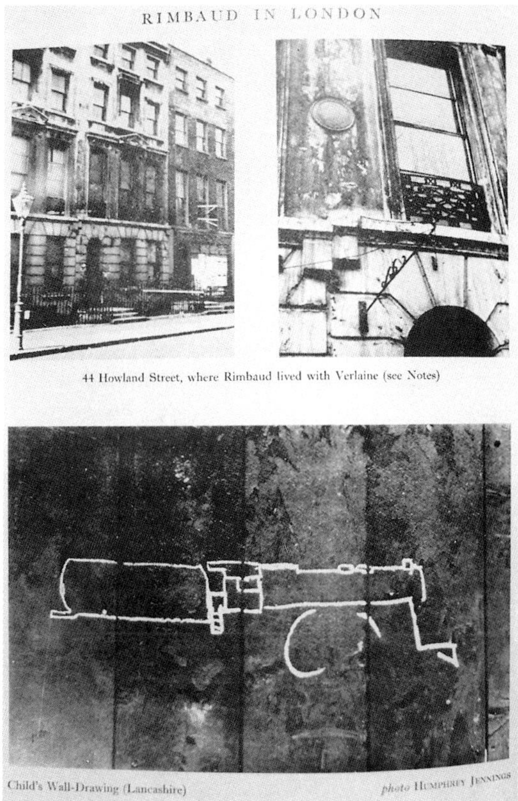

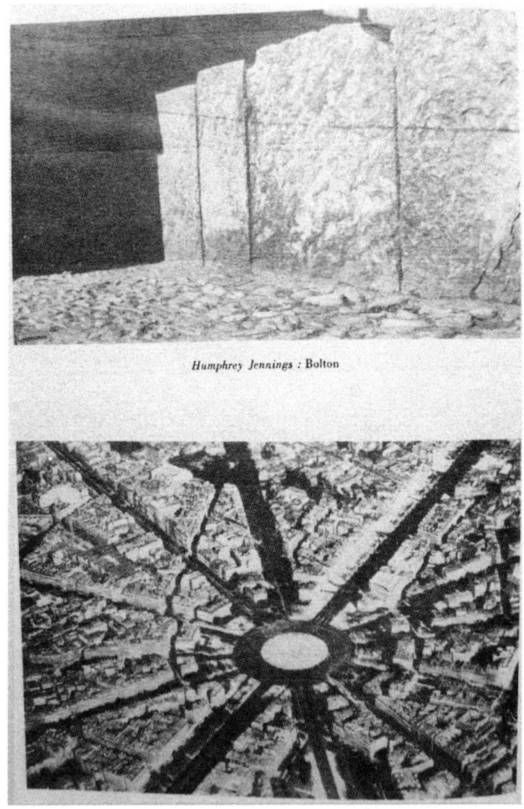

Fig 40 [*left*] 'Rimbaud in London' *London Bulletin*, 4-5 (July 1938). Humphrey Jennings, 'Child's Wall-Drawing (Lancashire)', © DACS 2006.

Fig 41 [*right*] Page from André Breton and Paul Eluard (eds), *Dictionnaire Abregé du Surréalisme*, 1938. Humphrey Jennings, 'Bolton', © DACS 2006; Max Ernst, 'La place de l'Etoile', © ADAGP, Paris and DACS, London.

Three photographs taken by Jennings in Bolton were reproduced in Surrealist publications, two of them in the *London Bulletin*. In one case, Jennings' image of a child's wall drawing of what is probably a railway engine but may be a gun (a potent confusion) was juxtaposed with photographs of the house in Howland Street where Rimbaud and Verlaine had lived (figure 40).[53] This connection would, for the Surrealists, have evoked Rimbaud's famous litany of disregarded aspects of popular culture: 'I liked stupid paintings ... signs, popular engravings ... ridiculous refrains, naive rhythms.'[54] Such also was the meaning of graffiti for the Surrealists, as an eruption of the repressed 'id' of the city, and Kathleen Raine wrote of Charles Madge: 'He saw the expression of the unconscious collective life of England literally in writings on the walls, telling of the hidden thoughts and dreams of the inarticulate masses.'[55] In Bolton, graffiti was also a significant subject for Harrisson and Spender.

The second Jennings photograph in *London Bulletin* was the image of a 'Persil' poster juxtaposed with Paul Nash's *Nocturnal Landscape* (figure 1, p. 6).

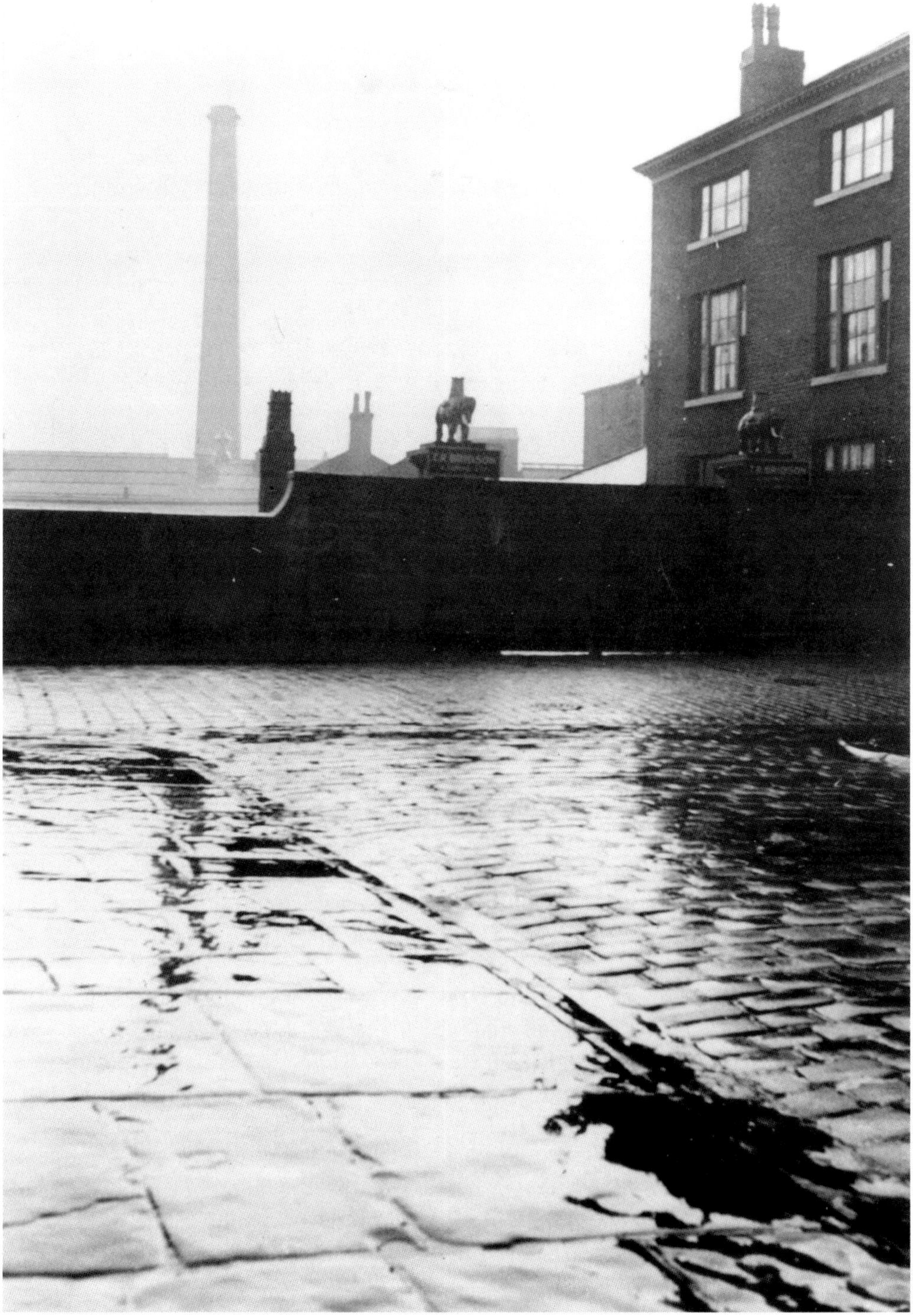

Fig 42 Humphrey Jennings, *Elephant Gate, Bolton*, 1939. Collection of Bolton Museums and Art Gallery. © DACS 2006.

This is one of many pictures by Surrealist-influenced documentary photographers of the period that juxtaposed the fantastic world of the billboard with the banality of reality. Others used such juxtapositions for political effect – one thinks particularly of the American photographers of the depression. (We know that Jennings had a copy of Walker Evans' *American Photographs*, published in 1938, in his library.[56]) It is also possible to read a political dimension into Jennings' picture, for the industrial landscape literally sits behind the seductive facade of consumerism which masks the actuality of how that desirable product is produced. Industrialisation hardly appeared in Parisian Surrealism for André Breton simply abhored the idea of work.[57] But Jennings (and Mass-Observation more generally) understood that new insights were possible by reading the industrial through Surrealism.

Jennings also had established links with the Parisian Surrealists and in 1938, another of his northern photographs was published in the *Dictionnaire abregé du Surréalisme*, edited by Breton and Eluard.[58] There, again, two very different pictures were juxtaposed (figure 41). Above was a crude wall made by slabs of stone seemingly blocking off a cobblestoned street: this was credited 'Humphrey Jennings: *Bolton*'. Below it was 'La place de l'Etoile' in Paris, photographed

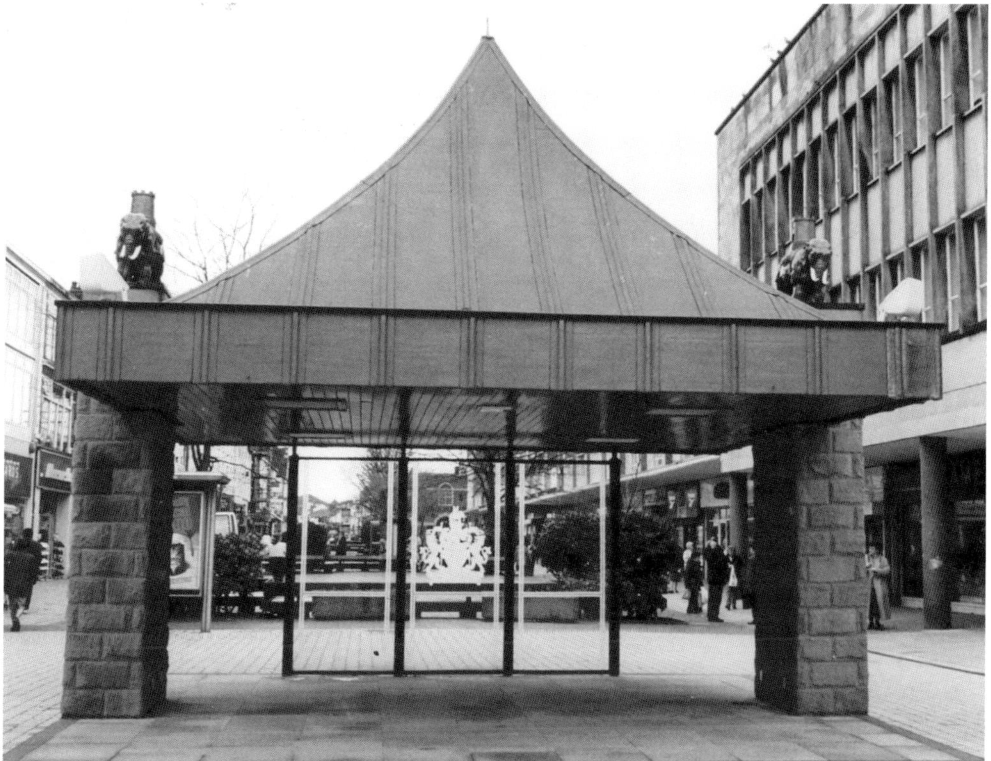

Fig 43 Ian Walker, *Bolton*, 2005. © Ian Walker.

from the air, but with the Arc de Triomphe 'removed'.[59] The contrast is striking – between a side-street in an industrial town and the ceremonial centre of a great city, and, formally, between the solid square stone blocks set on the ground and the elegant wheel of the Etoile seen from above. But without the title *Bolton*, one would be hard pushed to know where Jennings' photograph had been taken. There is no sense of context, the site could be urban or rural and the stones have a rough, primitive quality – almost like megaliths – which contrasts with the cultured setting of the Parisian right bank. Their crude solidity ironically echoes the block of the Arc de Triomphe which has been removed from the lower image.

Though these two images by Jennings – the Persil advert in the *London Bulletin* and the stones in the *Dictionnaire* – are otherwise very different, they have in common the way their meanings are created by the cutting of the image frame, what it includes and what it excludes. In the one case, a relationship is created between chimney and advert; in the other, the wall is cut off from whatever might explain its presence. Few images as we have by Jennings, these two examples nevertheless demonstrate that he well understood that documentary involves creation as well as reproduction.

Bolton Art Gallery owns a photograph by Jennings that shows the entrance to Bridson's Bleachworks, its gateposts topped by two elephants (figure 42). One can understand why Jennings would be so intrigued by the apparition of these exotic beasts on this grim street on this rainy day. (Those elephants are still in Bolton. When the Bleachworks were demolished in 1977, they were placed on a pavilion next to the main square (figure 43).) But why did Jennings stand so far away, making the elephants very small in the image? Why did he not move to the left so that we could see both elephants clearly? These are the simple mistakes of an amateur photographer and maybe that is what Jennings was. But perhaps his placement was deliberate and strategic – perhaps he wanted the obscurity, wanted the elephants to be almost lost in the townscape around them and wanted to capture that gleaming expanse of wet pavement in the foreground. Perhaps, here he was happy to sacrifice resolution for atmosphere.[60]

As we have seen, the Surrealists were fascinated by such hybrid, indefinable places – the *terrains vagues* that lay beyond the town centre.[61] Jennings found this uncertain landscape in industrial England. But the urban wasteland also featured large in British culture between the wars. T. S. Eliot's *The Waste Land* inspired a generation of artists and poets (like the young Louis MacNeice) who might never actually wish to visit such a landscape. This could cause a certain amount of sarcasm. Walking alongside the Tyne in 1933, J. B. Priestley was moved to comment: 'If T. S. Eliot ever wants to write a poem about a real wasteland instead of a metaphysical one, he should come up here.'[62] In the 1930s, these scenes of industrial dereliction came in turn to be known as 'Auden country', as W. H. Auden 'refined and systematically developed in his poems the idea of the landscape of Britain as semi-derelict'.[63] So ingrained was 'Auden country' in the consciousness of the decade that it could be parodied in Nicholas Blake's detective

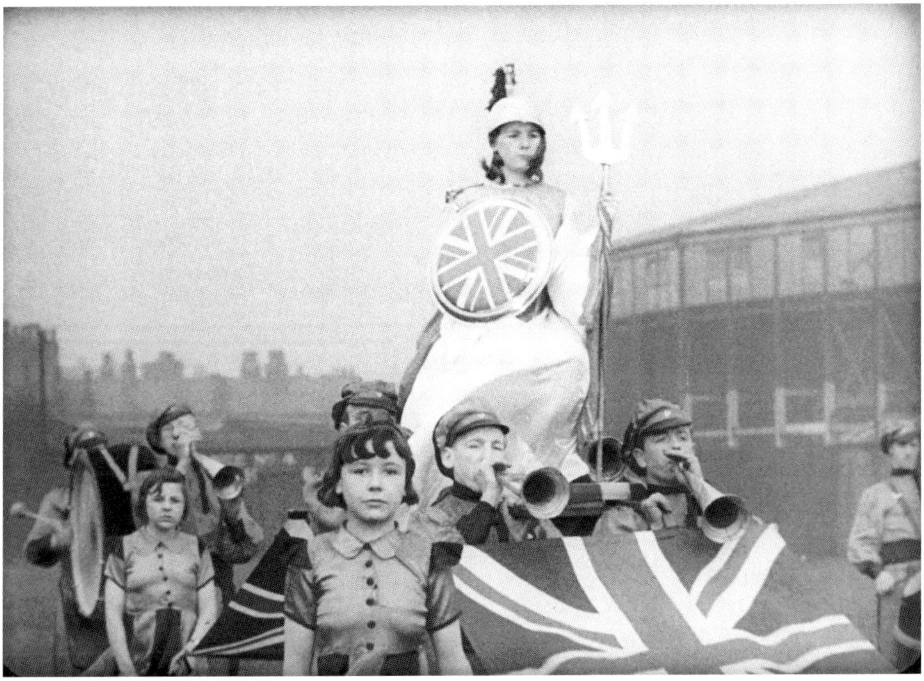

Fig 44 Humphrey Jennings, frame still from *Spare Time*, 1939.

story *Malice in Wonderland*, where the young Mass-Observer Mr Perry, travelling on a train past rusting factories, muses: 'There might be a certain romantic aspect in their decay; but with all deference to the early Auden, whose weakness for rusting metal and escaping steam was a notorious instance of the foibles of genius, one must insist that such fatal romanticism would not do.'[64]

We can again assume that Jennings would have known the photographs of Atget and Lotar as well as the poems of Eliot and Auden. His work, like that of Nash in a different context, brings together continental Surrealist influences and English culture and his insistence on a faithful reading of Bretonian Surrealism sits side by side with his fascination with concepts of Englishness. But he also pushes at the limits of both these positions. In his essay for Read's 1936 volume, Breton had written, 'Human psychism in its most universal aspect has found in the Gothic castle and its accessories a point of fixation so precise that it becomes essential to discover what would be the equivalent for our period. (Everything leads to believe that there is no question of it being a factory.)'[65] Probably not actually *in* the factory, but Jennings' photographs suggest that it need not be very far away, and in this he challenged the distaste of both Parisian Surrealism and English traditionalism for industrial labour.

The photograph of Bolton on a rainy day has been dated 1939, two years after Jennings first went there for Mass-Observation. If that dating is correct, it means it was taken when he returned to shoot some scenes for his film *Spare Time*.[66] Jennings had returned to the GPO Film Unit in 1938, when Grierson left for Canada to set up the National Film Board and his job passed to Alberto Cavalcanti. Cavalcanti's background was very different. Brazilian by birth, he had worked in the French avant-garde cinema in the 1920s and had an understanding of Surrealism. Elizabeth Sussex's remark that Cavalcanti's 'vision is surrealist rather than realist, and always therefore had the virtue of avoiding sentimentality' suggests the sympathy that he and Jennings would have had for each other's positions.[67] In 1939, he gave Jennings the job of directing what would be his first significant film.

Spare Time is often referred to as Jennings' 'Mass-Observation film', even though he no longer had any formal connections with the organisation. The film's theme is succinctly stated in the commentary by Laurie Lee: 'Between work and sleep comes the time we call our own. What do we do with it?' It concentrates on three industries in three places, each represented by a popular form of music. The first is steel in Sheffield and centres on a brass-band rehearsal. The last is coal in South Wales and features a male voice choir (of course). But it was the central sequence that caused the fuss. Filmed in Manchester, it featured a kazoo 'jazz band' rehearsing on yet another industrial wasteland (figure 44). As Dai Vaughan describes it, 'Photographed in a directionless grey light which emphasizes nothing, a formation of girls in shapeless and timeless grey trouser-suits parade in honour of a Britannia whose costume flaps in the wind as listlessly as a torn poster on a hoarding'.[68]

When the film was shown, this sequence caused great anger in documentary film circles. Basil Wright remembered, 'Humphrey seemed to show, in our opinion a patronizing, sometimes almost sneering attitude towards the efforts of the lower-income groups to entertain themselves.'[69] It would seem that, in the context of humanist documentary, a film that was not laudatory in its image of the working class was thought to be negative. But can one in fact tell – just from watching the film – what Jennings' attitude is to the kazoo band? If anything, the gaze of the camera in this sequence is steady, flat and rather neutral. Perhaps it was actually that impassive neutrality which unnerved the film's first viewers and it is an attitude that Jennings may have picked up from Surrealist documentary – Boiffard's photographs in *Nadja* or Buñuel's film *Land without Bread*.[70] Though it must be admitted that this gaze was that of an outsider, nevertheless, it did not necessarily assume a position of superiority.

In 1939, Jennings still had his major work ahead of him. When, after his death, the Cinémathèque Française mounted a season of films: 'Hommage au GPO Film Unit', the anonymous author of the publicity brochure made the comment: 'Humphrey Jennings était, pour les Anglais, leur Prévert.'[71] It seems a surprising comparison because the work of Humphrey Jennings and Jacques Prévert are so far apart – quintessentially English and French, we might say. Yet, upon reflection, the comparison is intriguing. Both were men whose intellectual and artistic beginnings were in the avant-garde and particularly in Surrealism. But both, without abandoning those foundations, moved into the heart of the popular culture of their retrospective countries. Jennings' wartime documentaries, Prévert's 'poetic realist' film scripts and book of poems *Paroles* now seem woven into their respective cultures, essential to their mythic sense of themselves.[72] Brian Winston called Jennings a 'Surrealist who became an arch-realist'.[73] But, in Jennings' case, the two ways of thinking always coexisted, too intimately bound together ever to be disentangled.

Notes

1 David Gascoyne, *A Short Survey of Surrealism* (London: Cobden-Sanderson, 1935).

2 David Gascoyne, *Journal 1936–37* (London: Enitharmon Press, 1980), p. 11.

3 Charles Madge and Tom Harrisson, *Mass-Observation* (London: Frederick Muller, 1937), p. 10.

4 Geoffrey Pyke, 'King and Country', *New Statesman and Nation*, 12:303 (12 December 1936), 974.

5 Charles Madge, 'Anthropology at Home', *New Statesman and Nation,* 13:306 (2 January 1937), 12.

6 For a biography of Harrisson, see Judith M. Heimann, *The Most Offending Soul Alive: Tom Harrisson and his Remarkable Life* (London: Aurum Press, 2002).

7 Tom Harrisson, *Savage Civilization* (London: Victor Gollancz, 1937). See also Gareth Stanton, 'In Defence of *Savage Civilization*: Tom Harrisson, Cultural Studies and Anthropology', in Stephen Nugent and Chris Shore (eds), *Anthropology and Cultural Studies* (London: Pluto Press, 1997), pp. 11–33.

8 Tom Harrisson, 'Preface', in Mass-Observation, *The Pub and The People* (Welwyn Garden City: Seven Dials Press, 1970), p. 5.

9 Tom Harrisson, *World Within: A Borneo Story* (London: Cresset Press, 1959), p. 159.

10 Tom Harrisson, Humphrey Jennings and Charles Madge, 'Anthropology at Home', *New Statesman and Nation*, 13:310 (30 January 1937), 155.

11 Kathleen Raine, *The Land Unknown* (London: Hamish Hamilton, 1975), p. 81.

12 Samuel Hynes, *The Auden Generation* (London: Bodley Head, 1976), p. 279.

13 Quoted in Anthony W. Hodgkinson and Rodney E. Sheratsky, *Humphrey Jennings: More than a Maker of Films* (Hanover: University Press of New England, 1982), p. 35.

14 Charles Madge, 'The Birth of Mass-Observation', *Times Literary Supplement* (5 November 1976), 1395. It is not possible to give an adequate account here of the difficult relationship between Mass-Observation and anthropology; see Jeremy MacClancy, 'Brief Encounter: The Meeting, in Mass-Observation, of British Surrealism and Popular Anthropology', *Journal of the Royal Anthropological Institute*, 1:3 (September 1995), 495–512.

15 Geoffrey Nowell-Smith, 'Humphrey Jennings: Surrealist Observer', in Charles Barr (ed.), *All Our Yesterdays: 90 Years of British Cinema* (London: British Film Institute, 1986), p. 324.

16 A Midwife, 'Anthropology at Home', *New Statesman and Nation,* 13:311 (6 February 1937), 201.

17 Charles Madge, 'Surrealism for the English', *New Verse* 6 (1933), 14–8, and 'The Meaning of Surrealism', *New Verse*, 10 (1934), 13–5.

18 Raine, *The Land Unknown*, p. 81.

19 Madge, 'The Meaning of Surrealism', 15. This is a review of Hugnet's *Petite Anthologie du surréalisme*.

20 Trevelyan archive, Trinity College Library, Cambridge, JOT 2/20: Letter from Humphrey Jennings in Cambridge, undated (c.1932).

21 Interview with Roland Penrose by Kevin Daly, 1981, quoted by Kevin Jackson, *Humphrey Jennings* (London: Picador, 2004), p. 159.

22 *Contemporary Poetry and Prose*, 8 (December 1936), reprinted in Kevin Jackson (ed.), *The Humphrey Jennings Film Reader* (Manchester: Carcanet, 1993), p. 220.

23 John Grierson, 'Propaganda', *Sight and Sound*, 2 (Winter 1933–34), 119. For a broader view, see Ian Aitken, *Film and Reform: John Grierson and the Documentary Film Movement* (London: Routledge, 1990).

24 Elizabeth Sussex, *The Rise and Fall of British Documentary* (Berkeley: University of California Press, 1975), pp. 110–1.

25 Nowell-Smith, 'Humphrey Jennings: Surrealist Observer', p. 324.

26 Madge and Harrisson, *Mass-Observation*, p. 34.

27 Charles Madge and Humphrey Jennings, 'Poetic Description and Mass-Observation', *New Verse*, 24 (February–March 1937), 2. The credits here are actually given as 'Examples collected by H.J., write-up by C.M.' The example referred to is an often cited contretemps on a Midland Red bus.

28 Madge and Jennings, 'Poetic Description and Mass-Observation', 3.

29 Tom Harrisson and Charles Madge (eds), *First Year's Work* (London: Lindsay Drummond, London, 1938), p. 66.

30 Ben Highmore, *Everyday Life and Cultural Theory* (London and New York: Routledge, 2002), p. 87.

31 Charles Madge, 'Oxford Collective Poem', *New Verse*, 25 (May, 1937), 17.

32 Interview in the film *Stranger than Fiction*, directed by Ian Potts (London: British Film Institute, 1985). Melville was then a member of the Surrealist group in Birmingham (see Tessa Sidey, *Surrealism in Birmingham 1935–1954* (Birmingham: Birmingham Museums and Art Gallery, 2001)).

33 George Pitman, 'Man in Our Time no. 8: Humphrey Jennings', *Our Time*, 3:12 (July 1944), 12–3.

34 Jackson, *Humphrey Jennings*, p. 328.

35 Jennings' day survey is in the Mass-Observation Archive, University of Sussex. It was reproduced as Appendix Two in Nick Stanley, *The Extra Dimension* (Birmingham Polytechnic: unpublished PhD dissertation, 1981), pp. 285–93. Extracts were reprinted in Mary-Lou Jennings (ed.), *Humphrey Jennings: Film-maker, Painter, Poet* (London: British Film Institute, 1982), pp. 17–18.

36 The negative photograph is reproduced in Mary-Lou Jennings (ed.), *Humphrey Jennings*, p. 18.

37 *London Bulletin*, 6 (October 1938), 21–2. The essay is reprinted in Mary-Lou Jennings (ed.), *Humphrey Jennings*, pp. 19–20, and Jackson (ed.), *The Humphrey Jennings Film Reader*, pp. 230–1.

38 David Mellor, 'Sketch for an Historical Portrait of Humphrey Jennings' in Mary-Lou Jennings (ed.), *Humphrey Jennings*, p. 68.

39 For example, Jackson, *Humphrey Jennings*, p. 379, and Hodgkinson and Sheratsky, *Humphrey Jennings*, pp. 89–90.

40 'Introduction', in Humphrey Jennings, *Pandaemonium* (London: André Deutsch, 1985), p. xxxv.

41 Pitman, 'Man in Our Time', 13.

42 J. B., 'Humphrey Jennings', *New Statesman and Nation* (3 March 1951), 246.

43 There are sixteen prints in the Victoria and Albert Museum and four in Bolton Art Gallery. Others are held in private collections.

44 Humphrey Jennings and Charles Madge (eds), *May 12: Mass-Observation Day Survey* (London: Faber & Faber, 1937). In the published version, Jennings' account is cut up; he is CM1. The original report is in the Mass-Observation Archive, University of Sussex and was reproduced in Stanley, *The Extra Dimension*, pp. 294–313.

45 The statue also later appears in his poetic evocation of the Blitz, *I See London*: 'I see in mind's eye the statue of Charles the First riding in double darkness of night and corrugated iron' (see Jackson, *The Humphrey Jennings Film Reader*, pp. 296–7).

46 Harrisson wrote to Geoffrey Gorer in 1938 that 'it was a crazy idea to have it edited by a whole bunch of intellectual poets' (quoted by David Pocock in his 'Afterword' to the 1987 reprint of *May 12*, p. 418). For Harrisson's retrospective view of Jennings, see Anthony W. Hodgkinson, 'Humphrey Jennings and Mass-Observation: a conversation with Tom Harrisson', *Journal of the University Film Assocation*, 27:4 (fall 1975), 31–5.

47 The three parts of *USA* were published in 1930, 1932 and 1936 respectively, and they appeared in one volume in 1938.

48 Letter to Cicely Jennings, 14 February 1944, in Jackson (ed.) *The Humphrey Jennings Film Reader*, p. 92.

49 Carol Shloss, *In Visible Light: Photography and the American writer 1840–1940* (New York: Oxford University Press, 1987), p. 149.

50 Madge, 'The Birth of Mass-Observation', 1395.

51 Pitman, 'Man in Our Time', 12.

52 Jackson, *Humphrey Jennings*, p. 186.

53 *London Bulletin*, 4–5 (July 1938), 22. (On the opposite page, there is appropriately a 'Hommage à Freud', who had arrived in London the month before.) The pictures of Howland Street were probably taken just before the house was demolished; the Post Office Tower stands on this site now. The original prints are in the Scottish National Gallery of Modern Art: Penrose collection, File 0970.

54 Arthur Rimbaud, *A Season in Hell*, Part II: 'Alchemy of the Word', translated by Wallace Fowlie in *Complete Works, Selected Letters* (Chicago: University of Chicago Press, 1966), p. 193.

55 Raine, *The Land Unknown*, p. 81.

56 My thanks to Charlotte Jennings for this information.

57 Talking to Nadja, Breton launches into a long diatribe on the subject: 'People cannot be interesting insofar as they endure their work … How I loathe the servitude people try to hold up to me as being so valuable' (*Nadja* (New York: Grove Press, 1960), p. 68). It is hard to imagine anything further from Jennings' feelings.

58 André Breton and Paul Eluard (eds), *Dictionnaire Abregé du Surréalisme* (Paris: Galerie des Beaux-Arts, 1938), p. 58.

59 Though anonymous, this image had been made by Max Ernst and published in *Variétés* in 1929, where it was juxtaposed with another aerial photograph of the Montparnasse cemetery (see Ian Walker, *City Gorged with Dreams* (Manchester: Manchester University Press, 2002), p. 42).

60 There is another photograph Jennings must have taken on the same day, which pushes this

irresolution even further; it is reproduced in Jackson (ed.) *The Humphrey Jennings Film Reader*, illus. 9.

61 On the Paris *terrain vague*, see Walker, *City Gorged with Dreams*, pp. 114–43.

62 J. B. Priestley, *English Journey* (London: William Heinemann, 1934), p. 310.

63 David Mellor, 'Mass-Observation: The Intellectual Climate', *Camerawork*, 11 (September 1978), 5.

64 Nicholas Blake, *Malice in Wonderland* (London: Collins, 1940), p. 11. There is a sly in-joke here, since Nicholas Blake was the pseudonym of the poet Cecil Day-Lewis and his detective hero Nigel Strangeways was based on his friend Auden.

65 Breton, 'Limits not Frontiers of Surrealism' in Herbert Read (ed.), *Surrealism* (London: Faber & Faber, 1936), p. 112.

66 There is a photograph by Jennings in the Victoria and Albert Museum of the top of a gasometer, which replicates a shot near the start of *Spare Time*, indicating that he was still at that point taking still photographs alongside his film work.

67 'Calvacanti in England', *Sight and Sound*, 44:4 (Autumn, 1975), 188, reprinted in part in Kevin Macdonald and Mark Cousins (eds), *Imagining Reality: The Faber Book of Documentary* (London: Faber & Faber, 1996), p. 116. See also Ian Aitken, *Alberto Cavalcanti: Realism, Surrealism and National Cinema* (Trowbridge: Flick Books, 2000).

68 Dai Vaughan, *Portrait of an Invisible Man* (London: British Film Institute, 1983), p. 37.

69 Sussex, *The Rise and Fall of British Documentary*, p. 110.

70 Though Jennings would have known *Nadja* well, there is no evidence that he knew *Land without Bread*. However, it is possible that he would have seen it when it was shown in London by the Film Society on 15 November 1937, or when it had a four-month run in Paris in 1936–37. (My thanks to Paul Hammond for this information.)

71 *Hommage au GPO Film Unit* (Paris: La Cinémathèque Française, no date), p. 14. (A copy is in the Jennings collection of the British Film Institute, File 20.)

72 *Spare Time* was first shown in London as support for Marcel Carné's 'poetic realist' film *Hotel du Nord*. It must have made a compelling comparison. (A copy of the cinema brochure is also in the BFI Jennings collection, File 20.)

73 Brian Winston, '*Fires were Started–*' (London: British Film Institute, 1999), p. 10.

6
Up north – Spender, Trevelyan and Brandt

In the 1938 Mass-Observation book *First Year's Work*, Bolton is called 'Northtown'.[1] This is an alternative to the more usual 'Worktown', though in the imagined geography of England, 'Northtown' and 'Worktown' mean much the same thing. The north is where the work gets done. These names operate in the tradition established by the great industrial novels of the mid-nineteenth century where, in Dickens' *Hard Times*, Preston became 'Coketown' and, in Mrs Gaskell's *North and South*, Manchester was 'Milton' (Milltown).[2]

All these names are, of course, meant to make these places stand for more than themselves. As Philip Dodd put it: '"The North" is less a number of particular places with specific histories than a Lowryscape, a settled place with an agreed iconography.'[3] But L. S. Lowry's paintings were already nostalgic for an industrial North whose iconography had been established for over a century. In *North and South*, the heroine Margaret Hale is forced by her father's changed circumstances to move from an idyllic village in the New Forest to Milton. But she feels 'almost a detestation for all she had ever heard of the North of England, the manufacturers, the people, the wild and bleak country'.[4] These three aspects would continue to be characteristic of the 'North' – it is industrial, inhabited by the working-class, and the urban desolation is matched by the harshness of the landscape. (Here *Wuthering Heights* can be added to the mix.)

It is, moreover, a place where light seems in short supply. In *North and South*, Lancashire is renamed 'Darkshire'. And whenever we hear William Blake's famous phrase 'dark satanic mills', we will almost certainly bring to mind an image of the mill-towns of the north. This is ironic, since Blake himself never travelled further north than Hampstead Heath and was most likely thinking of the new factories being built in London.[5] But for later generations, the phrase came to reinforce the space between the 'green and pleasant land' of the south and the 'dark satanic mills' of the north.

Evidently, this 'North' does not and cannot exist on its own – it is always placed in relationship to the 'South'. As Steve Edwards observed, 'North and South constitute two halves of an equation; they always presuppose each other and cannot be understood outside of their opposition.'[6] Even when the intention is to create a sense of social unity, the result still seems to emphasise difference.

The film *Nightmail*, produced by the GPO Film Unit in 1936, depicts the journey of the Postal Special train from London to Scotland and celebrates the way it brings the country together. Yet south and north are seen quite differently. The train travels through southern England in daylight but by the time it is moving through Lancashire, it is night and we see only the black massed shapes of industrial buildings and hear a litany of town names and their associated industries. The differing depiction of south and north may well have been the result of the train's actual journey, but this does not prevent it from also having a powerful ideological undertow.

Finally, this relationship between north and south has never been equal and reciprocal. Rob Shields has argued that in George Orwell's *The Road to Wigan Pier*, 'the *authority* to pronounce upon the "real" character of the British North is implicitly based on being not just a foreigner seeing the landscape with new eyes but a foreigner from "the South". Significantly, being from the North would not give one the same sort of authority to pronounce upon the character of the South.'[7] Thus one finds, again and again, visitors to the North remarking on its *strangeness*. Orwell, for example, wrote that 'when you go to the industrial North [the you is obviously another Southerner like himself] you are conscious, quite apart from the unfamiliar scenery, of entering a strange country'.[8]

It seems that to travel north was to travel to somewhere that was not really England at all: 'There is a real sense in which this excluded England is England's Other.'[9] And it is possible to read the books that were written during the 1930s about the North as 'travel books', parallel to those produced by other travellers at the time who had chosen the Mediterranean instead.[10] But one book was atypical in a number of respects, being neither just a tour of rural England (like Morton's *In Search of England*) nor a southerner's visit to the North (like *The Road to Wigan Pier*). This is J. B. Priestley's *English Journey*, published in 1934.[11] Though he visits his share of county towns, the last half of the book is spent in the industrial north, where he is both fascinated and appalled by what he finds. (It is also significant that, like Mrs Gaskell, Priestley actually came from the north; he was born in Bradford in 1894.)

It is hard to overestimate the impact of Priestley's book; most of those who subsequently travelled north in the 1930s would have read it and their vision of what they saw would have been predetermined by it. When Bill Brandt was asked if he had been surprised by what he found, he replied, 'No, I don't think so. I had read a book by Priestley describing the mining districts.'[12] The chronology takes a little untangling. Orwell went native in Lancashire in February–March, 1936; the resulting book *The Road to Wigan Pier* was published a year later in spring 1937. Tom Harrisson went to Bolton in October 1936, and Mass-Observation was established in the town early in 1937. Brandt finished photographing *The English at Home* in the summer of 1935 and published it in spring 1936; he travelled north a year later early in 1937.

As a Yorkshireman, Priestley naturally saw Lancashire in a different light to his home county. 'Between Manchester and Bolton', he wrote, 'the ugliness is so complete that it is almost exhilarating. It challenges you to live there.'[13] Bolton was where Tom Harrisson re-established himself after his contact with Madge and Jennings, organising the 'Worktown' survey from a terraced house in Davenport Street. Here he gathered a range of young observers, including the photographer Humphrey Spender, whose first visit to Bolton in April 1937 was followed by a number of subsequent trips over the next year. The 900 negatives that he took during that period were acquired by Bolton Museum and Art Gallery in 1994.[14] They thus have an altogether different status to the few fragments that have survived from Jennings' photography; despite his fragmented pattern of work, Spender produced a body of work which is both sustained and consistent. However, at the same time, there are some interesting fissures and ambiguities which reflect those which were fundamental to Mass-Observation more generally.

Spender, then working as 'Lensman' on the *Daily Mirror*, was invited to photograph in Bolton as part of Harrisson's obsession with gathering facts: 'It was factual data, of every kind, that he wanted from photos.'[15] This fundamental interest in factuality chimed with the spirit of the 1930s; reflecting back in 1940, Malcolm Muggeridge commented: 'Let us at all costs be factual, photographic, was the watchword'.[16] The most famous metaphorical use of photography was, of course, at the start of Christopher Isherwood's 'Berlin Diary', which was published for the first time in spring 1937: 'I am a camera with its shutter wide open, quite passive, recording, not thinking.'[17] Though Isherwood himself had probably picked up this image in Berlin, as a transposition of the objective 'camera-eye' espoused by photographers there, it also chimed with left-wing writers in Britain. In July 1937, Storm Jameson published a manifesto entitled 'Documents' and stating : 'As the photographer does, so must the writer keep himself out of the picture while working ceaselessly to present the *fact* from a striking (poignant, ironic, penetrating, significant) angle.'[18]

Even in 1970, Tom Harrisson could still say of Spender's images: 'The basis of this sort of photography is the camera as impartial, objective and, preferably, unobserved recorder.'[19] One wonders whether such faith in the photograph as objective record would have been shaken by Spender's later confessions about how much of a voyeur and intruder he felt in Bolton, spotted as a foreigner as soon as he opened his mouth: 'I was somebody from another planet.'[20] Nevertheless, Spender's work continues to be placed within a framework of 'social documentary' or 'humanist' photography, and this positioning has been emphasised in the choice of images made for the various publications of his work.[21] But this was a process which constructed Spender's oeuvre as much as it recorded it, and rendered other aspects invisible. Of course, humanist narrative was central to his work, but there were other elements as well and one of them was Surrealism. Indeed, with a certain degree of perversity, one could select an alternative set of images to construct a surrealist Spender to rival the dominant version.

Spender did not come to documentary photography unmarked by influences. He had learnt his craft in Weimar Germany, and the photograph he provided for the dust jacket of the first edition of Isherwood's *Farewell to Berlin* was a formalist view out of a window to the Lützowplatz below. In 1934, he had shared a London studio with William Edmiston, who had made 'surrealist' pictures to appear on the cover of *Architectural Review*.[22] Spender admired the work of Paul Nash, both his paintings and his photographs, which 'alerted me to the found object and its relationship or lack of relationship to its surroundings'.[23] And he was also a close friend of the Surrealist painter John Banting, whose influence he acknowledged, particularly in the use of deep perspectives.[24] All of these relationships suggest that Spender's eye was not an innocent one.

But these elements need to be placed within the overall thrust of his work. When Spender was asked much later about the incipient surrealism in his pictures, he replied,

> I was trying to be very objective and accepted surrealist elements when and where they cropped up, rather consciously avoiding pressures to seek out such elements. To say that surrealist elements were particularly evident in Mass-Observation's findings would be simply to say that such elements abound in everyday life, since my function was to document everyday life.[25]

Later, he added: 'I did not go round searching out such subjects but I was very aware they would turn up.'[26]

Spender's comments here are very finely balanced. On the one hand, he refuses an explicitly Surrealist approach which would actively 'seek out such elements' – the approach of Jennings, one suspects. But equally, he sets himself apart from a straightforwardly realist ethic into which his subject (and Harrisson's desires) would seem to have placed him. Spender shows a sophisticated understanding of how Surrealism is not separate from 'reality', but integrated within it. The 'sur' of Surrealism does not indicate that it is *beyond* reality, but rather that it is a heightened and deepened understanding of it. One can imagine Spender's excitement when he saw in Bolton Market the sign for a palmist which proclaimed 'TRUTH IS STRANGER THAN FICTION.'

When one starts to browse through Spender's images with Surrealism in mind (thus doing at one remove exactly what he himself resisted doing), many strange elements do indeed come out: underwear flying up in a back alley, a shrouded cart standing on the cobblestones, and, of course, the 'working man's hair specialist', whose hair takes on a demonic life of its own. In the allotments at Ashington in County Durham (where Spender went with a Mass-Observation delegation to meet with the miners' art group), one can see 'his Surrealist eye fancying the bedsteads used as pergolas'.[27] (The disjunction is reminiscent of the photograph by Nash of a bedhead that he found on the downs above Swanage.)[28] There are a number of individual shots like these, appearing in the middle of contact sheets taken up with other subjects. But to examine the surrealism of Spender's work in more depth, one needs to look closely at four subsets within it – his

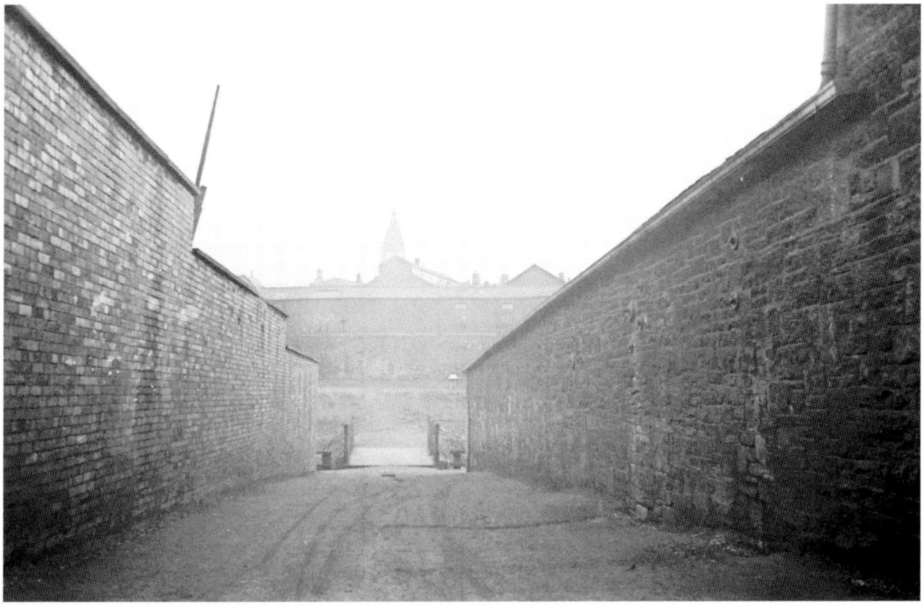

Fig 45 Humphrey Spender, *Bolton*, 1937–38. Collection of Bolton Museums and Art Gallery. © Bolton Metropolitan Borough Council.

representation of the industrialised *terrain vague*, his use of posters and adverts, the pictures of children's graffiti and, lastly, the images made in Blackpool.

Most of Spender's pictures are peopled, but there is a significant subset of images where we can see him exploring the sort of deserted, anomalous 'waste land' which had also interested Jennings. These pictures are much more precisely composed than his street shots (obviously he had more time and less fear of exposure) and this sometimes led him to make what he later dismissed as BPs ('beautiful pictures').[29] But the best of them also work on a more disquieting level, using abrupt perspectives, a disjunction between foreground and background and an eerie stillness in ways that are reminiscent of de Chirico (whose work lies behind so much Surrealist-influenced documentary photography) (figure 45). The sudden silence and stillness in a town dominated by the noise and bustle of 'work' is striking.

We have already seen an image by Jennings which juxtaposed the blandishments of advertising with the urban reality around it. Spender did the same in a number of photographs of which he said, 'The irony was deliberate. The contradictions, juxtapositions, seemed to us to be naturally surrealist.'[30] Particularly bleak is a shot of a desolate waste ground surrounded by a wall with a poster for the Harvest Festival in the top corner of the image (figure 46). There is also a photo of a white poster on the corner of a church proclaiming: 'Heaven above is Sweeter Blue. Earth Around is Sweeter Green'. The church is black and the street beyond it foggy. Harrisson seems in retrospect to have been incensed by this religious hypocrisy, writing in 1975, 'The children wrote on the walls, the churches plaster them with admonitions'.[31]

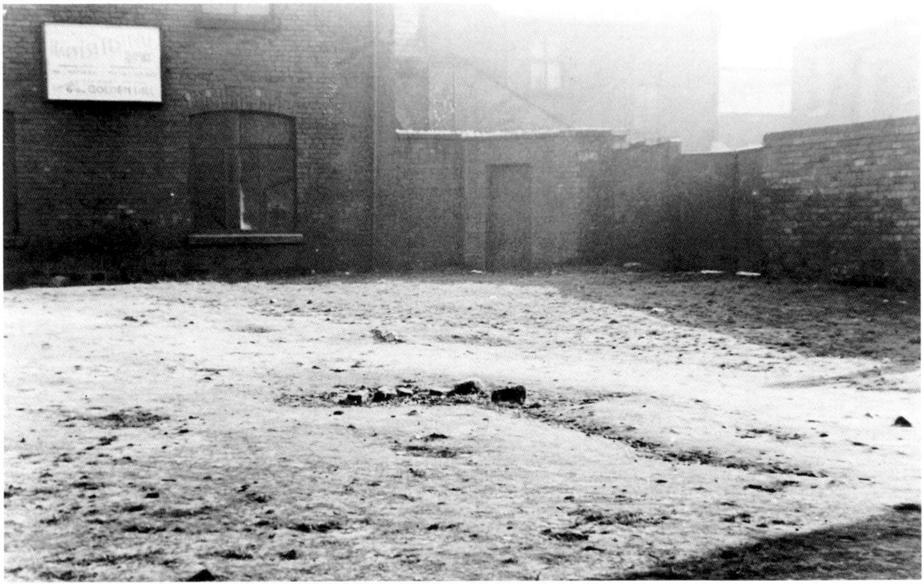

Fig 46 Humphrey Spender, *Wasteground, Bolton*, 1937–38. Collection of Bolton Museums and Art Gallery. © Bolton Metropolitan Borough Council.

This comment links the posters to graffiti as insertions into the otherwise unrelieved greyness of the town, but it also contrasts them – if the posters come into this environment as a cruel irony, graffiti comes out of it as an assertion of imaginative freedom. By the time that Spender went to Bolton, graffiti as a photographic subject was well established. The foundational work in the genre had been made by Brassaï and appeared in *Minotaure* in 1933 under the title 'From the Cave Wall to the Factory Wall'.[32] Spender later said that he had not known of Brassaï's graffiti photographs at the time,[33] but he would have seen at least one of them, which had featured prominently (if anonymously) on a poster for the 1936 International Surrealism Exhibition in London.[34] Spender's own work with graffiti was part of a larger interest within Mass-Observation. As we have seen, Jennings and Madge were both moved by it, and Spender's photographs of graffiti in Bolton came out of conversations with Tom Harrisson, who would tell Spender about ones he had seen.[35]

In 1975, Spender and Harrisson collaborated on a book, published in a limited edition at the Royal College of Art, which handled the relationship between image and text much more creatively than in any other Mass-Observation publication.[36] It is also the one public siting of Spender's graffiti images, accompanied by a text in which Harrisson emphasised the childlike innocence of the activity, 'Wall writing was an activity of excitement for kids ... You never saw an adult writing on a wall, it was a little kid's game.' This points to the difference between the graffiti that Spender photographed and that which Brassaï had found in the back streets of Paris. Brassaï's images were of primal gougings into the surface of the wall, most of them deeply imbued with sex or death or both. These seem

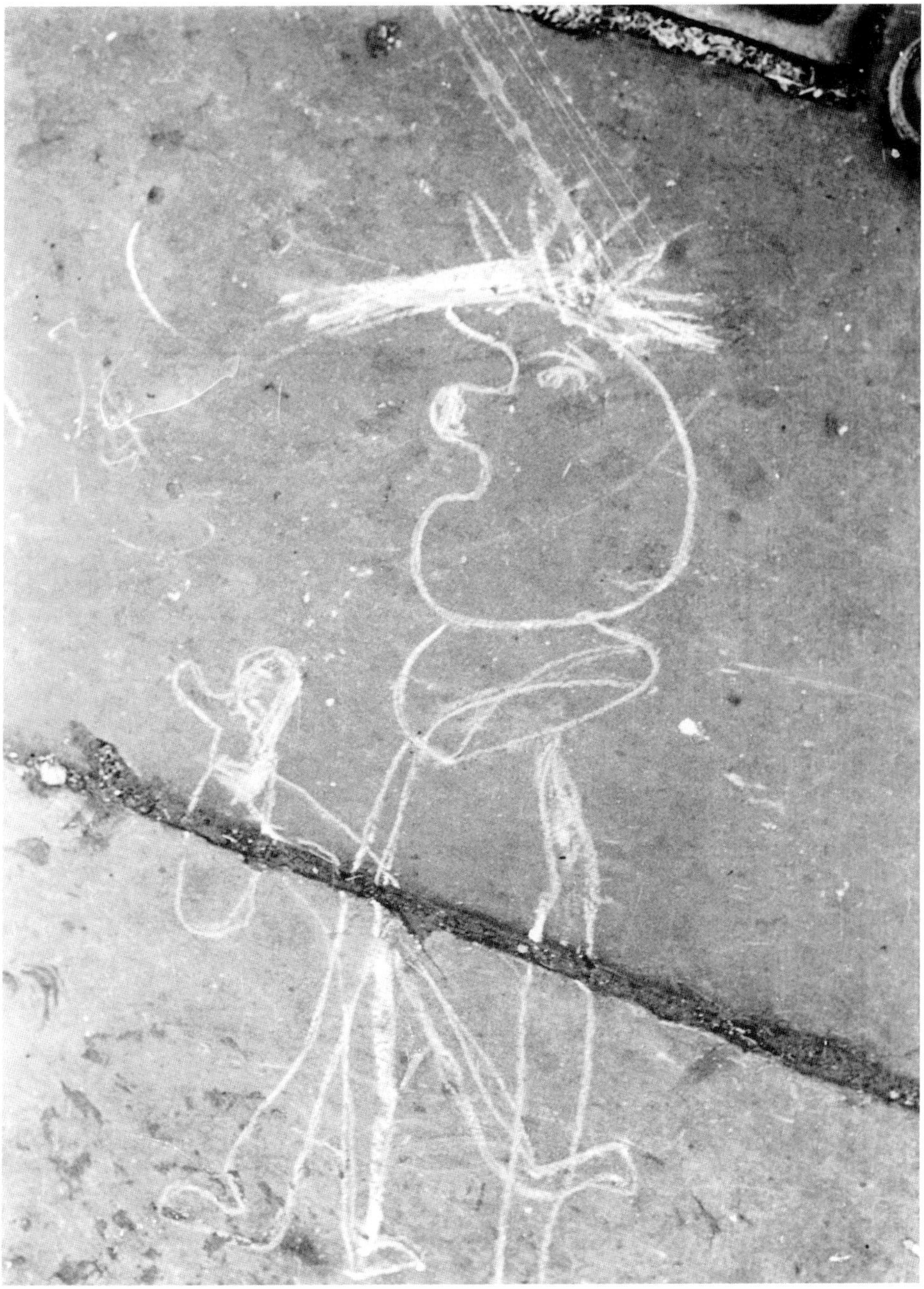

Fig 47 Humphrey Spender, *Graffiti, Bolton*, 1937–38. Collection of Bolton Museums and Art Gallery.

rather adult. But in the late 1930s, a number of photographers quite independently made images of the more common and temporary chalk drawings made by children; the work of Helen Levitt in New York stands out here.[37]

Spender photographed graffiti in two distinct ways. One was closer to Brassaï's tactics – to photograph it frontally, cropped closely to cut out any context. It is the graffiti itself which is emphasised. There are about 26 of these images. Spender printed up very few of them and they have to be searched for in the Bolton Archive, but, viewed as a group, one can almost see Spender trying to catalogue the range of graffiti. There are a couple which show abstract and 'automatic' free-flowing forms, there are comic ones, slightly threatening ones like a muzzled dog or a death's head, ones that echo popular culture (Popeye makes an appearance) and others that would have reminded Spender of the work of artists such as Miró, Picasso and Klee (figure 47). Finally, there are witty commentaries such as 'This egg was…' scrawled in chalk above a foundation stone proclaiming 'LAID BY JOSEPH HOLDEN'. While a couple would have appealed to Spender as a photographer: the injunction to 'Follow this Line and See your Photo' is followed by a crude drawing of a figure saying, 'This is your Photo.'

Spender's other tactic was to stand further back, at an angle, to include something of the context and the children themselves. This type of image, however, diminishes the direct power of the graffiti and makes it open to a greater sentimentality. It is how the humanist photographers of a later generation – Izis and Robert Doisneau in Paris, Roger Mayne in London – would represent children and their graffiti. Spender photographed some ragged urchins playing on a railway bridge next to a wooden fence on which is scrawled a range of graffiti. It is again typical of the way that Spender's work has been retrospectively constructed that it should have been these pictures that were included in his later books and not some of the more direct images of graffiti.

When Mass-Observation moved to Blackpool, there were again a number of distinct ways to approach the same experience. In discussing seaside resorts in his book *Places on the Margin*, Rob Shields placed alongside the idea of liminality (those moments of 'inbetween-ness' to which I referred in discussing Nash's work at Swanage) the more dynamic concept of the carnivalesque, originally articulated by the Russian theorist Mikhael Bakhtin. Shields wrote:

> The explosion of 'excessive' behaviour and social pleasures and leisure forms which is found in the seaside carnival is a mark of *resistant* bodies which at least temporarily escape or exceed moral propriety. Against the restraining empiricism, cerebral rationality, emphasis on control and economy, carnival produces a momentary social space based on the politics of pleasure and physical senses.[38]

However, Blackpool's most assiduous historian, John K. Walton, has sounded a warning against confusing Blackpool's feeling of 'carnival' with any Bakhtinian 'carnivalesque'. While restraints on eating, drinking and sex might be relaxed, 'authority was challenged implicitly rather than directly, and only up to consensually accepted points of tolerance … Blackpool was fun but it was no Rabelaisian carnival'.[39] Nevertheless, Blackpool did operate, in Tom Harrisson's words, 'as

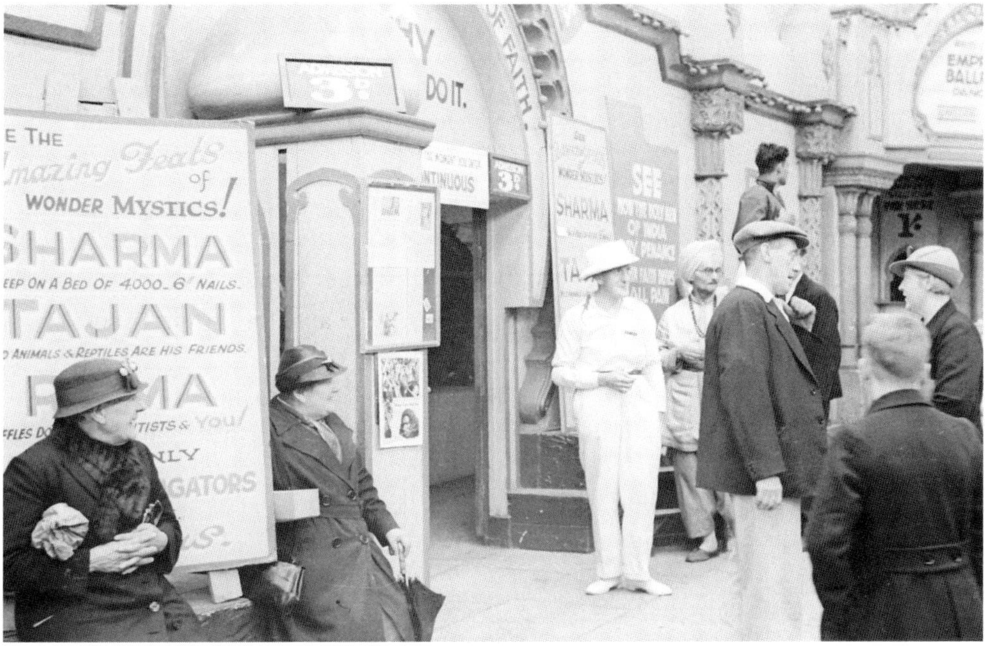

Fig 48 Humphrey Spender, *Blackpool*, 1937–38. Collection of Bolton Museums and Art Gallery. © Bolton Metropolitan Borough Council.

the fantasy outlet poised against the dark routine of the fifty-one weeks of the industrial year'.[40] In this respect, probably the most famous comment about Blackpool's visitors was made by an unidentified Lancashire businessman to the architect T. H. Mawson, who laid out many of Blackpool's gardens in the 1920s: 'men stick it out as long as they can and once a year they must either burst out or go to Blackpool; and there they go, and after a fortnight they come back quietened down and ready for work again. Blackpool stands between us and revolution. May it long continue as the protector of social order!'[41]

The theorists of Mass-Observation seem to have disagreed about how they should respond to Blackpool and the mass leisure it represented. For Tom Harrisson, it was part of an unthinking shift towards Fascism, which he linked with an excessive individualism, a rejection of science, a dependence on fantasy.[42] For Charles Madge on the other hand, 'fantasy has a function, in terms of the needs and desires of the human soul'.[43] This comment comes from an essay on the daily newspaper read as a form of 'popular poetry' – a reading no doubt based on Madge's own experience at the *Daily Mirror*. He further remarks: 'The function of the newspaper is to provide an area of strangeness within which strangeness has known limits.'[44] As much might be said for the exoticism of Blackpool.

In any case, Humphrey Spender seems to have enjoyed taking pictures in Blackpool, perhaps because he did not feel as inhibited as he had in Bolton. Later, he commented that, 'Some of the Blackpool stuff taken for Mass-Observation is sufficiently improbable as to be vaguely surrealist.'[45] Spender still made plenty of pictures of people, but he also photographed rows of staring dolls and laughing clowns, a display where 'Ali Baba discovers the Cave of Golden Shred', a robot and a laughing policeman, 'The Cow with 5 Legs' and a pseudo-Indian temple leading to Sharma the 'wonder mystic' lying on a bed of nails (figure 48). In one picture, there is just a sign proclaiming:

> THE FIRE EATING ARABS.
> THE KIDDIES RIDE.
> THE HEADLESS WOMAN.
> THE CROWN JEWELS.

Any Surrealist would have been happy to write that quatrain.

All of this could be (and was) analysed to demonstrate how popular leisure had become mechanised and fed the audience's baser emotions, exploiting a dubious exoticism to take them out of themselves. Since Harrisson was in charge of writing up Mass-Observation's findings, they inevitably present Blackpool as 'a symbol of the modernized primitivism of the working-class'.[46] On the other hand, Patrick Keiller has proposed that 'if Louis Aragon had come to England and someone had taken him to Blackpool, he might have been intrigued, and England wouldn't have been left off the Surrealist map of the world'.[47] But a Surrealist position here is by no means simple. While antagonistic to the anaesthetising effects of much mass culture, the Surrealists were also fascinated by its power and aware of how it could be subverted and used to more subjective ends. One might extend to the whole of Blackpool Tony Bennett's comment about the Pleasure Beach: 'If carnival enters the Pleasure Beach – and sometimes it does – it is through the people who tumble in from the promenade ... The Pleasure Beach is not a site of transgressions. It is a site to be transgressed but one which, to a degree, invites – incites even – its own transgression.'[48]

Spender's Blackpool photographs seem to have been the only ones he made for Mass-Observation which were published at the time. This was in the *Geographical Magazine* for April 1938, where 26 pictures were reproduced alongside a text written by Tom Harrisson.[49] A year later, Harrisson wrote another article for *Picture Post*, entitled 'So This is Blackpool'; this time a rather anonymous set of reportage images were used instead of Spender's pictures.[50] Although Harrisson's texts have a very similar 'breezy' tone, as Nick Stanley has called it,[51] the two sets of pictures create quite a different effect. While *Picture Post* used images of people, in crowds or as human interest close-ups, the *Geographical Magazine* reproduced many of Spender's images with a greater surrealist edge to them – photographs of displays, signs and illuminations. *Picture Post* emphasised Blackpool's air of familiarity while the *Geographical Magazine*, in the spirit of the original project of Mass-Observation, acknowledged its strangeness.

Aside from Spender (centrally) and Jennings (peripherally), there was a third photographer working for Mass-Observation in Bolton, though this was not his main purpose in being there. Julian Trevelyan came to Mass-Observation, like Jennings, from the experience of Surrealism (he had also shown in the 1936 exhibition), but like Spender, his contact was directly with Tom Harrisson. Trevelyan was mainly there to make paintings and collages, but he also took a set of photographs which offer a significantly different view of the place from Spender's. They worked quite separately, often after individual consultation with Harrisson, and only saw each other's pictures in retrospect.[52]

'Worktown had been the mythology of my childhood', wrote Trevelyan later.[53] Born in 1910 into a well-off family with branches in the north, Trevelyan as a child would 'cover sketch-books with drawings of imaginary cities, vast railway stations, and valleys full of smoking chimneys'.[54] After Cambridge (where he became friends with Jennings) he went to Paris in 1931 and stayed there till 1934. He gained first-hand knowledge of the *terrain vague* which surrounded the city: 'The cold winter wind cut through me as I sat drawing among the shacks in the "Zone"'.[55] He also photographed Parisian graffiti and indeed admired Brassaï's images when they were published in *Minotaure* in 1933.[56] Back in Britain, he showed in the 1936 Surrealist exhibition some etchings and drawings on slate titled 'Two Versions of Babylon', in which he created a sort of mythical city. Coming to Bolton in 1937 offered Trevelyan both a direct experience of industrialisation and a return to the world of his childhood imagination.

There still exist letters and cards from Harrisson to Trevelyan which capture something of the hectic and exhilarating mood of Mass-Observation in Bolton. Typed rather haphazardly on notecards, they exhort Trevelyan to come north. On 7 June 1937, Harrisson wrote, 'We have a Scotch Materialist, a Tramp

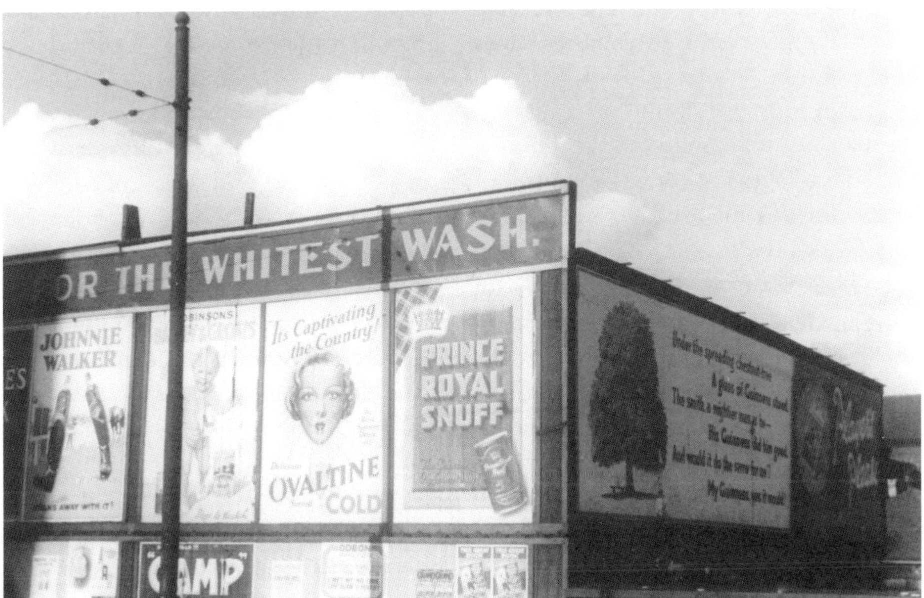

Fig 49 Julian Trevelyan, *Bolton*, 1937–38. Collection of Bolton Museums and Art Gallery. © The estate of the artist.

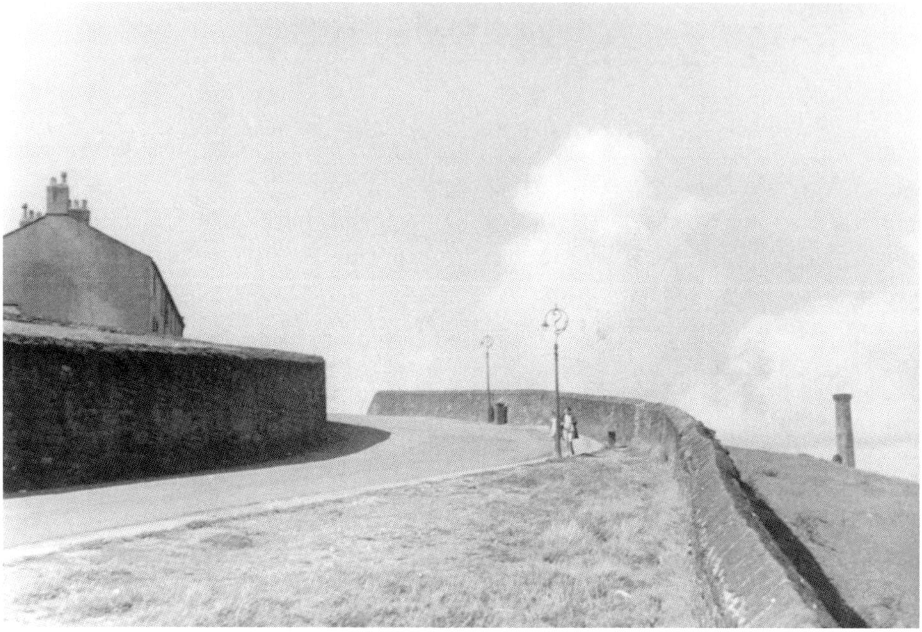

Fig 50 Julian Trevelyan, *Bolton*, 1937–38. Collection of Bolton Museums and Art Gallery. © The estate of the artist.

Recorder, a Harpo Marxist & a coalminer in the house at the moment ... You must paint some Bolton chimneys; they are like saltmines without the savour ... Bolton Art awaits you! You will enjoy it, I swear.'[57] Trevelyan later felt that his experience in Bolton was crucial in his subsequent shift away from Surrealism. 'We had arrived in Bolton in the dawn; the mills stood up gaunt & forbidding above the endless terraces of little slate-roofed houses. I was learning again to look and to forget about Surrealism.'[58] Yet there is still a substantial element of Surrealism in the images he made there, either as collages or photographs.

The collages are better known; made from newspapers and scraps of coloured paper, they bring together avant-garde technique and first-hand experience.[59] Trevelyan's photography in Bolton has not received the same attention, but the surviving pictures suggest that his image of the place was distinctly different from Spender's.[60] There are some photos which show people, often from behind or at a distance, but, generally, Trevelyan seems less interested in them than in their environment. Some images dwell, as Jennings and Spender had done, on the placement of advertising and publicity images. In one case, he photographs a building at an angle, so that the left side of the image is taken up by a wall of posters (figure 49). Above them, a white cloud seems to sit on top of the hoarding. Indeed, it is noticeable that Trevelyan prefers to photograph in sunlight (albeit rather wan and thin sunlight), giving his images a very different atmosphere from those of Spender.

Trevelyan also seems to avoid the town centre and in a number of pictures, he revisits the *terrain vague*, where the natural and the industrial merge. His

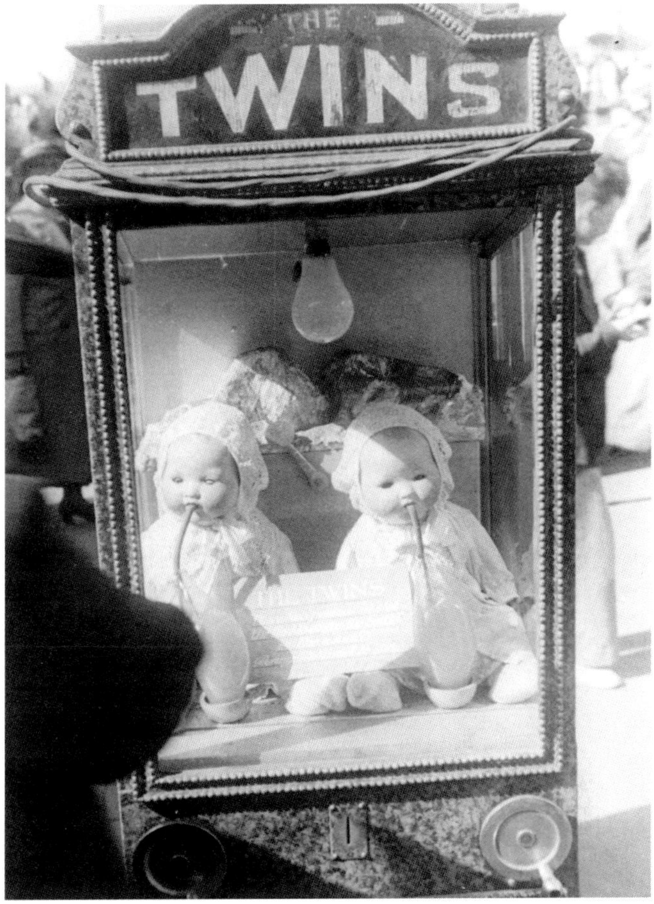

Fig 51 Julian Trevelyan, *Blackpool*, 1937–38. Collection of Bolton Museums and Art Gallery. © The estate of the artist.

method of photographing is also far from direct, sometimes throwing the composition off-centre (as with the wall of posters) or contrasting foreground and background. A sign saying 'Trespassers will be prosecuted. No fishing allowed', suggests that between it and the factory chimney in the distance, there must be a canal, but we cannot see it. There is a tension in such a picture between the rather graceful compositions that Trevelyan contrives and the indeterminate landscape he is depicting. He is able to make a haunting image out of very little – a road curving up round a bend between two walls, a chimney in the distance and two people walking past a surprisingly ornate lamp-post (figure 50).[61]

Trevelyan went to Blackpool on 14 August, and met Spender there. He returned the following Easter; on 16 March 1938, Harrisson had written to him: 'We are having a special drive at Balckpool [sic] and Bolton on leisure behaviour in the first fortnight of April, climax at easter … I really should be grateful if you could come up then, and youre due for a visit and Bolton is its dirty loveliest at that time.'[62] Trevelyan seems not to have been very enchanted

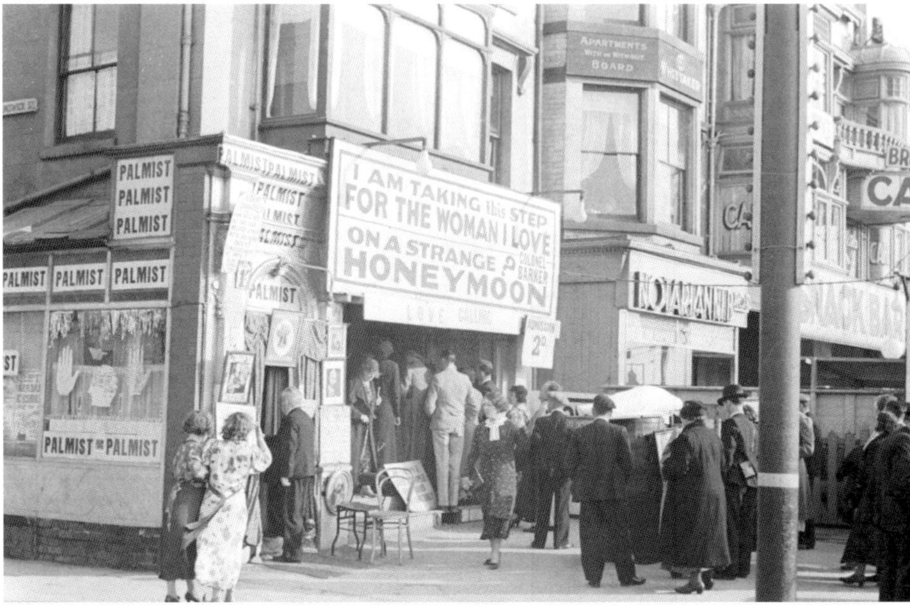

Fig 52 Humphrey Spender, *Exterior of Colonel Barker's Display, Blackpool*, 1937. Collection of Bolton Museums and Art Gallery. © Bolton Metropolitan Borough Council.

by Blackpool: 'The whole place was synthetic, a machine for pleasure in steel and concrete, dumped on the muddy shore of a muddy sea.'[63] Nevertheless, his Surrealist eye lit on a number of incongruities that were so extraordinary that he did not bother to compose as carefully as he had in Bolton. He photographed dummies in a sort of Punch and Judy show, a café on the seafront in the shape of a teapot and a glass case containing two baby dolls – 'The Twins' – each sucking liquid through a straw (figure 51). As Humphrey Spender commented, while he photographed the surrealism of Blackpool where he found it, Trevelyan went looking for it.[64]

A number of sights were photographed separately by both Spender and Trevelyan. In front of the entrance to the Sharma exhibit, for example, Trevelyan's stance is more frontal, perhaps less composed, where Spender's is oblique, a positioning which may be the result of either his greater photographic artistry or his unwillingness to confront his subject (or both). There is also one other point where Spender and Trevelyan photograph the same subject and their pictures are even more different. On the front, a shop had been taken over by a new sensation: 'Colonel Barker, whose famous sex-change from woman to man had previously filled all the headlines, was spending a strange honeymoon with his new bride in a cage into which one peered for sixpence.'[65] Unfortunately (or perhaps fortunately), neither Spender nor Trevelyan photographed the scene inside, but the pictures they took outside are again different. Spender stands some away along the road, to obliquely photograph the cornucopia of signage, the crowds milling around the pavement and the placement of this 'Strange Honeymoon' between a palmist's establishment and an ice-cream parlour (figure 52). Trevelyan moves in

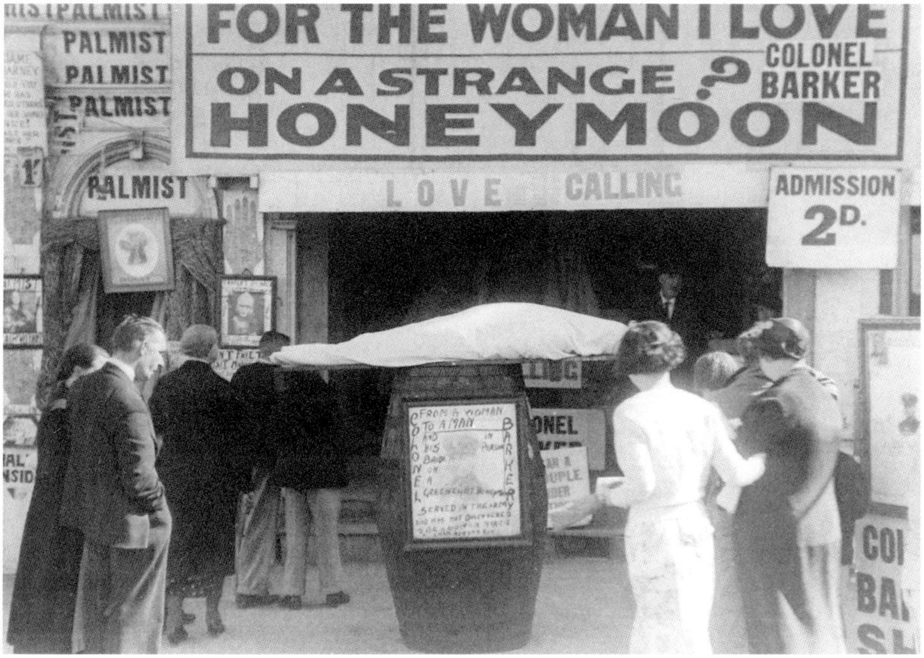

Fig 53 Julian Trevelyan, *Exterior of Colonel Barker's Display, Blackpool*, 1937. Collection of Bolton Museums and Art Gallery. © The estate of the artist.

closer and more frontally to focus on the mummy-like figure at the front of the display, both sinister and comic, draped in a white cloth and balanced precariously on top of a barrel (figure 53).

Another photographer came north in 1937. Bill Brandt also had a background in Surrealism and his work of the mid-1930s merged those concerns with social documentary. But the pictures that Brandt made in Yorkshire and the North-East look very different from those taken in Bolton by Spender and Trevelyan. Even before Brandt's printing became much heavier, late in life, these images were dark and dramatic, and have become established as 'mythic' representations of what the North felt like at that moment in history. As his biographer Paul Delany remarked, 'It is extraordinary that Brandt's pictures of the industrial North, which have done so much to define the thirties in the British imagination, were all taken on a single visit of a few weeks.'[66]

Brandt had published his first major monograph *The English at Home* in 1936 and it has often been taken to be Brandt's major contribution to the documentation of industrialisation. In fact, it might have been better (if less resonantly) titled 'Londoners at Home', since only two or three pictures were taken further away than a day trip's distance out of the city. These were made on a visit to the South Wales coalfields – the Welsh miners pretending to be English for the occasion. Otherwise, the poverty depicted in the book is that of the East End of London, rather than the northern industrial cities. Brandt went

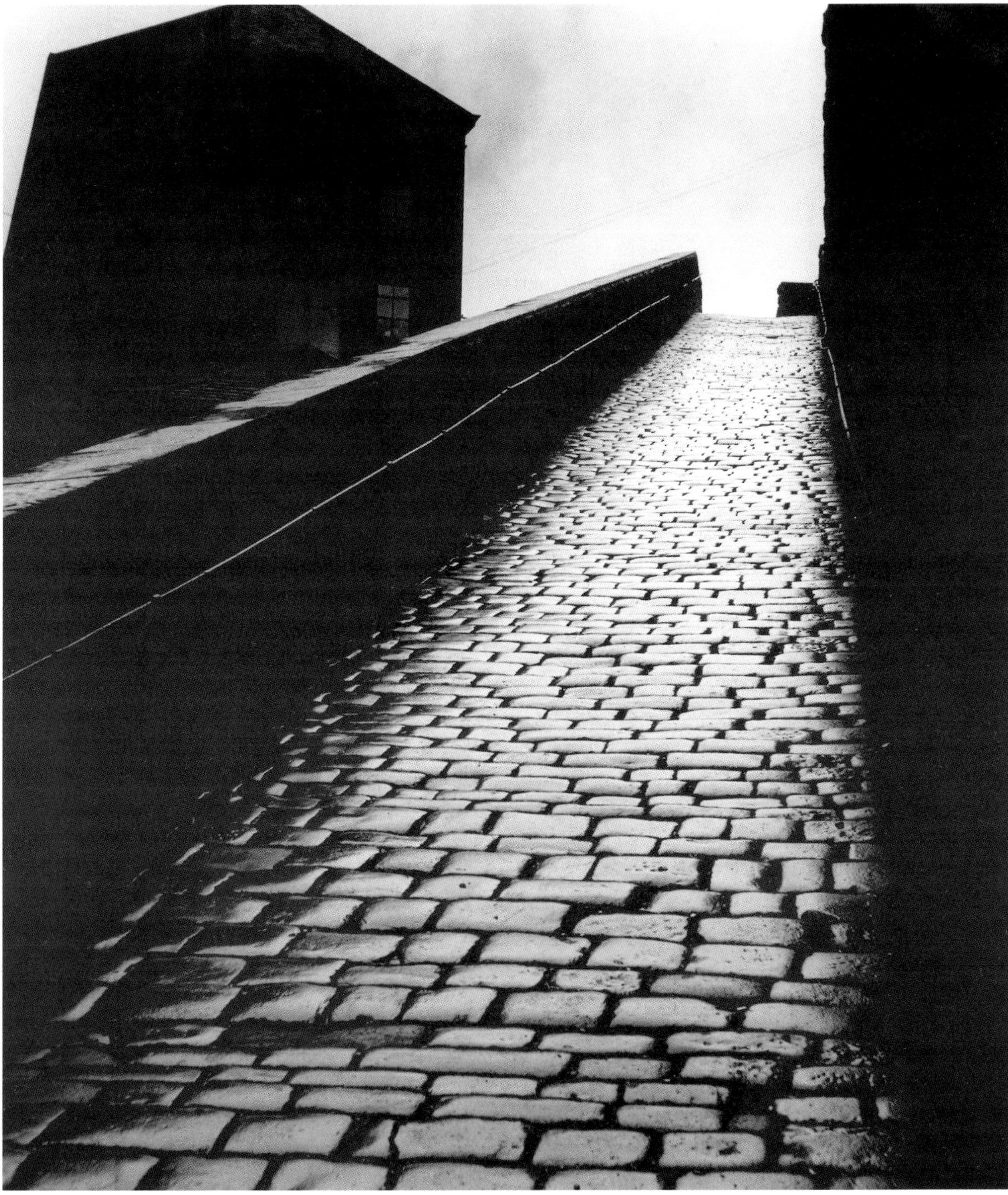

Fig 54 Bill Brandt, *A Snicket, Halifax*, 1937. © Bill Brandt Archive Ltd.

north in early 1937, almost a year after the publication of *The English at Home*, impelled both by his reading of Priestley and, more immediately, by the arrival of the Jarrow marchers in London on 8 November 1936. He travelled up the east side of the country through Yorkshire, probably because his eventual destination was Tyneside where the marchers had come from. But one might also wonder if Brandt yet knew about Orwell in Wigan and Mass-Observation in Bolton and thus stayed on the eastern side of the Pennines to keep clear of their territory. He would always remain independent in his work and attitudes.

The photographs that Brandt made are various in mood and tone. The close-up pictures of dirty children in a Sheffield slum or of unemployed miners picking over a Durham slag-heap are very different from the empty, haunted shots of a darkened city that he made in Newcastle and Halifax. It is those latter pictures which now have mythic resonance. As Brandt's partner Marjorie Beckett wrote in 1966 (presumably echoing his own words), 'Such towns as Newcastle, Sheffield and, particularly, Halifax looked to him as if they might have been built of coal.'[67] George Orwell had imagined Baudelaire writing a poem about a slag-heap;[68] in his own medium, that is what Brandt did, but by reducing what he actually told the viewer about the place.

Take, for example, Brandt's picture of a 'snicket', a steeply rising cobblestone pathway climbing up next to the gable end of a building (figure 54). The picture is radical, even for Brandt, in its lack of detail and context. Nothing tells us what building that is on the left. The dramatic narrowing of the perspective almost

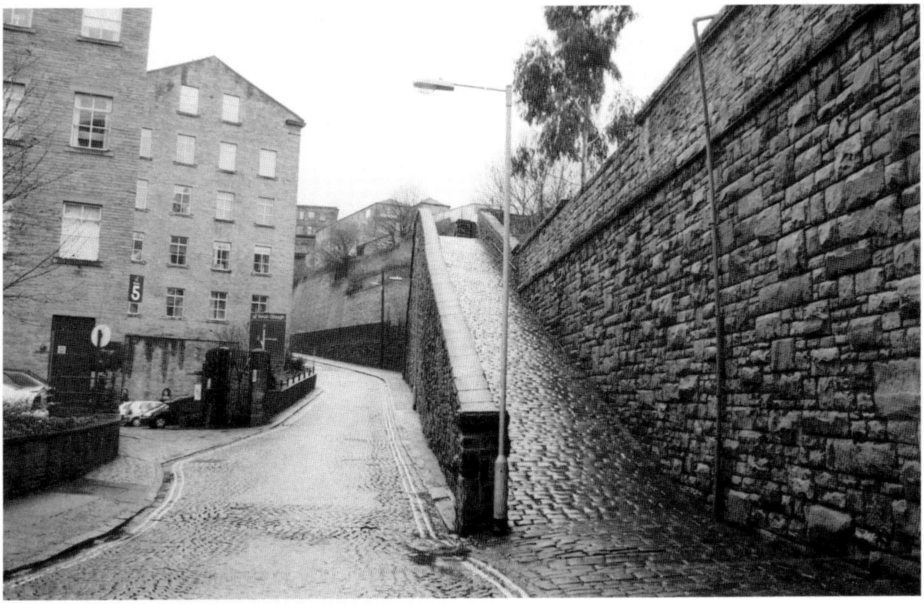

Fig 55 Ian Walker, *A Snicket, Halifax*, 2006. © Ian Walker.

seems to force our heads back as we view the picture and one feels as if one is already being forced to climb the snicket, even though it does not go anywhere. If Spender had photographed here, one can imagine that he would have wanted us to understand what the snicket does and where it goes, wanted us to see how a person might climb it and wanted us to know that the gable belongs to the largest mill in the town – Dean Clough, which extends to the left. As it is, all that information is only to be gained by visiting the site (figure 55) and not by looking at Brandt's picture, which by a combination of weather, light, a low camera position, a wide-angle lens and a printing technique that got darker and heavier over the next forty years, is both highly reductive and enormously expressive.[69]

Behind a picture such as this, there also lie influences from Brandt's time in Paris. One set of connections are photographic – to the books of Parisian photographs produced in the early 1930s by Kertész and (more particularly) Brassaï, both influenced in turn by the posthumous publication of the work of Eugéne Atget. It seems that Brandt, like other commentators of the time, also connected Atget's photographs with the paintings of Giorgio de Chirico. When Brandt was later asked about his feeling for Atget, he replied that he 'was enchanted by the steep perspective of his cobblestone streets'.[70] But in fact, while the cobblestones may be present in Atget's photographs, the steep perspective is not – that has been transposed from de Chirico's paintings. It is in the image of the snicket that Brandt himself placed Atget's cobblestones in a Chiricesque perspective.

If one climbs the snicket (and it is indeed very steep and, in wet weather, slippery) one comes to a bridge across a railway track, now removed. It was from here, on that same afternoon, that Brandt made another epic photograph – a view down on the track alongside which some boys are running, black smoking chimneys in the background.[71] Victor Burgin began his 1996 book *Some Cities* by recalling his own childhood in Sheffield in the 1940s and reproducing this photograph. He has never been to Halifax, he says, but 'I felt a shock of recognition when I first saw this photograph by Bill Brandt. I am one of those children running from school at "home time".'[72] How should we read this? Burgin has too sophisticated an understanding of photographic codes to propose that we should take this photograph to be simply a 'realistic' picture of a northern city. This scene might have looked like this late in the afternoon on a winter's day, but that is a very particular moment – one which Brandt has chosen for maximum visual, psychological and, we might say, mythic effect.

But northern cities could look very different. The light in Spender's pictures is characteristically flat and grey; 'there was a hell of lot of smog', he recalled.[73] Trevelyan photographed in sunlight while Jennings seems to have been there, not only on wet days like the one when he found the elephant gate, but also at times when (as he wrote in a later prose poem), 'Along plain streets of working-class houses ... pours the level sunlight of an evening in August. For an hour the hard edges of the mill-tied town alter and begin to open like a rose.'[74] Brandt's darkness is only one among many possible effects, which fitted what he *wanted* the place to look like.

If we are not to take Burgin too literally, then we must read his comments on an affective level. It is how he remembers the place – or perhaps it is rather how he wants to remember it. And in that his response is perhaps parallel to that of Brandt himself, whose photographs we should see as expressing how he imagined a place to be rather than – or as well as – what it actually looked like when he got there. Once, the narrative of Brandt's photography seemed linear – a move from artistic beginnings through a phase of social realism in the late 1930s and early 1940s and back to a more personal style after the war. But the situation has become more complicated as it has been demonstrated that even Brandt's images of the 1930s are what Charles Hagen called 'documentary fictions'. 'The essential mystery of the early photographs', he wrote in 1985, 'turns out to be not the Dickensian one of the city in industrial culture, but the Surrealist mystery of the remembering, dreaming self, imposing its emotional needs on the world around it.'[75] Perhaps we can say the same about the work that Brandt made in the north of England, particularly when Hagen goes on to connect Brandt's vision with the larger culture of the period: 'Brandt's England – whether discovered or invented – may have been shaped according to his own fantasies, but it also satisfied the idea of "England" held by many people of the time.'[76]

In terms of how Brandt's photographs came to fit into and reinforce that mythology, this effect was retrospective. It was not until 1948 when a set of six pictures from Halifax were published in *Lilliput*.[77] Even then, though, the photograph of the boys running alongside the railway line was not among the pictures reproduced. It would not appear until 1966, together with some of Brandt's other now classic shots from the north, in the first edition of *Shadow of Light*. But then, none of Spender's pictures was published until the 1960s either. The placement of all this work has been almost entirely retrospective, part of a collective process of memorisation, so that it is no longer possible to know where reality ends and myth starts. The two are now utterly merged and perhaps we can now no longer know just how black Halifax actually was – or how grey Bolton was – in 1937.

The photographs of Spender and Brandt operate in quite different domains, however, not least in terms of the access we can have to the pictures. It is impossible to imagine Brandt doing what Spender did and handing over all his negatives to the museum in the town where they were made. This suggests that Spender was comparatively lacking in ego, and content for his work to be seen as part of a larger research project in which even photographs that were undistinguished as pictures could carry vital factual information. Brandt, however, retained tight authorial control over his work at every stage and only about twenty of the images he made in the north in 1937 have ever been published. Each image becomes a condensed moment which seems to hold much more, yet in factual terms may tell us very little. We can read this difference between Brandt and Spender to either's advantage or disadvantage.

In 1993, the local photographer John McDonald exhibited his own contemporary photographs of Bolton alongside those of Spender under the title

From Worktown to Our Town. He ended his catalogue text by describing the 'Worktown' constructed by Mass-Observation as 'an imaginary place inhabited by real people'.[78] To an extent, that would be true of any attempt to encapsulate a place and its culture in images, whether they were made by locals or visitors. But the photographs taken in the 1930s by Spender, Jennings, Trevelyan and by Brandt reflect their particular positioning. They were all outsiders in terms of their southerness and class and they were all engaged with Surrealism. This does not invalidate their images, on the contrary, but it does inflect them – they are not a simple transposition of a familiar 'reality' but something rather more complex, ambiguous and estranged, filled with desire and now locked into memory.

Notes

1 Tom Harrisson and Charles Madge (eds), *First Year's Work* (London: Lindsay Drummond, 1938).

2 *Hard Times* and *North and South* were serialised in *Household Words* within months of each other in 1854–55. Dickens had visited Preston in February 1854 (see Peter Ackroyd, *Dickens* (London: Sinclair-Stevenson, 1990), p. 691).

3 Philip Dodd, 'Lowryscapes: recent writing about "the North"', *Critical Quarterly*, 32:2 (1990), 217.

4 Elizabeth Gaskell, *North and South* (London: Penguin, 2003), p. 40.

5 Peter Ackroyd has argued that Blake had in mind the (aptly named) Albion Mill, 'the first great factory in London', on Blackfriars Road near his home, which was burnt down in 1791 and remained as a blackened shell for the next eighteen years. See Peter Ackroyd, *Blake* (London: Sinclair-Stevenson, 1995), p. 130.

6 Steve Edwards, 'Disastrous Documents', *Ten.8*, 15 (1984), p. 15.

7 Rob Shields, *Places on the Margin: Alternative Geographies of Modernity* (London: Routledge, 1991), p. 213. Curiously, Shields uses the term 'British North' when he actually means 'English North'.

8 George Orwell, *The Road to Wigan Pier* (London: Penguin, 2001), p. 101.

9 Peter J. Taylor, 'Which Britain? Which England? Which North?', in David Morley and Kevin Robins (eds), *British Cultural Studies* (Oxford: Oxford University Press, 2001), p. 135.

10 Philip Dodd discusses Priestley and Orwell in 'The Views of Travellers: Travel Writing in the 1930s', in Dodd (ed.), *The Art of Travel* (London: Frank Cass, 1982), pp. 127–38.

11 J. B. Priestley, *English Journey* (London: William Heinemann, 1934).

12 'Bill Brandt: What do you Say', *The Image*, 9 (1973), p. 42.

13 Priestley, *English Journey*, p. 262.

14 These images can now be seen on the Museum's website though not as they appear on the contact sheets (see www.boltonmuseums.org.uk).

15 Humphrey Spender, *Worktown People* (Bristol: Falling Wall Press, 1982), p. 20.

16 Malcolm Muggeridge, *The Thirties* (London: Hamish Hamilton, 1940), p. 257.

17 Christopher Isherwood, 'A Berlin Diary', *New Writing*, 3 (Spring 1937), 11–26, reprinted in *Farewell to Berlin* (London: Chatto & Windus, 1939).

18 Storm Jameson, 'Documents', *Fact*, 4 (July 1937), p. 15.

19 Tom Harrisson, 'Preface' in Mass-Observation, *The Pub and The People* (Welwyn Garden

City: Seven Dials Press, 1970), p. 5.

20 Spender, *Worktown People*, p. 16.

21 As well as *Worktown People*, there are two other books featuring Spender's pictures: Humphrey Spender, *'Lensman': Photographs 1932–52* (London: Chatto & Windus, 1987) and Deborah Frizzell, *Humphrey Spender's Humanist Landscapes: Photo-Documents 1932–1942* (New Haven: Yale Centre for British Art/Paul Mellon Center for Studies in British Art, 1997).

22 Spender, *Worktown People*, p. 13.

23 Letter to the author, 21 November 2003.

24 David Mellor, 'Humphrey Spender and the Visual Imagination of Mass-Observation: A Descriptive Chronology' in *Humphrey Spender: Worktown* (Falmer: University of Sussex, 1977), unpaginated.

25 Letter to the author, 9 April 1986.

26 Letter to the author, 2003.

27 William Feaver, *Pitmen Painters: The Ashington Group 1934–1984* (London: Chatto & Windus, 1988), p. 90.

28 Reproduced in Pennie Denton, *Seaside Surrealism: Paul Nash in Swanage* (Swanage: Peveril Press, 2002), p. 38.

29 Spender, *'Lensman'*, p. 11.

30 Letter to the author, 2003.

31 Humphrey Spender and Tom Harrisson, *Britain in the 30s* (London: Lion And Unicorn Press, Royal College of Art, 1975), unpaginated.

32 Brassaï, 'Du mur des cavernes au mur d'usine', *Minotaure*, 3–4 (14 December 1933), 6–7. On Brassaï's photographs of graffiti, see Ian Walker, *City Gorged with Dreams* (Manchester: Manchester University Press, 2002), pp. 155–61.

33 Letter to the author, 2003.

34 The poster is reproduced in Michael Simpson, *In the Mind's Eye: Surrealist Works on Paper* (Manchester: Whitworth Art Gallery, 1996), p. 12.

35 Letter to the author, 2003. (Spender added that he wished he had taken more shots of graffiti.)

36 Spender and Harrisson, *Britain in the 30s*.

37 See Helen Levitt, *In the Street* (Durham NC: Duke University Press, 1987).

38 Shields, *Places on the Margin*, pp. 94–5.

39 John K. Walton, *Blackpool* (Edinburgh: Edinburgh University Press/Lancaster: Carnegie Publishing, 1998), pp. 79–80.

40 Spender and Harrisson, *Britain in the 30s*.

41 T. H. Mawson, *The Life and Work of an English Landscape Architect* (London: Richards, 1927), p. 344.

42 Tom Harrisson, 'A World's Brain Trust', *New Statesman and Nation* (10 September 1938), 375.

43 Charles Madge, 'Some reflections on popular poetry', *New Writing*, New Series, 3 (Christmas 1939), 66.

44 Madge, 'Some reflections on popular poetry', 70.

45 Letter to the author, 1986.

46 Gary Cross (ed.), *Worktowners at Blackpool* (London and New York: Routledge, 1990), p. 10.

47 Patrick Keiller, *Robinson in Space* (London: Reaktion, 1999), p. 230.

48 Tony Bennett, 'A Thousand and One Troubles: Blackpool Pleasure Beach', *Formations of Pleasure* (London: Routledge and Kegan Paul, 1983), 155.

49 Tom Harrisson, 'The Fifty-Second Week of the Year: Impressions of Blackpool', *Geographical Magazine* (April 1938), 387–402. For a detailed analysis, see Frizzell, *Humphrey Spender's Humanist Landscapes*, pp. 48–50.

50 Tom Harrisson, 'So This is Blackpool', *Picture Post* (1 July 1939), 26–32.

51 Nick Stanley, *The Extra Dimension* (Birmingham Polytechnic: unpublished PhD dissertation, 1981), p. 130.

52 Letter to the author, 2003.

53 Julian Trevelyan, *Indigo Days* (Aldershot: Scolar Press, 1996), p. 102.

54 Trevelyan, *Indigo Days*, p. 7.

55 Trevelyan, *Indigo Days*, p. 27.

56 Mel Gooding, 'Preface' in *The Imaginative Impulse: Julian Trevelyan 1910–88* (Henley-on-Thames: Bohun Gallery, 1998), p. 34.

57 Julian Trevelyan Archive, Trinity College Library, Cambridge: JOT 26/4.

58 Trevelyan Archive: JOT 60/1–3: Drafts for autobiography, 1, 58.

59 One of the collages *Bolton Mills, 1938* is in the collection of Bolton Museum and Art Gallery and another, dated 1937, is illustrated in Trevelyan, *Indigo Days*, fig. 5.

60 These comments are based on a set of 56 vintage prints acquired in 1993 by Bolton Museum and Art Gallery. The prints however are rather muddy, and this can make it difficult to assess the photographs.

61 These pictures are curiously reminiscent of photographs made by the Czech Surrealist photographers Miroslav Hák and Jírí Sever on the outskirts of Prague during the war; see Krzysztof Fijalkowski, 'Objective Poetry: Post-war Czech Surrealist Photography and the Everyday', *History of Photography*, 29:2 (Summer 2005), 163–73.

62 Trevelyan Archive: JOT 26/14. It would seem that, like Penrose, Harrisson was also somewhat dyslexic.

63 Trevelyan, *Indigo Days*, p. 100.

64 Letter to the author, 2003.

65 Trevelyan, *Indigo Days*, p. 99.

66 Paul Delany, *Bill Brandt: A Life* (London: Jonathan Cape, 2004), p. 137.

67 Marjorie Beckett, 'Notes on the Photographs' in Bill Brandt, *Shadow of Light* (London: Bodley Head, 1966), p. 11.

68 Orwell, *The Road to Wigan Pier*, p. 101.

69 For a detailed analysis of the different printings of 'A Snicket, Halifax', see Delany, *Bill Brandt*, pp. 269–73. See also Nigel Warburton, 'A Snicket, Halifax, 1937', in Sophie Howarth (ed.), *Singular Images* (London: Tate, 2005), pp. 57–63.

70 Letter of 8 April 1978 to Maria Morris Hambourg, quoted by John Szarkowski, 'Understandings of Atget', in Szarkowski and Hambourg, *The Work of Atget: Volume IV: Modern Times* (New York: Museum of Modern Art, 1985), p. 21.

71 Brandt reproduced the two Halifax pictures across from each other in the second edition of *Shadow of Light* (London: Gordon Fraser, 1977), nos 40 and 41.

72 Victor Burgin, *Some Cities* (London: Reaktion, 1996), p. 10.

73 Derek Smith, 'Interview with Humphrey Spender', *Humphrey Spender: Worktown*, unpaginated.

74 Humphrey Jennings, 'Summer 1940' in Kevin Jackson (ed.), *The Humphrey Jennings Film Reader* (Manchester: Carcanet, 1993), p. 295.

75 Charles Hagen, 'Bill Brandt's Documentary Fiction', *Artforum* (September 1985), 112. On Brandt's constructed documentary, see Nigel Warburton, 'Brandt's Pictorialism' in Warburton (ed.), *Bill Brandt* (Oxford: Clio Press, 1993), pp. 1–26.

76 Hagen, 'Bill Brandt's Documentary Fiction', 114.

77 Bill Brandt, 'Hail, Hell and Halifax', *Lilliput* (February 1948), 151–6.

78 John McDonald and Humphrey Spender, *From Worktown to Our Town* (Bolton: Bolton Museum and Art Gallery, 1993), p. 5.

7
Revenge on culture – the Surrealism of the Blitz

In the summer of 1938, when Paul Nash was discovering the Monster Field and Roland Penrose was in Greece, George Bowling, a dissatisfied middle-aged insurance salesman, decided to revisit his childhood home at Lower Binfield in Oxfordshire. He found it much changed – the rural idyll destroyed by industry and urbanisation.

George is, of course, the hero of *Coming Up for Air* by George Orwell, a book filled not only with the disaffections of the present but also apprehension for the future. The fear of war hovers throughout – Lower Binfield is close to an aerodrome and is being constantly overflown by bombers on training sorties. Near the end, that fear comes crashing to the ground when a bomb is accidentally dropped on the town. Along with the rest of the population, George rushes to the scene, to discover that the kitchen of one house has taken the force of the explosion: 'A jar of marmalade had rolled across the floor, leaving a long streak of marmalade behind, and running side by side with it there was a ribbon of blood. But in among the broken crockery there was lying a leg. Just a leg, with the trouser still on it and a black boot with a Wood-Milne rubber heel ... The blood was beginning to get mixed up with the marmalade.'[1]

Orwell's fictional description is an extraordinary mix of normality and violence – marmalade and blood. His biographers have viewed this scene as an extension into England of his experiences in Spain, but a couple of years later, similar sights would become actual when the war finally did come to England. On 24 September 1940, Orwell wrote in his diary: 'Oxford Street yesterday ... Outside John Lewis's, a pile of plaster dress models, very pink and realistic, looking so like a pile of corpses that one could mistake them for that at a little distance. Just the same sight in Barcelona, only there it was plaster saints from desecrated churches.'[2] Orwell was no Surrealist but elements of surrealism, nevertheless, enter here – the unsettling combination of the ordinary and the strange with the dummies standing in for real human bodies, as mannequins had done throughout Surrealist art. Now though the dummies resembled dead bodies, not living ones.

The Blitz that ravaged London along with other British cities between September 1940 and May 1941 has been the subject of countless books and I do not intend to provide an overall view, even if that were possible.[3] Instead, I want to concentrate on the Blitz as it was experienced in one place – London, from one perspective – Surrealist. This is not to discount the experience of other cities, but the Blitz in London was more intense and prolonged than anywhere else and much of the representation of the Blitz was London-based. In addition, it is apt that this text, having travelled through the rural south and the industrial north should now arrive back in the metropolis against which those other sites of Englishness must be placed.

In concentrating on the Blitz as a surrealist experience, it might seem uncaring to treat so much human loss as if it were merely an artistic effect. One is reminded of the comment made by Ed Murrow, the straight-talking American journalist, in a broadcast on 12 September 1940: 'Miss Dorothy Thompson [the American writer] made a broadcast to Britain last night ... She informed the British that the poets of the world were lined up on their side ... I'm not sure that Londoners agreed that the poets would be much assistance, as they grabbed their blankets and headed for the air-raid shelters.'[4] Quite, and the population of the city had first and foremost to survive. Nevertheless, the 'surrealism' of the blitz was widely remarked, a constant referencing which was ripe for parody. In *Put Out More Flags*, Evelyn Waugh has his hero Basil Seal say to the ersatsz Surrealist painter Poppet Green: 'You know I should have thought an air raid was just the thing for a surrealist: it ought to give you plenty of compositions – limbs and things lying about in odd places, you know.'[5]

If Surrealism affected the response to the Blitz, so the Blitz affected the response to Surrealism. In June 1940, a week after the evacuation from Dunkirk, the exhibition 'Surrealism Today' opened at Zwemmer's Gallery. According to William Plomer, writing in the *New Statesman*, soldiers returned from France saw the work in a new light after the battle: '"This isn't strange to us," they said. "It's just like what we've been seeing over there."'[6] But critics differed as to whether this made Surrealism outmoded or all the more relevant. Thomas McGreevy in *The Studio* remarked: 'One cannot help wondering whether the surrealists did not instinctively sense whither the European society in which they lived was tending, and whether their movement was not, in fact, a criticism of that society' while the reviewer in *The Times* argued that 'nothing that you can do on canvas will stand up to what is going on in the world'.[7]

Some of those who had participated in Surrealism before the war agreed. Julian Trevelyan argued that it 'became absurd to compose Surrealist confections when high explosives could do it so much better, and when German soldiers with Tommy-guns descended from the clouds on parachutes dressed as nuns. Life had caught up with Surrealism or Surrealism with life, and for a giddy moment we in England lived the irrational movement to its death.'[8] (The German parachutists dressed as nuns were one of the more colourful myths of 1940. Ruskin Spear made a delightful drawing imagining what they might look like.)[9] Nigel Henderson – who was to become an important figure after the war – seems to have agreed: 'Surrealism was everywhere in a sense. Houses chopped by bombs while ladies were still sitting on the lavatory, the rest of the house gone but the wallpaper and fires still burning in the grate. Who can hold a candle to that kind of real life Surrealism? It must have spelled the end of it in a way.'[10]

On the first night of war – 3 September 1939 – 'a strange hush fell upon London such as no man had known since the days of the Great Plague. It was as if most of the capital's seven million souls had suddenly died.'[11] The experience that most defined Londoners' new awareness of their city during the year between the declaration of war and the beginning of the Blitz was the blackout. As well as any writer, Elizabeth Bowen caught the strangely detached air of London as it waited for the inevitable attack. In her best-known short story 'Mysterious Kôr', she evoked the blackout: 'Full moonlight drenched the city and searched it; there was not a niche left to stand in. The effect was remorseless: London looked like the moon's capital – shallow, cratered, extinct.'[12] When this story was printed after the war in the American edition of *Harper's Bazaar* in April 1946, it was accompanied by a portrait of the author by Bill Brandt, who greatly admired her work.[13]

It was also Brandt who made the most remarkable set of photographs of the darkened city. Brandt had already worked by night – indeed, one of his books *A Night in London*, published in 1938, was entirely devoted to it.[14] But the blackout intensified the darkness and the stillness of the city. 'London appeared to be a vast, deserted necropolis', wrote Rupert Martin of Brandt's pictures. 'The unreality of the scene, the deserted streets and the quality of light recall the enigmatic townscapes of de Chirico.'[15] We have already seen this inevitable analogy used with Brandt's images of Halifax; here again, Brandt found himself a subject which would enable him to reread his adopted country in terms of the uncanny and strange.

Brandt produced two portfolios of blackout pictures for *Lilliput*, the little magazine where much of his work was published. The first appeared in December 1939, only three months after war had been declared and thus represented Brandt's response to the initial period of blackout.[16] 'Night after night, in that unforgettably fine September of 1939, Bill Brandt photographed the deserted streets with their houses looking as unsubstantial as painted scenery.'[17] However, anyone with a knowledge of *A Night in London* might have spotted something rather familiar in three of the pictures in the *Lilliput* spread. The picture of a house façade in Mayfair was surely the same picture that Brandt had reproduced the year before as 'Late Lights in London', but with the lights in the windows now touched out of the photograph. Likewise, a shot of a Bermondsey warehouse had lost its street lamps, while a shot of the turrets of the Houses of Parliament also appeared in both *A Night in London* and *Lilliput*. (Here, no retouching was needed but, of course, the resonance of the building had changed with wartime.)[18]

One has by now got used to the argument that Brandt was not so much a documentarian as a pictorialist, and would go to any lengths of staging or manipulation to obtain his picture. Still, there is something disturbing about this particular piece of sleight of hand. Did no one notice the rather blatant recycling? It does somehow (even with our post-hoc sophistication about the constructedness of documentary) seem to diminish the pictures and such a feeling would surely have been overwhelming at the time when the new urgency of wartime had made things matter more. But to turn the argument round: why aren't Brandt's tactics a legitimate response to the subject? Then the lights were on, now they are off. Might we not see this as a sort of rephotography via the retoucher's brush?

Moreover, Brandt was not alone in his sleight of hand. Six months later, *Lilliput* published a portfolio of 'Blackout in Paris' by Brandt's friend and rival Brassaï.[19] But at least one picture – here titled 'Suburb' – had a previous life, having been reproduced in *Minotaure* in 1933 as the view across the rooftops of Paris seen from Picasso's studio.[20] Compared with Brandt's discreet bits of retouching, the changes made in the picture are rather dramatic. What was originally a horizontal picture, with the Eiffel Tower seen in the distance on the right, becomes a vertical image, with the tower cropped out, a mass of dense black filled in at the bottom and a moon added for good measure. This does indeed make Brandt's changes seem rather minor.

Brandt's second portfolio of blackout photographs appeared in *Lilliput* two and a half years later in August 1942, after the city has been ravaged by bombing (though, in fact, only three of the ten pictures show this damage).[21] Below one picture, Brandt commented, 'Half these effects are got in the darkroom.' Undoubtedly, there is more legerdemain here, and one might suspect that the lighting conditions in a few pictures were not quite as they seem. Nevertheless, there are several photos here which were among Brandt's best, images pared down to an elegant simplicity, such as the picture that would later become known as 'Deserted Street in Bloomsbury'.[22] In its use of masses of black poised against a deep perspective, it is reminiscent of 'A Snicket, Halifax', but the circumstances of its taking, the fact that the water glittering in the gutter is as likely to be from a fire hose as from rain, gives its emptiness and silence a charge of expectancy.

For a few nights in November 1940, Brandt also went underground to photograph people sleeping in London shelters. After the war, he started to combine these two sets of pictures, bringing the images of deserted streets above ground and cramped sleepers below into dialogue with each other. In *Camera in London* (1948), the caption to the shelter pictures also seeks to connect the images: 'The people who used to live in the houses'.[23] (This is not strictly true, of course, since the working class who crammed into the tube stations at Liverpool Street and the Elephant and Castle were not the people who lived in the Adelphi or Park Crescent.) Later, in the two editions of *Shadow of Light*, Brandt would more thoroughly mix up the two sets of pictures.

The shelter photographs were commissioned by the Ministry of Information (MoI) and from 4 to 12 November, Brandt went out every night to visit tube stations, church crypts and cellars. The negatives that Brandt took (or at least most of them) were handed over to the MoI and later deposited in the Imperial

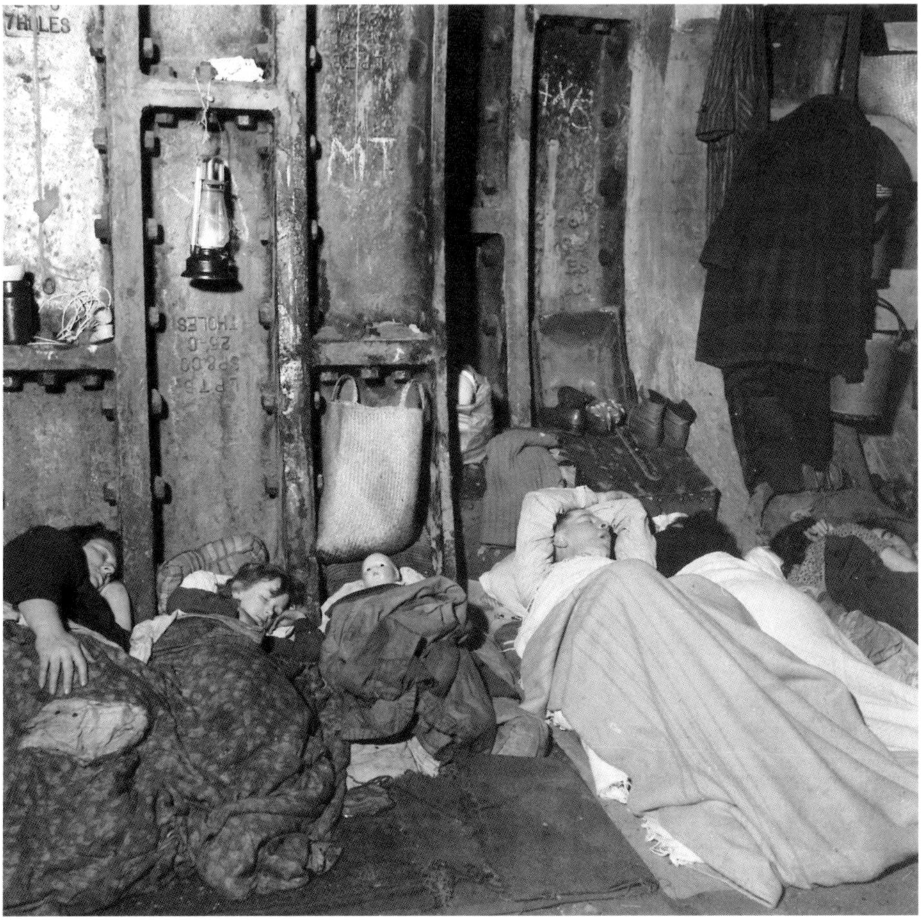

Fig 56 Bill Brandt, *A Family Asleep in Liverpool Street Underground Station, 12 November 1940.* © Imperial War Museum, neg. no. D1582.

War Museum.[24] To look at the 41 pictures by Brandt now in the Museum Archive is to have quite a different relationship with them than one can experience with the rest of his work. They are to be found in the middle of a vast number of other images, many by anonymous photographers; from the Home Front alone, there are 149 albums of pictures filled with 38,143 photographs.[25] The shelter pictures as they are sited in the Imperial War Museum raise a series of questions about authorship and the balance between fact and myth.

The prints in the Museum albums are surprising, especially when one has become used to the versions that Brandt made for *Shadow of Light*. They are sharp, clear, hard, well-lit and full of telling details, which convey something of the roughness and the dampness of the conditions underground. There is often an echoing space around the figures which Brandt may always have intended to crop out but which now add to their effect. It is still possible to find surprising images here: an image of a family asleep, for example, below the graffitied wall of the tube tunnel, their belongings hung or propped carefully above them. And

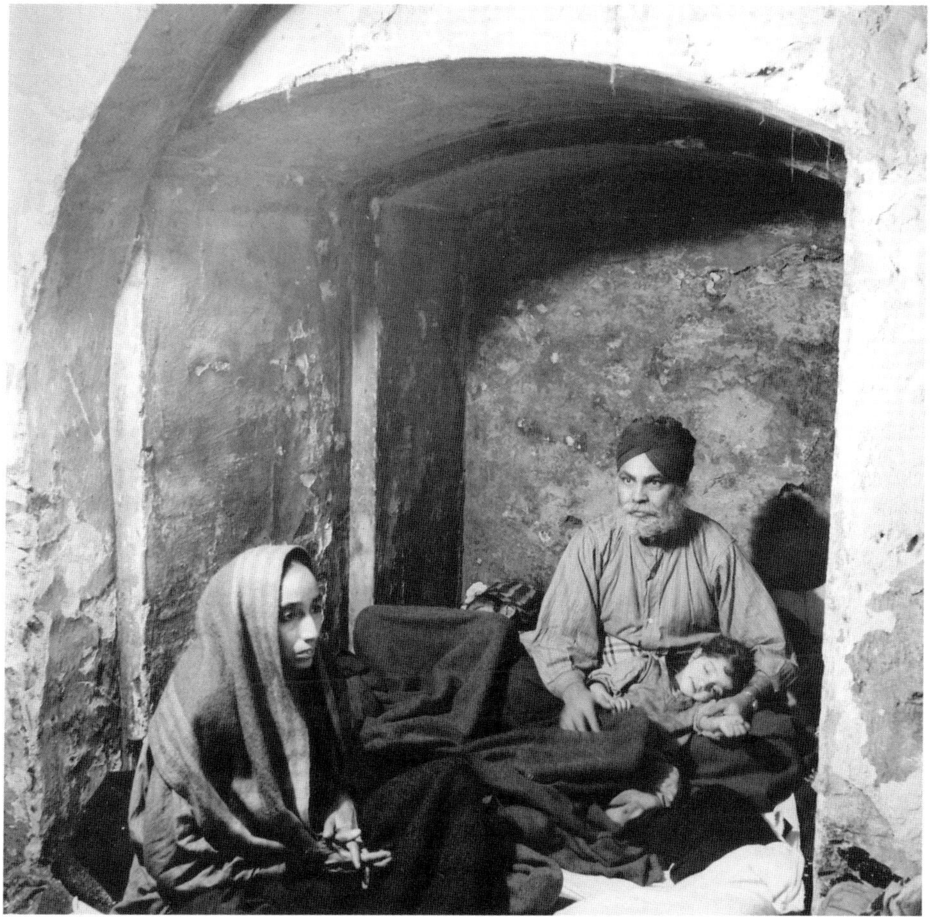

Fig 57 Bill Brandt, *A Sikh family sheltering in the Crypt of Christ Church, Spitalfields, 6 November 1940*. © Imperial War Museum, neg. no. D1516.

in the middle of the row of heads emerging from beneath the bedclothes, the staring, unsleeping face of a doll (figure 56).

Other pictures would be transformed by the time they appeared in *Shadow Of Light* in 1966. One of the most remarkable images is of a Sikh family who Brandt found in the crypt of Christ Church, Spitalfields, and whom he photographed as if they were the Holy Family (figure 57).[26] To look at this picture as Brandt later reworked it next to the original negative is to see how the echoing space above their heads has been closed in, how the figures now loom out of the darkening shadows and the details of the surfaces around them have been erased. Of course, they are posed, though to what extent one cannot tell. The journalist Ritchie Calder must have come across the same family:

> As I climbed the ladder I was confronted by a brown baby face with startled black eyes, under a turban, staring at me for a moment in the flickering candlelight before it disappeared under the bedclothes

> beside its Indian mother. Stretched on the rough floor was a tall figure of an ex-Bengal Lancer, his magnificent shovel beard draped over a blanket, his head turbaned and looking, in sleep, like a breathing monument of an ancient Crusader.[27]

The actual fighting of the fires was by its very nature difficult to depict. Perhaps it is in stories by writers such as William Sansom and Henry Green who worked in the fire service during the Blitz where one finds the most intense accounts of what it was like. Stephen Spender, another fireman-writer, wrote that Sansom's stories 'reveal his fascination with what was often a surreal experience ... an almost privileged entry into an elemental world of a reality completely different from everything outside it'.[28] Nevertheless, these accounts cannot be the same as the experience itself. At the end of Green's novel *Caught*, when his alter-ego Richard is trying to tell his sister-in-law about his experience fighting fires, his narrative is interrupted by an inner voice repeating, 'It had not been like that at all.'[29]

It is ironic but perhaps inevitable that the most powerful representation of the fire service at work during the Blitz should be a film that is at once a 'documentary' and a 'fiction', made almost a year after the worst of the bombing: Humphrey Jennings' *Fires were Started*. The film tells its story with such reticence and naturalism that, on the whole, one would not know that its director was known for his intellectualism and artiness and had once been so heavily involved with Surrealism. Yet there are a few moments when the realist surface of the film cracks a little. Near the end, for example, a one-legged man is seen moving slowly through the rubble (figure 58). A year earlier, he had appeared in Jennings' finest poem 'I See London' written in the spring of 1941,

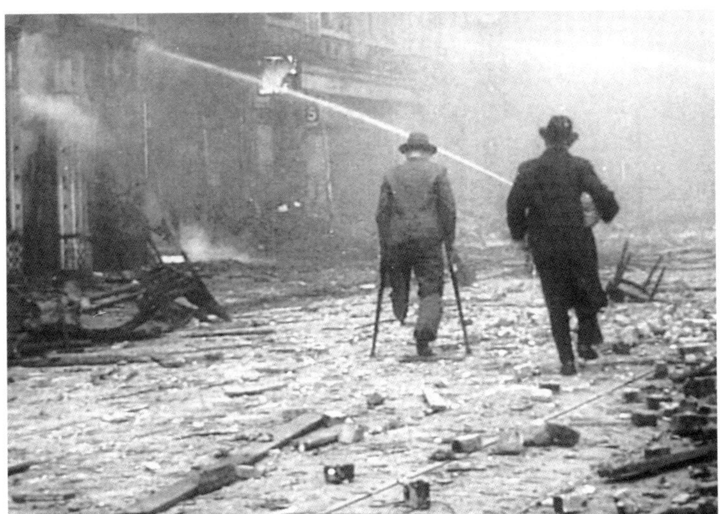

Fig 58 Humphrey Jennings, frame still from *Fires were Started*, 1942.

in which the sense of personal testimony is emphasised by the repetition of 'I see ... I see', culminating with, 'I see a thousand strange sights in the streets of London.'[30] As well as the 'one-legged man crossing the fire on crutches', these include 'the clock on Bow Church burning in daytime' and 'an ambulance girl with her arms full of roses'.

Kathleen Raine remembered, during the Blitz,

> walking with Humphrey among the wreckage of houses, where rain dripped down from charred beams and wallpaper hung in tatters, through Blake's Golden Square and the streets of Soho, Humphrey all the time talking of Blake, so that we seemed to be walking within those very blood-vessels of the city to which Blake had likened 'London's darkening streets'.[31]

This is doubtless filtered through Raine's own mystical readings of Blake, but even so, it gives a sense of how excitement and horror, history and the present, the real and the imaginative could become so thoroughly dissolved together during the Blitz, particularly as it was lived by an artist like Jennings.

The most extraordinary of these moments of 'surreality' in *Fires were Started* occurs at the height of the fire, when suddenly a large dray-horse gallops across the frame past the film's central character, played by William Sansom (figure 59). It is often stated that the scene is in the script, but in fact, what *is* there is different. The fifth treatment (dated 27 January 1942) says: 'Out of the darkness a man running towards him leading three dray horses whose frightened eyes reflect the fire and the gun flashes.'[32] Sansom also described something like this being shot: 'I remember having to run five times in front of two fire-maddened

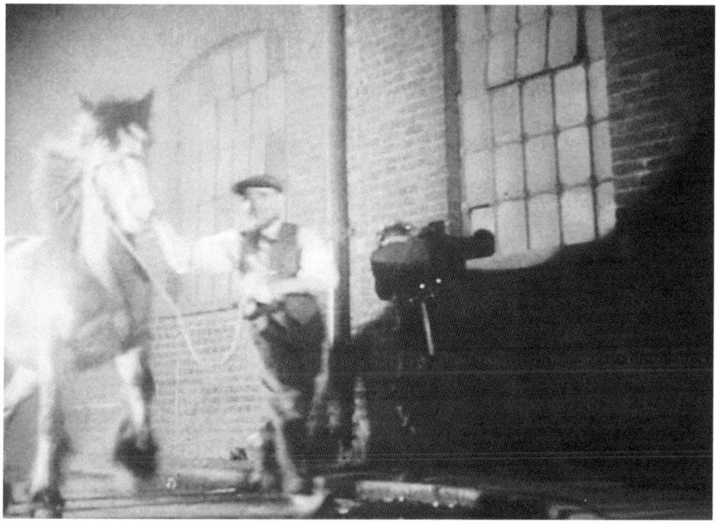

Fig 59 Humphrey Jennings, frame still from *Fires were Started*, 1942.

dray-horses who then had to rear back to miss me, rolling their awful eyes, hammering the air with their giant hoofs a few feet from my tender tin hat.'[33] If shot, this was not used and the image of the single horse is the more effective for its lack of such overt drama.

In their book *London's Burning*, Peter Stansky and William Abrahams call this 'a surrealist moment, surely, but a suggestion too of the timeless, historical part of ordinary, English life'.[34] Horses had been a perennially fascinating subject for Jennings; he had written about them, painted them and filmed them. Charles Madge once described Jennings as if he were himself a horse: 'full of nervous energy and ready to gallop off at any moment'.[35] But this is a description of a thoroughbred and the horse in *Fires were Started* is a workhorse. It is not an abstract emblem, like the white horse that Nash photographed at Uffington, but a real horse, like the one that Constable painted at Flatford. It is a country horse brought to the city. It is also a vision.

There is another, less celebrated, horse which also appeared at the height of the Blitz. James Hanley's novel *No Directions*, published in 1943, is an intense, almost hallucinatory account of a night in a house in Chelsea. At the height of the raid, the artist Clem wanders out into the street to witness for himself the awesome power of destruction. Suddenly, he sees 'something white threshing in the black moving sea'. It is a stallion; he grabs its bridle as the horse drags him through the burning streets. Finally, he calms it down and leads it out into the green fields, 'older than steel and stone, where this beast belonged'.[36] There is nothing in the text that explicitly tells us that this is more of a hallucination than the other excessive events of that night and it is only the unlikelihood of finding green fields in central London that suggest that it is. As much as Jennings, Hanley exploits the mythic presence of the horse, but coming as it were from the other direction. If Hanley's horse is a hallucination that has the power of the real, then Jennings' horse is real, but appears, bursting through the night, like a hallucination – vanishing almost before we see it.

Other animals might also be found in the blitzed city. In a memoir of his father, Henry Green's son wrote that, 'Henry once entered a burning house, axe in hand, to find a naked girl, oblivious of smoke and flames, making love to a Great Dane.'[37] No further explanation is given and the event did not make it into any of Green's stories about the Blitz. Apparently, the juddering power of the bombing could indeed cause heightened sexual excitement (unless this was another hopeful myth). Perhaps Lee Miller was referencing this effect when she photographed a chalked sign on a London street proclaiming 'One Night of Love'. It was presumably an advert for a film or entertainment, though Miller would have known that it was also the title of a painting by Max Ernst.

The next morning, the city awoke and at that moment – in the apparent clarity of daylight – the strange montage that the destruction produced was at its most potent. Everyone, it seems, had their own moment of horror or humour. 'The great sweep of Regent Street ... stared gauntly like a thoroughfare in a dead city', wrote Mollie Panter-Downes in one of her columns for the *New Yorker*. 'It would have been no surprise to see grass growing up out of the pavements, which were covered instead with a fine, frosty glitter of powdered glass.'[38] The shattered glass struck many observers; the narrator in Nigel Balchin's novel *Darkness Falls from the Air* recounts, 'Just as I was crossing into Soho a window fell out of a shop on the corner of Burlington Street. Nothing was actually firing at that moment. It just fell out by itself ... There was a bobby walking along Beak Street. I said, "Did that fall or was it pushed?" He said, "They often do that."'[39]

Vera Brittain noticed that, 'In one elegant furniture shop where the plate-glass windows have been completely destroyed, two beautiful yellow porcelain vases stand untouched on their pedestal.'[40] In the East End, Graham Sutherland found that 'even a mattress that had been blown out of a house into the middle of a street looked more like a body than a mattress. From butchers' shops which had been hit the meat spewed on the road, and I remember when seeing this for the first time I thought that here was a body that hadn't been picked up.'[41] Ed Murrow recalled: 'One night I stood in front of a smashed grocery store and heard a dripping inside. It was the only sound in all London. Two cans of peaches had been drilled through by flying glass and the juice was dripping on the floor.'[42] (One is reminded of Orwell's image of blood and marmalade.)

In her novel *The Heat of the Day*, Elizabeth Bowen wrote of the sense that the blitzed city was haunted: 'Most of all the dead, from mortuaries, from under cataracts of rubble, made their anonymous presence – not as today's dead but as yesterday's living – felt through London. Uncounted, they continued to move in shoals through the city day, pervading everything with their torn-off senses.'[43] The presence of the dead was not only something to be imagined; one observer, Robert Herring, felt it to be all too real: 'The air itself, as we walked, smelt of burning. Gritty, it grated in my lungs. I felt cannibal – inhaling, with each breath, skeleton cinders.'[44] Graham Greene was not the only one to be reminded of another destroyed city in describing 'the strange torn landscape where London shops were reduced to a stone ground-plan like those of Pompeii'.[45]

Some of these accounts are factual, though filtered through memory and imagination. Others are fictional, though presumably based in observation or experience. It can be hard to tell the difference. As Dai Vaughan remarked of the documentary films of the period:

> In a bombed hospital, an umbrella might very well encounter a sewing machine on a dissecting table. If the goal of surrealism was *changer la vie*, life was now changing before everyone's eyes ... [these changes] were generating their own imagery at a pace which left the artist no need to trawl his or her subconscious for symbols of flux and transcendence. Surrealism and the documentary imperative were united.[46]

There was a wide range of photographs made in the aftermath of the Blitz, many with no thought of artistry and the better for it. Even so, there were

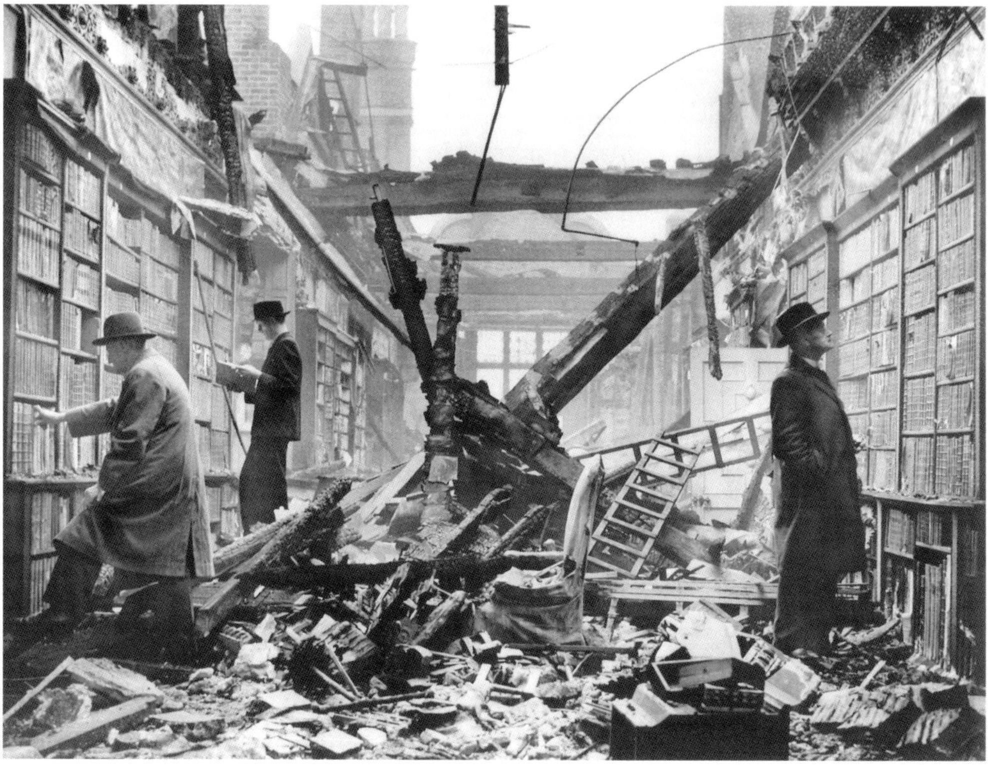

Fig 60 Photographer unknown, *The Library, Holland House, Kensington, London*, 1940. © English Heritage, National Monuments Record.

moments when photographers could not help but record the sheer strangeness of the scene before them. That most straightforward of photographers Bert Hardy photographed a woman working at her sewing machine next to a shattered window so that, as Angus Calder wrote, the glass that's left 'might be seen as the angelically shimmering cape of the Air Raid Precautions man outside, whose body it covers with apparent exactitude'.[47] Hardy himself said of this picture that he hesitated to photograph it 'in case it didn't look "real" enough'.[48] But in fact, many of the best-known images of the Blitz work on that line between the normal and its disruption to create an everyday 'surrealism'.

One of the most remarkable pictures of this type was taken in the library of Holland House after a bomb fell on it in October, 1940 (figure 60). It has been seen in many different contexts since.[49] The picture is almost perfectly symmetrical, an order which balances against the chaos of the destruction, in the midst of which three men stoically regard the intact books on the shelves. Their absorption seems both bizarre (how can they carry on reading books in the middle of this?) and resolute (what can be more important than to still value books?). The photographer is unknown and the picture must be staged but, as Susan Sontag remarked, 'It is pleasing to imagine that ... the three gents were observed indulging their bookish habits in the destroyed mansion and the photographer did little more

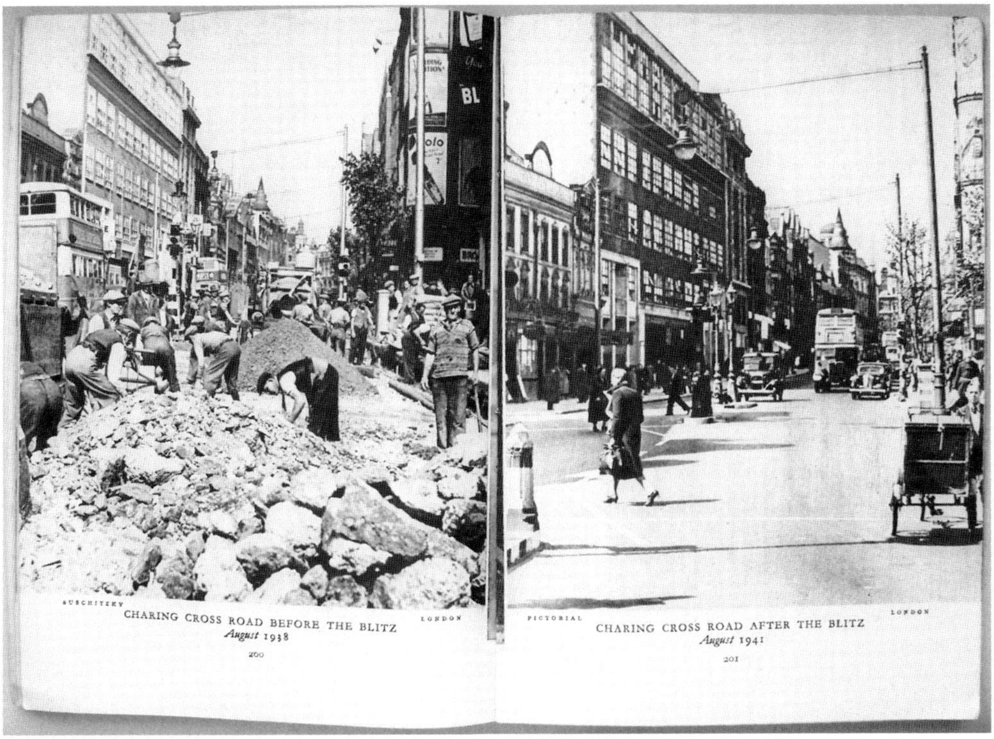

Fig 61 Spread from *Lilliput* (September 1941). Photograph on left © Wolfgang Suschitzky.

than space them differently to make a more incisive picture.'[50]

The expectation of what a Blitz photograph should look like was so prevalent that it was possible to trick the audience. In September 1941, when the worst of the bombing was obviously over and attitudes were a little more relaxed, *Lilliput* reproduced across a double-spread two shots of Charing Cross Road taken from near the same spot, one before the Blitz, the other after (figure 61). In one, all is clean and orderly, full of bustling pedestrians and traffic; in the other, the street has piles of debris strewn across it, which workmen are struggling to sort out. The joke is that the debris picture is the 'Before' shot, taken in 1938 (and the debris is just road workings), the 'After' shot of 1941 is the clean one.[51]

In a little feature in May 1941, British *Vogue* celebrated new books by two of the magazine's leading photographers.[52] These did not contain pictures of fashionable couture but of Blitz damage. Yet Lee Miller's work in *Grim Glory* was very different from Cecil Beaton's photographs in his book *History Under Fire*. Beaton collaborated with James Pope-Hennessy on *History Under Fire* as a record of the destruction of buildings in the City.[53] John Piper reviewed the book on its publication and commented: 'Mr Cecil Beaton is an old hand. The war, he decides, has played enough tricks without the artist and photographer adding to them. He has taken some excellent, straight photographs of buildings and parts of buildings, selecting carefully, rearranging subjects laudably to make them tell better.'[54] There is a certain irony in Piper's praise of Beaton's 'straightness', for, just as Beaton's photographs are theatrical, full of framings and reframings, so much the same might be said of the Piper's own paintings of the Blitz, which 'resemble stage sets or backcloths to ballets to an extent that it is sometimes difficult to associate them with real events'.[55] This, we might say, was the Blitz as 'picturesque'.

But not all of Beaton's Blitz photographs were so 'straight' and in his diary, he recorded the following:

> I went to Albemarle Street to see if the wax head I had seen among the debris of a former hairdressing establishment was still there ... I clambered over the rubble to find a new wax head lying, bald but still smiling, among the cracked mirrors, glass fragments and wreckage of the ladies' beauty shop. The men working on the job were very helpful and when I asked one if he had seen the head with the golden hair flying wild, he said he thought it could be unearthed. It was. The ghoulish head was produced from a mound of rubbish, and I proceeded to photograph it against the dreadful surroundings (figure 62).[56]

Then the watching crowd got edgy, Beaton was asked to show his papers, told he shouldn't photograph that subject and escorted from the scene by a policeman. It was as if he were photographing a real body. When a variation on the picture was reproduced in the *Sketch* on 13 November, its caption read: 'The blast of the Blitzkrieg has bombed London into surrealism! Cecil Beaton has only to take his camera out after the "All Clear" has sounded to find well posed subjects on every hand.'[57]

Well-tuned commercial photographer that he was, Beaton was also able to incorporate the Blitz into his fashion photography. He took a model dressed in a Digby Morton suit to the Temple, photographed her in front of the rubble, and, when the picture was printed in *Vogue*, it carried the caption 'Fashion is Indestructible'.[58] It is curious now to look through copies of British *Vogue* for 1940–41. There is certainly a war going on and it is constantly referred to, but it is largely out of sight. 'Do you still need *Vogue*?' asks an editorial in November 1940 and the answer is, 'Yes, more than ever' (for that vital information about how to be chic without showing off). A few pages later, the magazine reproduces some pictures of its own offices wrecked by bomb damage.

Those photographs were taken by Lee Miller, whose presence in the magazine had been largely through her regular contributions as a photographer of fashion. When she arrived in London in June 1939, one of her first actions had been to approach *Vogue* for work. Miller's work for *Vogue* is well made and usually unostentatious; only a knowing viewer might spot the odd trick picked up from

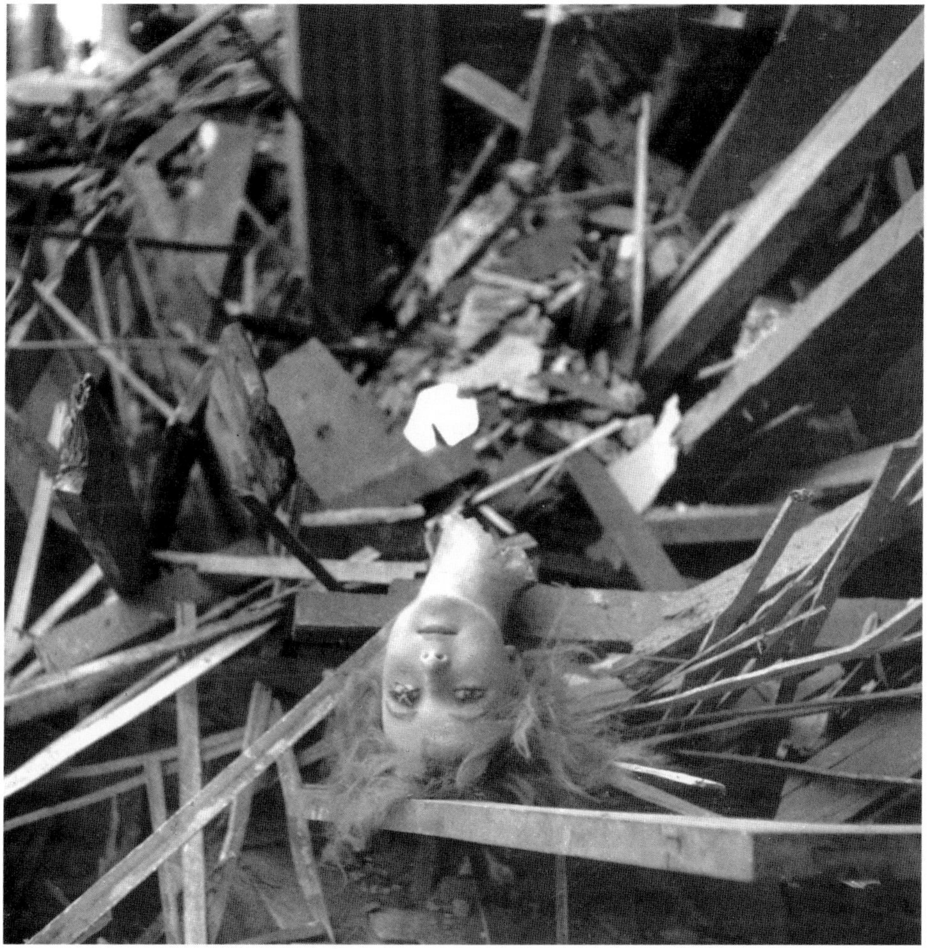

Fig 62 Cecil Beaton, *London bomb damage*, 1940. © Cecil Beaton Archive, Sotheby's London.

her days with Man Ray. But at the same time as she was making these pictures, so perfectly poised, she was also out in the streets photographing the far-from-perfect reality of the Blitz. Miller's picturing of the damage probably began as she travelled to work between Hampstead, where the Penroses lived, and the *Vogue* office in Bond Street. She would also have developed and printed the pictures in the *Vogue* darkrooms, and subsequently shown them to friends and acquaintances. It was probably in this way that the writer Ernestine Carter saw them.[59]

Like Miller, Carter was an American expatriate married to an Englishman. They had first met in New York, when Carter was working at the Museum of Modern Art and Miller had attended a screening of Cocteau's film *Le Sang d'un poète*, in which she had appeared. In London in 1940, they both found themselves wanting 'something to do'. Carter wrote later:

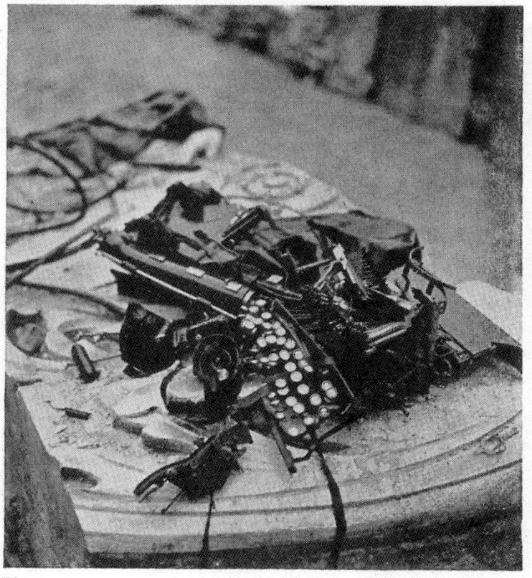

72 **Remington silent**

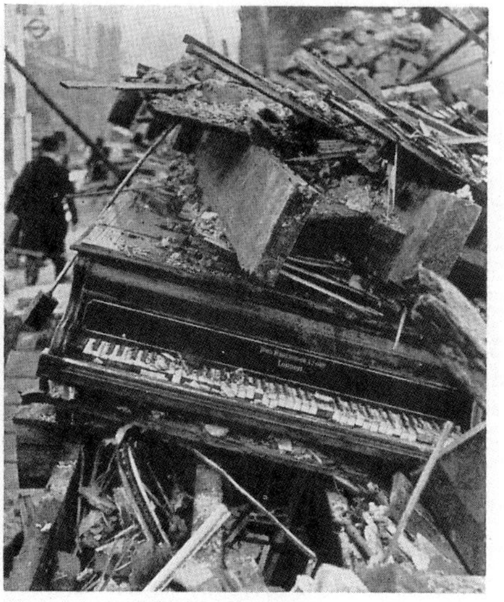

73 **Piano by Broadwood**

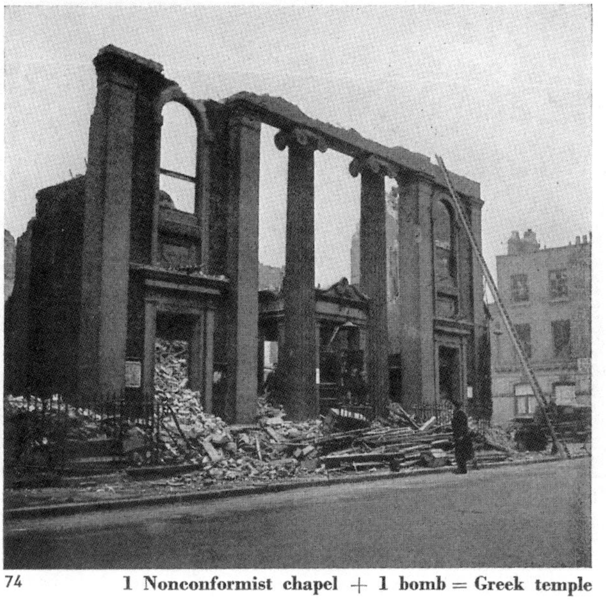

74 **1 Nonconformist chapel + 1 bomb = Greek temple**

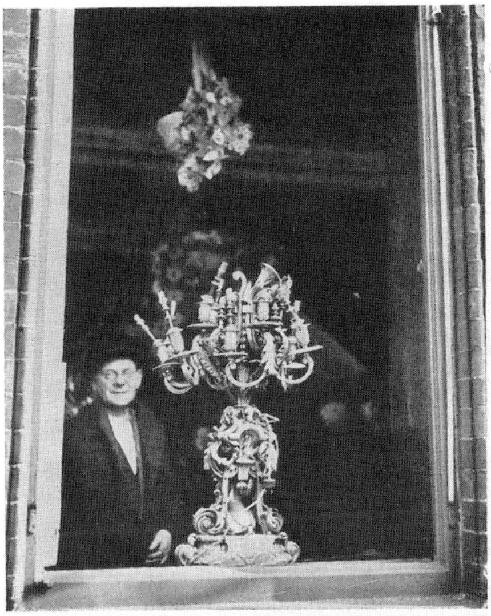

75 **Baroque made rococo**

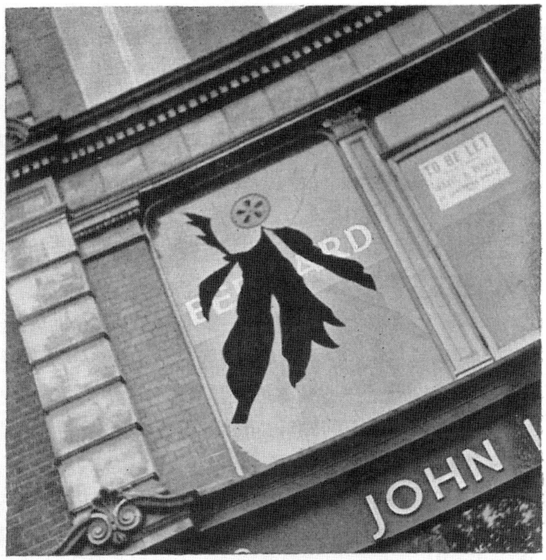

76 **Blast pays deserved tribute to the Gas Light & Coke Company's trade-mark, Mr. Therm**

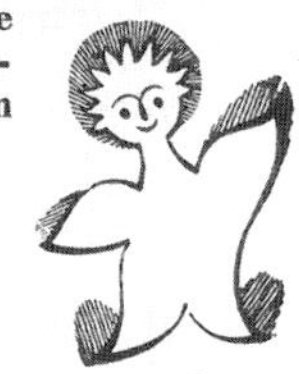

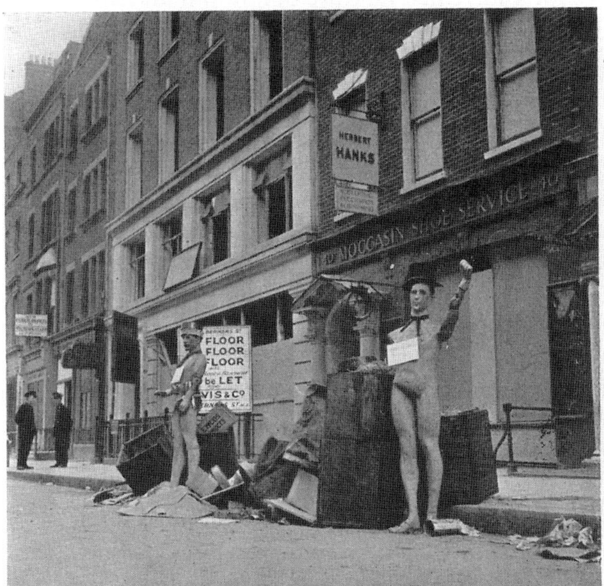

77 **Indecent exposure?**

Fig 63 Spread of photographs by Lee Miller from *Grim Glory*, 1941. © Lee Miller Archives, England 2007.

profile resembles Lee Miller herself.[68] As always with Miller, it seems that the personal cannot be disentangled from the broader cultural and pictorial issues of her images. But perhaps this is a necessary element in giving her pictures the undertow they have.

It is interesting to place 'Revenge on Culture' alongside the photograph that Cecil Beaton took in Albemarle Street. Though one is of a classical statue and the other of a hairdresser's wax dummy, the pictures both present surrogate images of women under attack. (In the great mass of photography of the Blitz, there are very few pictures of actual bodies, largely because of self-censorship. Rather, buildings, statues, objects and mannequins become metaphors for the destruction wrought on real bodies.) The shock effect of Beaton's picture is more dramatic, of course, but it is rather superficial. Miller also wants to disorientate the viewer, but more gently, by removing the background and tilting the camera.

Part of this effect is also formal. Beaton's composition is centralised with a spiral of diagonal lines around the head. 'Revenge on Culture' on the other hand works through a shifting set of diagonal planes moving back into space and trapping the nude figure between them. The black bar holds her down, the brick seems to be crushing her breast (even though we are aware it is made of stone) and she seems to be holding out her hand to resist the pressure from the sharp edge of the block in front of her. Yet it seems a gentle gesture. There is a tenderness in the way that Miller approaches the threatened figure and – whether triggered by cultural, gendered or personal associations – this makes the image resonate in ways that Beaton's picture does not. For him, the dummy is just another mannequin with which to make a photograph.

There is much more that might be said and many other examples that might be cited of the 'surrealism' of the Blitz, but one thing, I hope, is evident. While this aspect of the experience may not have been central to what Angus Calder has called 'The Myth of the Blitz', it was a significant element, both as it was lived and as it was turned into words and pictures. Of all the works cited here, one might say, as Angus Wilson did of Elizabeth Bowen's short stories, that they provide 'moments of sudden vision just as the bombs themselves exploded London's surface beauty or squalor to reveal long-forgotten depths beneath'.[69] For Surrealism, it was a period when the dark horrors that fascinated it were no longer imagined but actual, when it was not the hidden recesses of the individual psyche that was under scrutiny but the unconscious of the larger culture. Surrealism was real and reality surreal: the rhetoric and imagery of Surrealism were constantly invoked in the attempt to render palpable the intensity of the experience of the Blitz. But what this did to Surrealism itself – what role Surrealism could have after that moment when it had come together so intensely with real life – was open to question.

Notes

1 George Orwell, *Coming up for Air* (London: Penguin, 2000), pp. 235–6.

2 George Orwell, 'War-time Diary: 1940', in Sonia Orwell and Ian Angus (eds), *Collected Essays, Journalism and Letters of George Orwell, Vol. II: My Country Right or Left 1940–1943* (Harmondsworth: Penguin, 1970), p. 375.

3 As well as the other books cited here, there are important general accounts of the Blitz in Angus Calder, *The People's War* (London: Cape, 1969); Constantine Fitzgibbon, *The Blitz* (London: Macdonald, 1970) and M. J. Gaskin, *Blitz: the story of 29th December 1940* (London: Faber & Faber, 2005). Mass-Observation's reading of the Blitz can be found in Tom Harrisson, *Living Through the Blitz* (London: Collins, 1976), while Robert Hewison, *Under Siege* (London: Weidenfeld & Nicolson, 1977) gives an account of artistic life in London during the period.

4 Edward R. Murrow, *This is London* (London: Cassell, 1941), p. 186.

5 Evelyn Waugh, *Put Out More Flags* (London: Penguin, 2000), p. 31.

6 William Plomer, 'Surrealism To-Day', *New Statesman and Nation*, 19:488 (29 June 1940), 794.

7 For an account of the exhibition, including the comments of critics, see Nigel Vaux Halliday, *More than a Bookshop: Zwemmer's and Art in the 20th Century* (London: Philip Wilson, 1991), pp. 157–66.

8 Julian Trevelyan, *Indigo Days* (Aldershot: Scolar Press, 1996), p. 80.

9 Ruskin Spear's watercolour titled 'Home Guard's Dream' is reproduced in Martin Harrison, *Transition: The London Art Scene in the Fifties* (London: Merrell, 2002), p. 13.

10 Dave Hoffmann and Shirley Read, 'Nigel Henderson' (interview), *Camerawork*, 11 (September 1978), 12.

11 Leonard Mosley, *Backs to the Wall: London Under Fire 1939–45* (London: Weidenfeld & Nicolson, 1971), p. 1.

12 Elizabeth Bowen, *The Demon Lover and Other Stories* (London: Jonathan Cape, 1945), p. 173.

13 Mark Haworth-Booth, 'Introduction' in Mark Haworth-Booth and David Mellor, *Bill Brandt: Behind the Camera* (Oxford: Phaidon, 1985), p. 37.

14 Bill Brandt, *A Night in London* (London: Country Life, 1938).

15 Rupert Martin, *Bill Brandt: War Work* (London: The Photographers' Gallery, 1983), reprinted in Nigel Warburton (ed.), *Bill Brandt* (Oxford: Clio Press, 1993), p. 48.

16 Bill Brandt, 'Blackout in London', *Lilliput* (December 1939), 551–8.

17 Marjorie Beckett, 'Notes on the Photographs' in Bill Brandt, *Shadow of Light* (London: Bodley Head, 1966), p. 11.

18 The first writer to spot this reuse seems to have been David Mellor in his essay 'Brandt's Phantasms', in Haworth-Booth and Mellor, *Bill Brandt: Behind the Camera*, p. 78.

19 Brassaï, 'Blackout in Paris', *Lilliput*, 36 (June, 1940), 509–16.

20 This is one of the many photographs by Brassaï illustrating André Breton's article 'Picasso dans son élément', *Minotaure*, 1 (1933), 4–22. The picture of the rooftops titled 'La Fenêtre' is on page 11.

21 Bill Brandt, 'London by Moonlight', *Lilliput* (August 1942), 131–40.

22 In *Lilliput*, 137, it was captioned 'Street in a Bombed Area' and had also been reversed,

presumably for compositional reasons.

23 Bill Brandt, *Camera in London* (London: Focal Press, 1948), pp. 86–7.

24 A photograph of a man asleep in a stone sarcophagus in *Shadow of Light* comes from a different negative than the image in the Imperial War Museum – one Brandt had presumably kept back for himself.

25 A number of Brandt's images are placed in the context of images by other unrecorded photographers in Mike Seaborne, *Shelters: Living Underground in the London Blitz* (London: Dirk Nishen, 1988).

26 This analogy is made by Mark Haworth-Booth in his 'Introduction' to the second edition of *Shadow of Light* (London: Gordon Fraser, 1977), p. 19.

27 Ritchie Calder, *Carry On London* (London: English Universities Press, 1941), p. 38.

28 Stephen Spender, foreword to William Sansom, *The Blitz: Westminster at War* (Oxford: Oxford University Press, 1989), p. ix. Sansom's stories of the Blitz were collected in *Fireman Flower and Other Stories* (London: Hogarth Press, 1944).

29 Henry Green, *Caught* (London: Harvill Press, 2001), pp. 173–98.

30 The poem is reprinted in Kevin Jackson (ed.) *The Humphrey Jennings Film Reader* (Manchester: Carcanet, 1993), pp. 296–7.

31 Kathleen Raine, *The Land Unknown* (London: Hamish Hamilton, 1975), p. 167.

32 Jennings Collection, British Film Institute, File 6.

33 William Sansom, 'The Making of *Fires were Started*', *Film Quarterly*, 15:2 (Winter 1961–2), 28.

34 Peter Stansky and William Abrahams, *London's Burning* (London: Constable, 1994), p. 109.

35 Quoted in Stansky and Abrahams, *London's Burning*, p. 72.

36 James Hanley, *No Directions* (London: André Deutsch, 1990), pp. 136–7.

37 Sebastian Yorke, 'A Memoir' in Matthew Yorke (ed.), *Surviving: the Uncollected Writings of Henry Green* (London: Chatto & Windus, 1992), p. 297.

38 Mollie Panter-Downes, *London War Notes 1939–1945* (London: Longman, 1972), p. 100.

39 Nigel Balchin, *Darkness Falls from the Air* (London: Cassell, 2002), p. 32.

40 Vera Brittain, *England's Hour* (London: Macmillan, 1941), pp. 200–1.

41 Roberto Tassi, *Sutherland: The Wartime Drawings* (London: Sotheby Parke Bernet, 1980), p. 19.

42 Murrow, *This is London*, p. 189.

43 Elizabeth Bowen, *The Heat of the Day* (London: Vintage, 1998), p. 91.

44 Quoted by Philip Ziegler, *London at War 1939–1945* (London: Pimlico, 2002), p. 145.

45 Graham Greene, *The Ministry of Fear* (London: Vintage, 2001), p. 40

46 Dai Vaughan, *Portrait of an Invisible Man* (London: British Film Institute, 1983), p. 68.

47 Angus Calder, *The Myth of the Blitz* (London: Jonathan Cape, 1991), p. 142. Hardy's picture is reproduced as Plate 14.

48 Bert Hardy, *My Life* (London: Gordon Fraser, 1985), p. 40.

49 One of the most intriguing sitings of this photograph is in Eduardo Cadava's book *Words of Light: Theses on the Photography of History* (Princeton: Princeton University Press, 1997), p. 62. The book is about Walter Benjamin's concept of history and photography and it is hard in that context not to connect the picture with Benjamin's own work on (and in)

libraries, and his suicide on 26 September (days before the library was bombed) while trying to escape the same forces of Fascism that had caused the bombing.

50 Susan Sontag, *Regarding the Pain of Others* (New York: Farrar, Straus and Giroux, 2003), p. 57.

51 *Lilliput* (September 1941), 200–1. The pre-war picture is by Wolfgang Suschitzky from his extended series of photographs on Charing Cross Road (it is reproduced in his book, *Charing Cross Road in the Thirties* (London: Dirk Nishen, 1989), p. 14).

52 Lesley Blanch, 'Vogue's Spotlight', *Vogue* (May 1941), 41.

53 Cecil Beaton, *History Under Fire*, with a commentary by James Pope-Hennessy (London: Batsford, 1941). For a discussion of the book, see John Taylor, *A Dream of England* (Manchester: Manchester University Press, 1994), pp. 193–5.

54 John Piper, 'A War-Artist on War-Photographs', *The Spectator*, 5898 (11 July 1941), 38.

55 Alan Ross, *Colours of War* (London: Jonathan Cape, 1983), p. 50. On the theatricality of Beaton's Blitz photographs, see David Mellor (ed.), *Cecil Beaton* (London: Barbican Art Gallery, 1986), p. 35.

56 Cecil Beaton, *The Years Between: Diaries 1939–44* (London: Weidenfeld & Nicolson, 1965), pp. 39–40.

57 Cecil Beaton, 'Blast of Modern Art! London bombed into Surrealism', *The Sketch* (13 November 1940), 209. The dummy's head in this published picture is on a different part of the rubble, demonstrating how Beaton moved the head around as he photographed it.

58 Cecil Beaton, 'Fashion is Indestructible', *Vogue* (September 1941), 32.

59 My thanks to Antony Penrose for these speculations (interview with the author, 20 July 2005).

60 Ernestine Carter, *With Tongue in Chic* (London: Michael Joseph, 1974), p. 56.

61 Ernestine Carter (ed.), *Grim Glory* (London: Lund Humphries, 1941), preface by Edward R. Murrow, photographs by Lee Miller and others. Published in the USA as *Bloody but Unbowed* (New York: Scribners, 1941).

62 Piper, 'A War-Artist on War-Photographs', 38.

63 Roland Penrose, *Scrapbook 1900–1981* (London: Thames & Hudson, 1981), p. 128.

64 Jane Livingston, *Lee Miller: Photographer* (London: Thames & Hudson, 1989), p. 58.

65 Benjamin Péret, 'Ruines: Ruine des Ruines', *Minotaure*, 12–13 (May 1939), 57–61.

66 Antony Penrose, *The Lives of Lee Miller* (London: Thames & Hudson, 1985), p. 104.

67 Gwen Raaberg, 'The Problematics of Women and Surrealism', in Mary Ann Caws, Rudolf E. Kuenzli and Gwen Raaberg (eds), *Surrealism and Women* (Cambridge, Mass: MIT Press), p. 6.

68 Carolyn Burke, *Lee Miller* (London: Bloomsbury, 2005), p. 207.

69 Angus Wilson, 'Introduction' in Elizabeth Bowen, *Collected Stories* (London: Vintage, 1999), p. 7.

8
The street and the beach

'Wildflowers had spread over the bomb sites: rose-bay willowherb, coltsfoot, groundsel, Oxford ragwort, Canadian fleabane and Thanet cress.'[1] This image from *The Times* in 1945 is an apt metaphor both for the exhausted culture left at the end of the war and the way that culture was beginning to renew itself in new and curious ways. The post-war period would be a time of change for all three of the elements traced in this book: Englishness, Documentary and Surrealism. The values of Englishness had underpinned much wartime propaganda, yet the relationship this country now had with Europe, with its diminishing Empire and with the dominant power of the USA had fundamentally changed. For the duration of the conflict, Documentary had been elided with propaganda; after the war, there would be a need to reassert its criticality. Surrealism as a movement was tired and disorganised, albeit that its core values had, for many writers and artists, been validated in their experience of the war.

These three strands also continued to interweave through the second half of the twentieth century, but in ways that were often fragmentary and irregular. An account of this period could follow many avenues. David Briers has suggested that echoes of Mass-Observation's fascination with the strangely normal could be traced in post-war culture:

> shot through with humour, and influenced by popular entertainment and the particularities of everyday life in postwar urban Britain ... a history of these currently disregarded manifestations would have to take on board an interrogation of a field of activity that encompassed such things as Stephen Potter's *Lifemanship* guide, I-Spy books, *The Goon Show* and *Candid Camera*.[2]

Such an investigation would be fascinating, a reminder of how complex culture is and how much gets lost in any one retelling. But while this everyday culture forms a broad background here, I concentrate on the work of just a handful of individual artists, photographers and film-makers, whose work stands in a significant but varying relation to the main themes of this book. As the title of this chapter suggests, we, again, shift between the city centre and the margins of the coast: between the photographs taken by Nigel Henderson, Ian Breakwell and Richard Wentworth in Bethnal Green, Smithfield and Islington respectively, and images of the English seaside by Lindsay Anderson, Tony Ray-Jones, Susan Hiller and Martin Parr. The films of Patrick Keiller and photographs of John Davies map the landscapes between the two; Ralph Rumney's Venetian photo-story is a single excursion into Europe.

This is by no means a definitive account – nor could it be – but rather an attempt to trace some broader ideas as they move through individual bodies of work. It is a story that largely starts anew after the war, for none of the protagonists whose work we have studied so far would play an active part in it. Paul Nash died in 1946 at the age of 57, while Humphrey Jennings fell to his death researching a film on the Greek island of Poros in 1950. He was 43. Eileen Agar, Humphrey Spender and Julian Trevelyan continued to work as painters and printmakers but not (with any seriousness) in photography. Cecil Beaton returned to the world of glamour and fashion. Roland Penrose devoted his energy to the setting up of the Institute of Contemporary Art and the task of bringing modern art to a broader audience. In 1966 he was knighted.

Lee Miller had chased the war across Europe, ending up back in Romania in 1946. The gypsies who had entranced her eight years earlier were gone; burnt out, she returned to England and marriage. When she died in 1977, her obituary in *The Times* read: 'Lady Penrose, wife of Sir Roland Penrose, Chairman of the Institute of Contemporary Arts, died on July 21. She was Lee Miller, an American who had been a photographer and had worked for Paris Vogue.'[3] Her reputation in her own right would be established posthumously.

Only Bill Brandt would significantly extend his photographic practice in the post-war period, but his move to a melodramatic printing style and self-conscious artistry was not to everyone's taste. Nigel Henderson, for example, 'admired Brandt's earlier social reportage ... but found the wide-angle nudes of the Fifties sterile'.[4] The dominant photographic taste of the post-war period was rather for roughness, crudeness and a refusal of artistry. Peter Rose Pulham, who a decade before had been making elegant, studio-bound portraits of 'surrealist' artists,[5] said in 1952: 'the best photo is of a national calamity, when the camera is knocked out of the photographer's hand, develops itself in the gutter and is immediately published in the newspapers, where its impact as a smudged image is immediate. Afterwards, the negative is stored in the police archives.'[6] Or is, perhaps, found in the studio of Francis Bacon, who apparently much admired Pulham's celebration of inartistic photography. It was this sort of photography which, of course, fed into Bacon's own work, alongside the undoubted influence of Surrealism, though he himself always played down the link.

This combination of indebtedness to and dismissal of Surrealism was common to the period. One central forum for artistic debate was the ICA, which had been founded in 1946 by Roland Penrose together with other members of the pre-war Surrealist group, Herbert Read and E. L. T. Mesens. Indeed, according to Penrose, the roots of the ICA went back to the 1936 exhibition.[7] But these erstwhile rebels were evolving into establishment figures, concerned to make the, by now, great tradition of European modernism respectable. So we have the curious situation of Surrealism (or at least a rather stale post-war version of it) being seen as the Establishment against which a younger generation had to rebel.

Within the ICA itself, the focus for this rebellion was the Independent Group, who met between 1952 and 1955. They looked back to the anti-art positionings of Dada. They re-examined those elements of modernism which had responded to developments in science and technology. Most famously, they looked across the Atlantic to American culture, both high (Jackson Pollock) and low (comic books). This does not mean, however, that Surrealism was altogether absent from this debate, and for two artists involved with the Independent Group – Nigel Henderson and his close friend Eduardo Paolozzi – Surrealism remained an important element in their work. Paolozzi is an important figure in this respect as the only major post-war artist to admit wholly to the influence of Surrealism. Looking back in 1995, he said: 'I'm like a curious kind of hybrid on the English landscape; I still find Surrealism the big important seed that has been planted in me. I still find that it's a kind of petrol that makes me do things.'[8]

Paolozzi had moved from his native Edinburgh in 1945 to study at the Slade School of Art. There he met Henderson, who was older and from a very different – upper-class – background; his wife Judith was Virginia Woolf's niece. For Paolozzi, he was 'a symbol of a rapidly vanishing England, deeply scarred by war'.[9] Unlike the other members of the Independent Group, Henderson had known the pre-war art world. His mother Wyn Henderson had run the Guggenheim Jeune gallery in London, through which Henderson had met significant artists including Marcel Duchamp. An early interest in Surrealism had included 'reading Lautréamont, Eluard and Aragon in uncut editions which his mother got from Paris'.[10] He also knew some of the English Surrealists and especially admired Jennings: 'He was trying to put down something about his vision of England. A poet really. I liked that very much.'[11]

In 1945, the Hendersons moved to the working-class East End, where Judith Henderson worked as an anthropologist on a project called 'Discover Your Neighbour'. (Tom Harrisson gave her encouragement with this.) Henderson developed his own fascination with the area and acquired a Rolleicord 6 x 6 cm to photograph it. The pictures he made on the streets of Bethnal Green between 1949 and 1953 are a ragged bunch of images – battered walls, peeling posters, scratched graffiti, shop windows piled high with adverts for tobacco and ice cream, children playing, people seen through the windows of pubs and cafes, street entertainers, market stalls. They follow no single narrative and, as James Lingwood has noted, 'the influences on Henderson were remarkably diverse, and in no way restricted to a specifically British tradition or to a snapshot aesthetic'.[12] In the library at the Slade, he had come across books of photographs by Atget and Walker Evans, he knew Brassaï's pictures from *Minotaure* and admired the street photography of Cartier-Bresson. (Henderson guided Cartier-Bresson round the East End on a visit in 1951.)

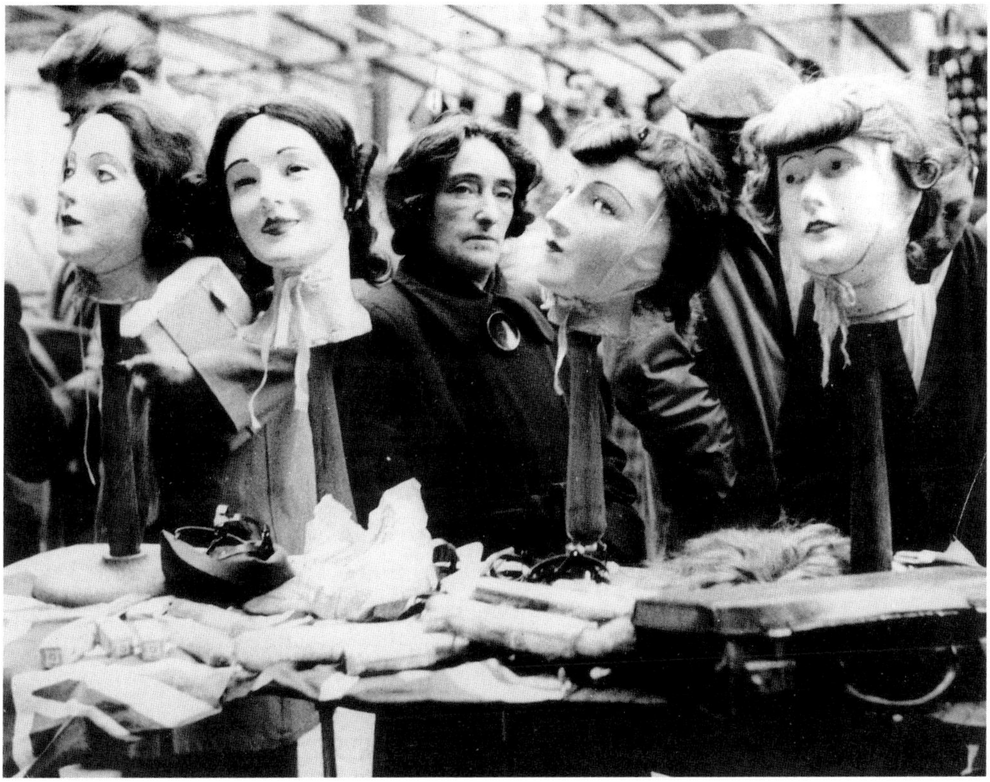

Fig 65 Nigel Henderson, *Wig Stall, Petticoat Lane*, 1952. © The Henderson Estate, courtesy Mayor Gallery, London.

Sometimes, single pictures appear to bring various genres together. The photo Henderson took of a wig stall on Petticoat Lane in 1952 seems at first glance an extension of the Surrealist genre of mannequin photography (figure 65). It may take a second or two to notice the real woman whose face fits so perfectly in the row of heads, a woman whom Spender or Brandt might have photographed in the 1930s. Whereas the mannequins all gaze blissfully out of frame, she fixes the photographer with a gaze that is sad, resigned and a little reproachful. The camera has drawn her and the mannequins into a relationship that is fleeting yet now as fixed as the smiles on the mannequins' faces.

Ignored and almost unknown for a long time, Henderson's pictures can in retrospect look like a missing link between the heroic days of 1930s documentary and a later generation of 1960s photographers dubbed by Martin Harrison the 'young meteors'.[13] But Henderson himself had no great ambitions for his work: 'his aim was simply to make a collection of different shots around the very strong and coherent (and to the middle class young man, highly exotic) image of Bethnal Green where he lived'.[14] It is true that many of Henderson's pictures operate on a recordative level and are now historically valuable for that alone. But certain pictures move beyond that, almost into a state of reverie, where a young girl hovers like a ghost in front of a bead curtain, two heads seen through a pub window are transformed into white biomorphs, the haunted face of a housewife suddenly appears in a row of mannequins, and it is as if the surface of the world has dissolved.

In 1953, the year that the Hendersons moved out of London to live in Essex, the film-maker Lindsay Anderson was in Margate, Kent making a short documentary about a school for deaf children. Up to that point, Anderson had mainly made his mark as a film critic; his influential essay on Humphrey Jennings, 'Only Connect', would be published the following year.[15] Now, with some spare film and a 16 mm camera, he made a short film about Dreamland, the largest funfair in the south of England. (Twenty years later, the teenage Tracey Emin worked there as a waitress, describing Dreamland as 'a wild Victorian fun-fair where the Catch-a-duck and Shoot-a-coconut mixed with the sounds of the Wurlitzer and Eddie Cochran'.)[16]

Anderson's film, *O Dreamland*, just 12 minutes long, would not be shown publicly until 1956, as part of the first 'Free Cinema' programme. Roughly shot in grainy black and white with unsynchronised sound laid over the top, the film has attracted controversy for its unflinching image of Dreamland as a crude, bleak place populated by alienated visitors (figure 66). Raphael Samuel called it a film 'in which pleasuregoing is represented as repulsive'.[17] This sounds a familiar note. As Dai Vaughan has remarked, 'in simply refusing that convention whereby all working-class enjoyments must be pressed into the symbolization of wholesome leisure, [*O Dreamland*] sounded that alien key, neither major nor minor, which had not been heard in a British documentary since the kazoo band sequence in *Spare Time* seventeen years earlier'.[18]

Anderson is evidently repulsed by Dreamland but he is also fascinated. His friend Gavin Lambert wrote of the film: 'The first time it is like a blow in the face;

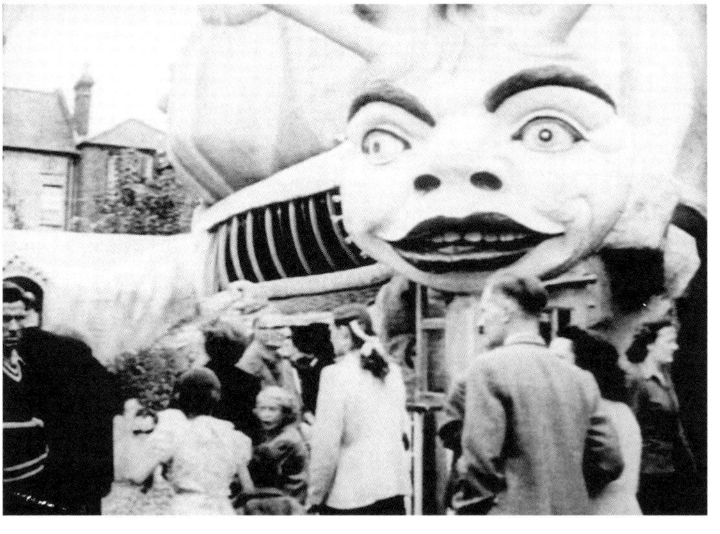

Fig 66 Lindsay Anderson, frame still from *O Dreamland*, 1953. By kind permission of British Film Institute.

the second, one approaches it with a kind of eager dread.'[19] Anderson followed Jennings in the direction of a subjective and critical documentary, yet he went well beyond him in his emphasis on the pleasures of darkness and violence; in the film's sardonic coolness, it is rather Buñuel who comes to mind. (In 1952, Anderson had reviewed *Los Olvidados*, the film that had re-established Buñuel's reputation).[20] Alan Lovell also made a comparison between *O Dreamland* and a film by another 'surrealist' film-maker, *A propos de Nice* by Jean Vigo, but remarked, 'The essential difference between the two films is the surrealism which encourages Vigo to go beyond direct reportage.'[21]

Nevertheless, there are elements of surrealism embedded in *O Dreamland.* Anderson would in later films like *The White Bus* and, more famously, *If...*, show himself fully willing and adept at shifting between social reality and moments of extravagant fantasy. *O Dreamland* is not so overt, but in its sharp, almost vicious juxtapositions, its claustrophobia, the unnerving disassociation of image and sound, it is a film which disorientates and undermines one's sense of separation between fantasy and reality. Near the end of the film, a cut-out dwarf appears holding a sign which might almost be a Surrealist slogan: 'The dreams I see are yours to see. Over there in reality'. Anderson may have been justified in believing that Dreamland offered nightmares rather than dreams, but a nightmare is also a state of mind in which excess leads to the destabilisation of a sense of normality.

If Nigel Henderson and Lindsay Anderson extended the pre-war Surrealist interest in the street and the seaside and reinvigorated it with a new directness and even bruteness, another work of the period took up the Surrealist theme of the relationship between the homely and the exotic. In the mid-1950s, the magazine *Ark*, published at the Royal College of Art, began to include photography. No. 17 in 1956 included work by Nigel Henderson while no. 23 contained some of Humphrey Spender's photographs from Bolton (perhaps the first publication of his Mass-Observation work).[22] In the next issue, however, there was something rather different: a new piece by a young English artist Ralph Rumney, entitled *The Leaning Tower of Venice*, also known by the alternative title *Psychogeography of Venice*.[23]

Born in 1934, Rumney grew up in Halifax, the son of a vicar. He discovered Surrealism as a teenager when he came across the 1936 volume *Surrealism*, edited by Herbert Read; this led him to request books by the Marquis de Sade from the town library, resulting in a miniature scandal.[24] In Paris in the early 1950s, he met the Lettriste group, led by Guy Debord. Among many other things, they were in revolt against the dogmas of latter-day Surrealism, though many of their central ideas such as the exploration of 'psychogeography' through a process of *dérive* – drifting through the city – were founded on the practices of the early Surrealists. Rumney begins *The Leaning Tower of Venice* with a definition from Debord: 'Psychogeography is the study of the exact effects of geographic environment, controlled or otherwise, on the affective behaviour of individuals...'[25]

about England with the detached curiosity of a man investigating the customs of some remote and unfamiliar tribe.'[38] The analogy Mortimer made with anthropology is tempting, as it is with other photographers discussed here from Nigel Henderson to Martin Parr, but it must be treated with care. Like Brandt, Ray-Jones was more interested in making pictures than recording facts and there is a persistent desire, not to understand the scene he is recording, but rather to render its strangeness.

It is easy to conjure up Surrealism as an influence on Ray-Jones and harder to pin it down. His friend David Burch recalled that 'of all the photographers I think that Bill Brandt held a special place with him. Robert Frank was one of his favourite photographers and he greatly admired the earlier Cartier-Bresson photographs.'[39] (This emphasis on Cartier-Bresson's early work is significant, since that was when he had been most influenced by Surrealism.) Ray-Jones also knew the Surrealist journal *Minotaure*,[40] and in 1970, he interviewed its main photographer Brassaï.[41]

Among Ray-Jones' favourite painters were de Chirico and Magritte but also Brueghel, Goya and Hopper. He had a particular interest in cinema, which ranged from Fellini to Tati. Again, though, two Surrealist directors were important as reference points. According to his wife, Anna, his favourite film was Jean Vigo's *L'Atalante*, while he once told Ainslie Ellis, 'I want my pictures to bite like the images in Buñuel's films which disturb you while making you think.'[42] Surrealism then, was certainly in Ray-Jones' mix of influences, even if it was there alongside a great many other things.

Ray-Jones' photography of the English covered a number of themes but the largest set of pictures was made at the seaside. 'I chose the seaside resort because it is a world unto itself, with its own moral code and set of values, where the behaviour of the vacationers is far less inhibited than in their town life.'[43] Between 1966 and 1970, Ray-Jones visited seaside resorts around the coast of England. He photographed on the beaches and the promenades, in gardens and on piers and in one case, on a boat off Beachy Head.[44] At Margate, he photographed three rather awkward girls in bikinis with sashes saying 'Dreamland: Go-Go Girl 1969'.

In 1968, on a visit to Butlin's Holiday Camp at Clacton-on-Sea, Ray-Jones made one of his best 'surrealist' images, where a young man in an indoor swimming pool looks through a viewing window into the eyes of a girl standing outside the pool, in the same space as the photographer (figure 67).[45] Their faces are only inches apart, yet they are in separate worlds. (There is, though, also a little bit of leakage, both cultural – the crudely painted seaplants – and natural – where water has run down from the window and stained the wall.) When Tony Ray-Jones put together a book dummy of 'England by the Sea', he paired the photographs very carefully. He placed this swimming pool picture opposite an image of a group of people relaxing in the sun – one woman is also pictured as a blurred shape seen through a glass screen.[46] In both cases, reality seems refracted by the frame within the frame, shifted to the other side of the looking glass. It

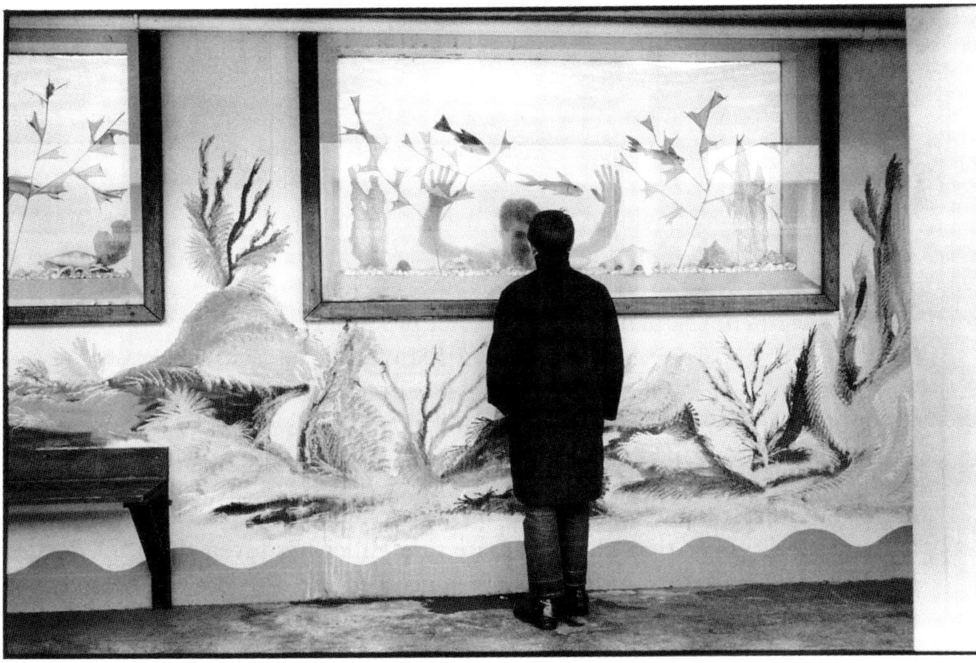

Fig 67 Tony Ray-Jones, *Butlin's Holiday Camp, Clacton-on-Sea, 1968*. © National Museum of Photography, Film and Television/Science & Society Picture Library.

is as if Ray-Jones subliminally alludes to the fact that, as we look through a camera, the reality on the other side of the glass is also somewhat refracted.

As part of his extensive research process, Tony Ray-Jones collected seaside postcards and, according to David Burch, 'hoped the postcards might be published alongside his own work'.[47] Although this did not happen, it is intriguing to place Tony Ray-Jones' Butlin's photographs opposite another set of pictures taken during the same period by the John Hinde postcard company. (There is, for example, an image of a similar indoor swimming pool taken by Hinde's photographer Elmar Ludwig at the Butlin's, Ayr.)[48] The 'surrealism' of these images is of quite another order than that of Ray-Jones' pictures – smooth and even, full of hyperrealist detail, saturated colour and endless fixed poses. Back in 1941, George Orwell had said that seaside postcards 'are a sort of diary upon which the English people have unconsciously recorded themselves'.[49] Orwell was specifically referring to the vulgar comic cards of Donald McGill, but his sense that postcards might represent the collective unconscious of English culture can be more generally applied. As the artist Tom Phillips once remarked, 'The postcard is to the world as the dream is to the individual.'[50]

Whereas Roland Penrose in 1937 had recruited picture postcards to his own subjective ends, it might now be appropriate to allow the cards to speak for themselves. This was the task undertaken by Susan Hiller in her work *Dedicated to the Unknown Artists*, which comprised 305 postcards of 'Rough Seas', collected from seaside resorts around the country. In the exhibition, first shown

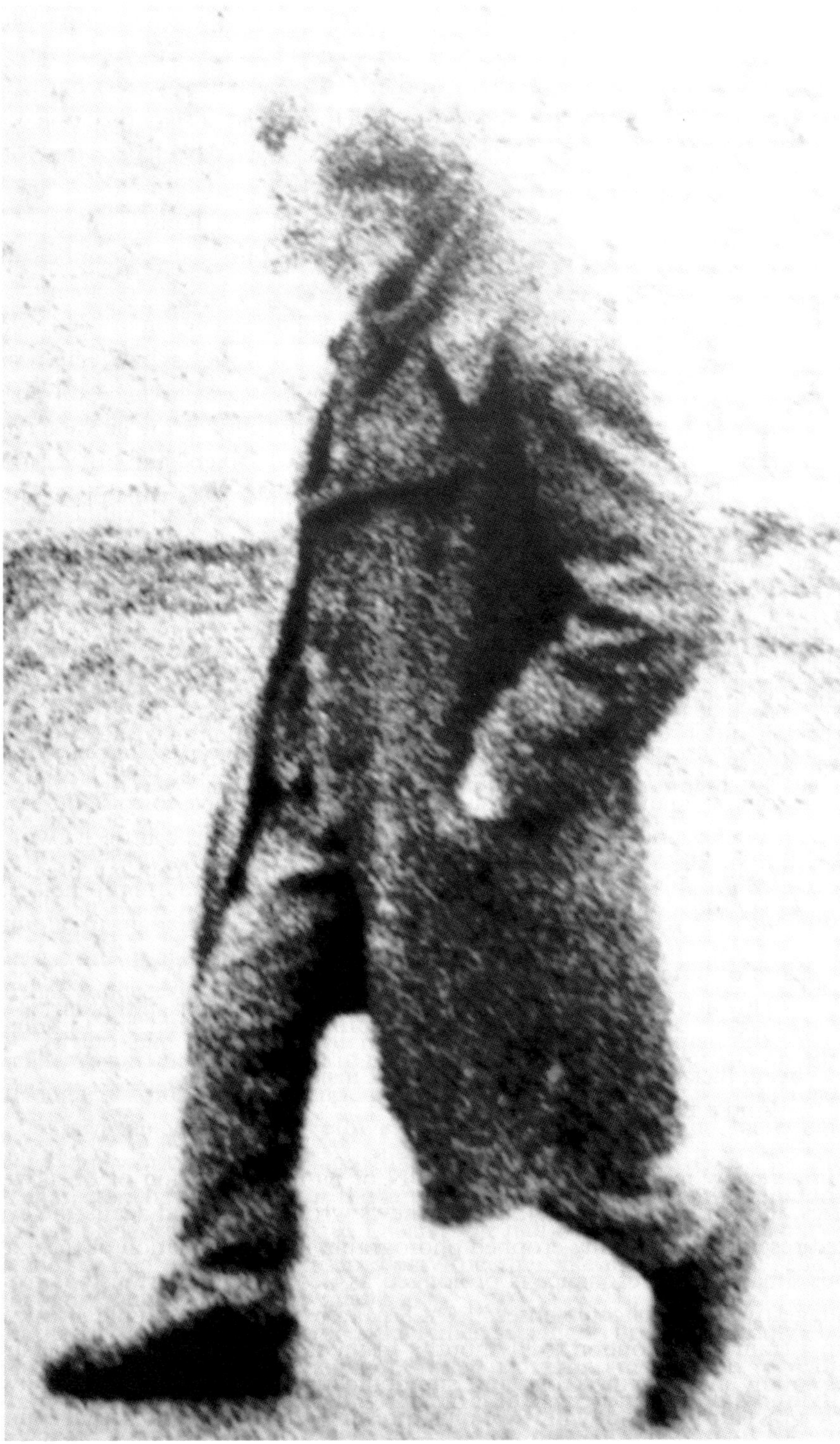

Fig 69 Ian Breakwell, *The Walking Man Diary*, 1975–78 (detail). © The artist's estate, courtesy Anthony Reynolds Gallery, London.

photograph.

Breakwell did frequently incorporate photographs into the diary, but photography became central in one extended piece that he made in the mid-1970s: *The Walking Man Diary*. Then living on the third floor of a former bacon factory in Smithfield, Breakwell observed the street from above. One day in 1975, he noticed a man 'just as purposeful as those around him but not engaged in any business except that of walking continuously on a circuitous and regular route'. Breakwell photographed him whenever he saw him. 'Then one day he was not there any more.'[63]

The photographs are necessarily distanced, of course, and sometimes it is even hard to spot the man, though one knows he must be there. This reflects the artist's own relationship with him, for he gets to know the man very well at the same time as he does not know him at all. At one point, Breakwell zooms into a big blow-up of the man made from the centre of a negative but, of course, the closer we get, the more the image breaks up and the less we know (figure 69). In one sense, *The Walking Man Diary* is very different from the other diary materials, in so far as it adopts a distant viewpoint and concentrates on just one figure. Yet it emphasises the sense of selection that is at work throughout and the coolness and distance which renders the scene strange. Most of the hilarious, grotesque and dreadful things that Breakwell reported would not have seemed hilarious, grotesque or dreadful to the participants.

Breakwell realised that the man below him was not a tramp, since he carried

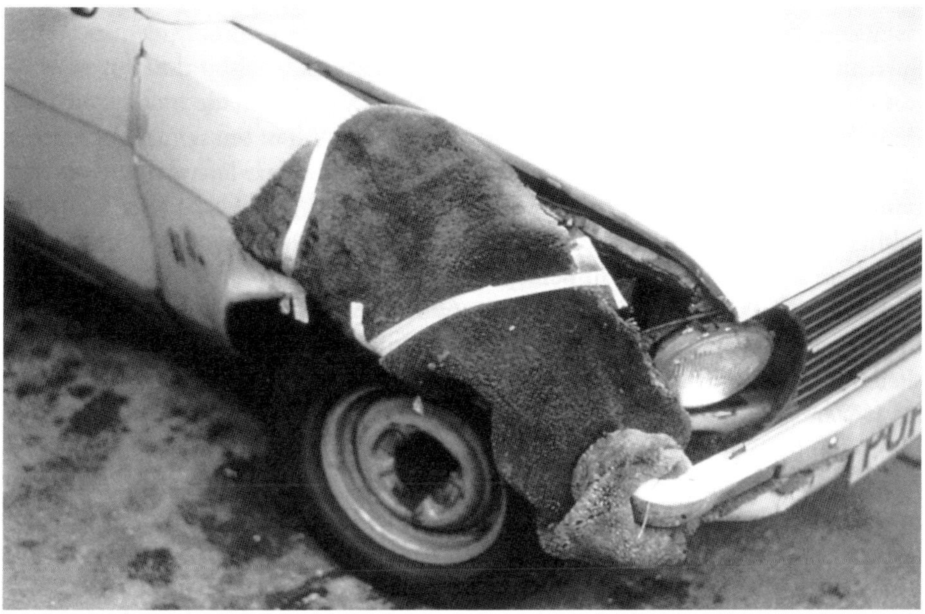

Fig 70 Richard Wentworth, *London, 1977*, from the series *Making Do and Getting By*. Courtesy Lisson Gallery, London, and the artist.

While, in his 1999 film *Think of England*, he arrives at Blackpool in a howling gale.[83] One hefty girl flashes her bra at the camera, but most people struggle just to stand up in the wind. It is as if Susan Hiller's 'Rough Seas' had returned with a vengeance.

Martin Parr has also been a keen collector of postcards, as well as many other objects, and in the interweaving between his own photography and his collection of artefacts, one can see a relationship that threads through this account. Nash, Agar, Penrose, Jennings and Henderson were all both makers and collectors, and this duality connects with the Surrealist interest in the found object as a revelatory force. As the Surrealist scholar Roger Cardinal put it: 'To collect is to launch individual desire across the intertext of environment and history. Every acquisition, whether crucial or trivial, marks an unrepeatable conjuncture of subject, found object, place and moment.'[84]

Parr's specific interest in postcards has however been various. On the one hand, he was a prime mover in the rediscovery and publication of the hyper-real John Hinde cards from Butlin's. But he has also published a selection of 'boring postcards' – flat, impassive images of shopping centres, housing estates and motorways from the 1950s and 1960s.[85] Of course, when gathered together, these images are anything but boring; beautiful yet also sinister, the very impassivity of the photographs allows a multitude of meanings to coexist and renders them strange.

'There is nothing so mysterious as a fact clearly described.' This often-cited maxim from the American photographer Garry Winogrand sounds an echo, of course, of Paul Nash's belief that 'the greatest mystery comes of the greatest definiteness'.[86] In 1986, Richard Ehrlich quoted Winogrand in a text about the landscape photographs of John Davies, alongside a comment from Davies himself: 'I'm as interested in the mysteries of the world as the next person, but I choose not to make images that amplify the mystery.'[87] Davies was one of a generation of landscape photographers who moved away from the dark drama of Brandt's photographs to a clearer, cooler visual effect, concentrating on the complexities and ambiguities that a modern landscape photography should entail.[88]

It may seem curious, looking at the crisp delineation of a photograph by John Davies to learn that Surrealism had been one of his major influences, but this was so. Born in County Durham, Davies went to London in the late 1960s – a time of revolution, drugs and squatting – and discovered Surrealism, particularly the work of Magritte.[89] What particularly engaged his interest was its political dimension, challenging habit and tradition, proposing a change in thought that might lead to a change in life itself. Though his subsequent work has shifted through many different landscapes – from the dappled light of the Lake District to the uncanny brightness of the sunlit city centre spaces in his more recent colour work, there has always been a sense of unspoken connections moving beneath the precisely captured surface.

In the 1980s, Davies' reaction to the shifting social pressures of the time was to photograph on the margins, between city and country, in areas of Britain that

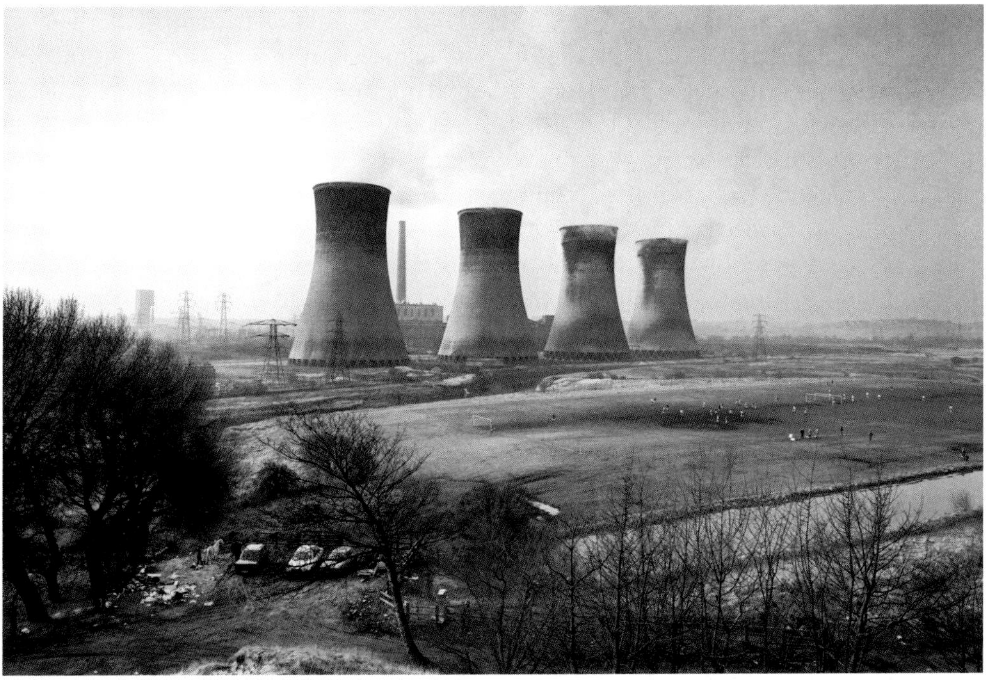

Fig 72 John Davies, *Agecroft Power Station, Pendlebury, Greater Manchester*, 1983. © John Davies.

were being rapidly deindustrialised. The resulting book was ironically titled *A Green and Pleasant Land*.[90] A key picture in the series was taken on the outskirts of Manchester in 1983 (figure 72). In the background are the four cooling towers of Agecroft Power Station and beyond that the colliery that provides its fuel. Davies first visited the scene in mid-week and climbed the embankment from which he would take the shot. (Many of his photographs are taken from these raised positions which allow for an analytical reading of the scene, a certain distance and removal.) Discovering that the works' football team would be playing on Sunday morning, he returned to get his picture.

The photograph plays off the monolithic, modernist geometries of the cooling towers, receding in stately procession, against the scrappy, ill-defined *terrain vague* that lies in front of them – the football pitch where it looks as if the grass has a hard time covering the black mud, a canal that ends abruptly in a clump of winter trees, the tyre tracks in the foreground. And there, tiny, in the bottom left, is the detail that transforms the scene – a white horse standing in a scattering of rubbish. Not a horse carved into a hillside or galloping through the city streets, but discovered in this wasteland, as if it had wandered in from somewhere more rural, settled and certain. A fragile moment, but then everything in this landscape is subject to change. Those cooling towers have gone now – the colliery closed down, of course – and in their place, there is a prison.

The phrase 'It's so exotic, so homemade' at the start of Patrick Keiller's 1994 film *London* is delivered by the film's unnamed narrator who has returned to London to rejoin his former companion, Robinson, in a quest to investigate the 'problem of London'. Together, the two men conduct a series of journeys through the city, sometimes dictated by news events – the re-election of the Conservative government, a series of IRA bombings – more often by a tradition of literature written in and about the city, by both English and European writers.

In conversation with Colin Sorensen, Keiller was explicit about the Surrealist sources for *London*: 'I suppose the whole film stems from an interest in Surrealism. One of the traditions that I try to connect myself with is the Surrealist literature of the city, most of which is French.'[91] In an earlier essay published in 1982, Keiller had discussed in some detail the urban geography established within the tradition of the *flâneur*, referencing the writings of Poe, Baudelaire, Apollinaire, Breton and Aragon as well as the photography of Atget and Lotar.[92] *Flânerie* involves a double and contradictory process of immersion and isolation. The *flâneur* is in the crowd, but not of it. It is an irony in Keiller's film that, whereas the voice-over talks of walking the city, subjectively engaging with its histories, the camera stays resolutely still, impassively recording.

In one sense, *London* is a documentary, for there is nothing we see that was not already there before the camera as it filmed. Yet these images are overlaid by the fictionalised narrative of the relationship between Robinson and the narrator. In previous films like *Stonebridge Park* (1981) and *Norwood* (1983), Keiller had juxtaposed images of the flat London suburbs of the films' titles with first-person tales of robbery, deceit and murder. These films offer a lesson that we can never live in the objective world without overlaying our own subjective and sometimes fantastical interpretation. Robinson, for example, lives in Vauxhall where, we

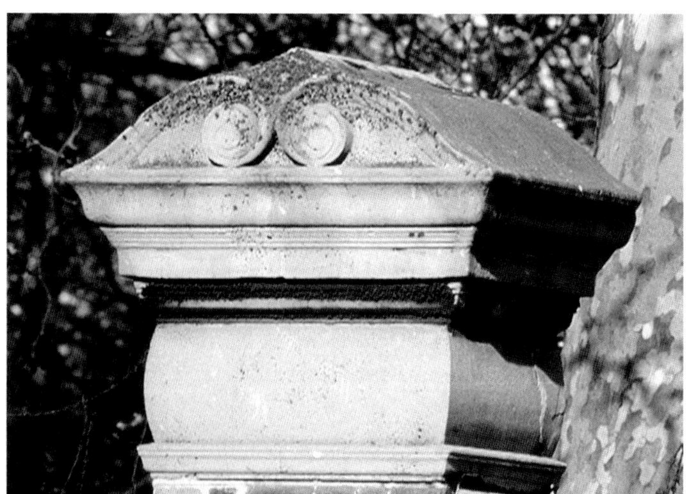

Fig 73 Patrick Keiller, 'Gatepost, Vauxhall Park, London SW8', frame still from *London*, 1994. By kind permission of British Film Institute.

are told, 'he listens to the gateposts at the entrance to the park'. In large close-up we see the gateposts, glowing a rich red in the afternoon sun as if they were urban versions of the 'object-personages' that Nash found some sixty years earlier (figure 73). The scrolls on top look like eyes watching us as we watch them – a moment of almost Lacanian intensity animating the banality of the inner city.

Keiller's next film after *London* was *Robinson in Space* (1997), which took Robinson and his friend on a parallel journey across England. Here the contrast is between eighteenth-century writers such as Defoe and Sterne and the contemporary industrialisation of the country. Surrealism has a less obvious place in this, until, near the end of the film, the pair arrive in Blackpool, where it turns out Robinson was born. (So was Keiller, but the parallel should not be extended too far.) Keiller had been there before, in 1987, for his film *Valtos*; then Blackpool, filmed at a distance, had glittered in the summer sunlight through which visitors moved as if in a trance. In *Robinson in Space*, the Narrator tells us: 'Robinson says that Blackpool holds the key to his Utopia.' Keiller commented, 'Robinson says what he says in Blackpool because he is a surrealist and believes in the carnivalization of life. Blackpool is probably the nearest you get to that.'[93]

The artist Jeremy Deller has remarked that 'Blackpool is where the English go so they don't need to feel English.'[94] Patrick Keiller and Martin Parr, despite the great differences in their approach, would probably both turn that around to say that Blackpool is rather a place where the English go to be *really* English. But perhaps those positions are not so far apart; it tells us something about the nature of Englishness that somewhere like Blackpool can be both quintessentially English and not English at all, both central and marginal at the same time. Blackpool's exoticism is thoroughly homegrown, yet just as much as any other site of carnival, it can offer a site of release and escape – if not utopia.

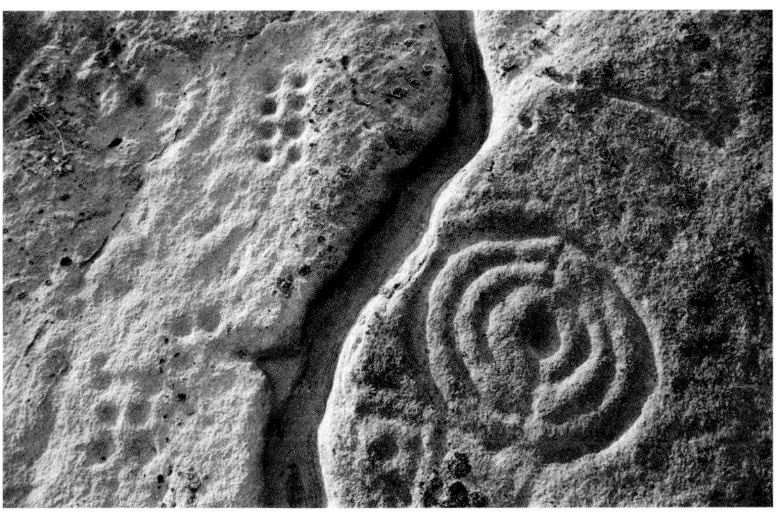

Fig 74 Patrick Keiller, 'Detail of Rock Carving, Chatton Park, Northumberland', pre-production photograph for *Robinson in Space*, 1997. By kind permission of British Film Institute.

Indeed, at the end of *Robinson in Space*, the Narrator remarks, 'I cannot tell you where Robinson finally found his Utopia.' These words are followed by large close-ups of prehistoric rock carvings from the moors of Northumberland – repetitive patterns of circles, labyrinths and hollows (figure 74). These had previously appeared at the end of Keiller's short film *The Clouds* (1989); he had also wanted to make a specific study of them, linking them to the manifestation of the primitive in modern art – what Len Lye called the 'old brain'.

In one sense, this is a return to where we started, with Nash walking through the field at Avebury, looking for the points of connection between ancient and modern. But much has changed since Nash first caught the bus to Avebury in 1933 and belief in such a connection has often been difficult to sustain. Can Robinson really connect with the distant past and immerse himself in it? Or is it only fantasy, wish-fulfilment, an escape from reality?

1933 was also the year that J. B. Priestley travelled north and it is over seventy years since he wrote that he had seen 'a lot of Englands'. Now there are even more. And in that period, there have also been many different versions of Surrealism (and indeed 'surrealism') and many reinventions of documentary. The account in this book of the relationship between Surrealism, Englishness and documentary has been partial – there is much more that could have been said. And it has been fragmentary. The elements described here cannot be forced into a unity – rather they must sit side by side, to rub against each other as parallel routes through the history of English culture. There is also no real conclusion to this story – it continues into a new century.

English artists took Surrealism out for a walk – into the fields, past the factories and along the beach, places it hadn't been to before, and they used photography to document what happened there. All these juxtapositions of ancient and modern, urban and rural, man-made and natural, the centre and the margin, home and abroad, the obvious and the unknown, the important and the trivial, the so exotic and the so homemade, point forward to yet more possibilities that remain both provocative and productive.

Notes

1 *The Times* (3 May 1945), quoted by Brian Appleyard, *The Pleasures of Peace* (London: Faber & Faber, 1989), p. 3.

2 David Briers, 'Insignificance', *Art Monthly*, 295 (April 2006), 9.

3 'Lady Penrose', *The Times* (25 July 1977), 14.

4 Letter from Nigel Henderson to Mark Haworth-Booth, *c.*1976, quoted in Martin Harrison, *Transition: The London Art Scene in the Fifties* (London: Merrell, 2002), p. 54.

5 See Peter Rose Pulham, 'Surrealist Artists', *Lilliput* (October 1943), 323–30. Pulham's portfolio follows a text by Ruthven Todd, 'Where are the Surrealists Now?', 319–22.

6 Transcript of talk at the ICA, March 1952, quoted by Harrison, *Transition*, p. 55.

7 Interview with Roland Penrose, 1983, referenced in Anne Massey, *The Independent Group* (Manchester: Manchester University Press, 1995), p. 9.

8 'Glynn Williams talks to Eduardo Paolozzi', *Sotheby's Art at Auction: The Art Market*

Review (London, 1995), reprinted in Robin Spencer (ed.), *Eduardo Paolozzi: Writings and Interviews* (Oxford: Oxford University Press, 2000), p. 327.

9 Spencer (ed.), *Eduardo Paolozzi: Writings and Interviews*, p. 14. For a fuller account of Henderson's life and work, see Virginia Walsh, *Nigel Henderson: Parallel of Life and Art* (London: Thames & Hudson, 2001).

10 'Notes towards a chronology based on conversations with the artist', *Nigel Henderson: Paintings, Collages and Photographs* (London: Anthony D'Offay Gallery, 1977), unpaginated.

11 Dave Hoffmann and Shirley Read, 'Nigel Henderson', *Camerawork*, 11 (September 1978), 13.

12 James Lingwood, 'Nigel Henderson' in David Robbins (ed.), *The Independent Group* (Cambridge, Mass: MIT Press, 1990), p. 76.

13 Martin Harrison, *Young Meteors: British Photojournalism 1957–1965* (London: Jonathan Cape, 1998).

14 'Notes towards a chronology based on conversations with the artist'.

15 Lindsay Anderson, 'Only Connect: Some Aspects of the Work of Humphrey Jennings', *Sight and Sound*, 4 (April–June 1954), pp. 181–3, 186. The essay has often been reprinted, including Mary-Lou Jennings (ed.), *Humphrey Jennings: Film-maker, Painter, Poet* (London: British Film Institute, 1982), pp. 53–9.

16 Tracey Emin, *Strangeland* (London: Sceptre, 2005), p. 29. At the time of writing, Dreamland is threatened with closure.

17 Raphael Samuel, *Theatres of Memory, Vol I: Past and Present in Popular Culture* (London: Verso, 1994), pp. 267–8.

18 Dai Vaughan, *Portrait of an Invisible Man* (London: British Film Institute, 1983), p. 177.

19 Gavin Lambert, 'Free Cinema', *Sight and Sound* (Spring 1956), reprinted in Kevin Macdonald and Mark Cousins (eds), *Imagining Reality: The Faber Book of Documentary* (London: Faber & Faber, 1996), p. 212.

20 L. G. A., 'Los Olvidados', *Monthly Film Review*, 19 (June 1952), 76. (My thanks to Paul Hammond for drawing my attention to this review.)

21 Alan Lovell, 'Free Cinema', in Alan Lovell and Jim Hillier, *Studies in Documentary* (London: Secker & Warburg/ British Film Institute, 1972), p. 140.

22 See Nigel Henderson, 'Photographs', *Ark*, 17 (1956), 48–51; Humphrey Spender, 'Mass-Observation', *Ark* , 23 (1958), 16–7.

23 Ralph Rumney, 'The Leaning Tower of Venice', *Ark*, 24 (1958), between 20 and 21. The full work is reproduced in Iwona Blaswick (ed.), *An Endless Adventure … an Endless Passion … an Endless Banquet: a Situationist Scrapbook* (London: Verso/ICA, 1989), pp. 45–9.

24 See Ralph Rumney, *The Consul* (London: Verso, 2002), pp. 8–9. See also Alan Woods, *Ralph Rumney: The Map is Not the Territory* (Manchester: Manchester University Press, 2000).

25 This is translated from Debord's 'Introduction à une critique de la géographie urbaine', in the journal edited by the Belgian Surrealist Marcel Mariën, *Les Lèvres nues*, 6 (November 1955), 11.

26 Rumney, *The Consul*, p. 47.

27 Rumney, *The Consul*, p. 46.

28 Simon Sadler, *The Situationist City* (Cambridge, Mass: MIT Press, 1998), p. 78.

29 David Mellor, *The Sixties Art Scene in London* (London: Phaidon, 1993), p. 59.

30 See Ian Walker, *City Gorged with Dreams* (Manchester: Manchester University Press, 2002), p. 55.

31 'Venise a vaincu Ralph Rumney', *Internationale Situationniste*, 1 (June 1958), 28. The broader context is explored by Andrew Hussey, *The Game of War* (London: Jonathan Cape, 2001), pp. 128–30.

32 From a review of Patrick Waldberg's *Surrealism* and Marcel Jean's *The History of Surrealist Painting*, published in *New Worlds*, 1966; reprinted in *A User's Guide to the Millenium* (London: HarperCollins, 1996), p. 88.

33 J. G. Ballard, *The Unlimited Dream Company* (London: Flamingo, 2000), p. 35.

34 This often-quoted statement was originally written by Ray-Jones for the exhibition *Personal Views* at the ICA in 1970.

35 For an allied discussion of these questions, see my essay 'Through the Picture-Plane: On Looking into Photographs' in Martha Langford (ed.), *Image And Imagination* (Montreal: McGill-Queens University Press, 2005), pp. 17–25.

36 Russell Roberts, *Tony Ray-Jones* (London: Chris Boot, 2004), p. 16.

37 Tony Ray-Jones, 'Photographs from England and America', *Creative Camera* (October 1968), 349.

38 Raymond Mortimer, 'Introduction', in Bill Brandt, *The English at Home* (London: Batsford, 1936), p. 4.

39 Letter from David Burch to Ainslie Ellis, 31 March 1972, in the Tony Ray-Jones collection, Insight Research Centre, National Museum of Photography, Film and Television, Bradford.

40 Information from Peter Turner cited by Ainslie Ellis, 'Introduction', in Tony Ray-Jones, *A Day Off: an English Journal* (London: Thames & Hudson, 1974), p. 8.

41 Tony Ray-Jones, 'Brassaï talking about Photography', *Creative Camera* (April 1970), 121.

42 Ellis, 'Introduction', p. 6.

43 This comes before the reference to 'the sadness and the humour in a gentle madness' in his 1970 statement.

44 See Ian Walker, 'Summer of Love: A Photograph by Tony Ray-Jones', *Source*, 40 (autumn 2004), 16–21.

45 In *A Day Off*, the picture is given as 'Butlin's Holiday Camp, Scarborough', one of many mistitlings in that posthumous volume.

46 See Roberts, *Tony Ray-Jones*, p. 37.

47 Letter to Ainslie Ellis. Ray-Jones mounted a set of seaside postcards in an Artist's Sketchbook (see Roberts, *Tony Ray-Jones*, p. 31).

48 *Our True Intent is All for your Delight: the John Hinde Butlin's Photographs*, introduction by Martin Parr (London: Chris Boot, 2002), p. 83.

49 George Orwell, *The Lion and the Unicorn* (London: Secker & Warburg, 1941), reprinted in Sonia Orwell and Ian Angus (eds), *Collected Essays, Journalism and Letters of George Orwell, Vol. II: My Country Right or Left 1940–1943* (Harmondsworth: Penguin, 1970), p. 60. Orwell's essay 'The Art of Donald McGill', first published in *Horizon* (September 1941), is in the same collection, pp. 155–65.

50 Tom Phillips, 'The Postcard Vision', in *Works, Texts to 1974* (Stuttgart: Hansjörg Mayer, 1975), p. 233.

51 Hiller also published a small artist's book: *Rough Sea* (Sussex: Gardner Art Centre, 1976).

52 Richard Cork, 'Storm in a Postcard', *Evening Standard*, 17 March 1977, reprinted in *Every-*

thing Seemed Possible: Art in the 1970s (New Haven and London: Yale University Press, 2003), p. 173.

53 Susan Hiller, 'Dedicated to the Unknown Artists: an interview with Rozsika Parker', first published in *Spare Rib*, 72 (July 1978), 28–30, reprinted in Barbara Einzig (ed.), *Thinking about Art: Conversations with Susan Hiller* (Manchester: Manchester University Press, 1996), p. 28.

54 'Looking at New Work: an interview with Rozsika Parker, 20 December 1983', in Susan Hiller, *The Muse My Sister* (Londonderry: Orchard Gallery, 1984), p. 23.

55 John Roberts, 'Lucid Dreams', in Hiller, *The Muse My Sister*, p. 38.

56 Einzig (ed.), *Thinking about Art,* pp. 27–8.

57 John Lyle, 'Little England: Ian Breakwell's Diary 1964–1985', *City Limits* (July 17–24, 1986), 93.

58 Nick Kimberley, 'Introduction', *Ian Breakwell's Diary 1964–1985* (London: Pluto, 1986), p. 8.

59 Angus Calder and Dorothy Sheridan (eds), *Speak for Yourself: A Mass-Observation Anthology, 1937–1949* (Oxford: Oxford University Press, 1985), pp. 1–2.

60 *Ian Breakwell's Diary 1964–1985*, p. 90.

61 J. H. Matthews, '*Diary Extracts 1968–1976* by Ian Breakwell', *TRANSFORMAcTION*, 8 (1977), 38–9. *Diary Extracts 1968–1976* was published by Midland Group, Nottingham, 1977.

62 *Ian Breakwell's Diary 1964–1985*, p. 31.

63 Ian Breakwell, *Continuous Diary and Related Works 1965–1978* (Glasgow: Third Eye Centre, 1978), p. 25. More recently, images from *The Walking Man Diary* were published in Nick Barley (ed.), *Breathing Cities* (Basel: Birkhäuser, 2000), pp. 26–9.

64 Simon Groom, 'In Media Res', in *Richard Wentworth* (Liverpool: Tate, 2005), p. 73.

65 Richard Wentworth, *Making Do and Getting By*, with music by Ry Cooder (London: Whitechapel Art Gallery, 1985), video, 20 minutes.

66 Marina Warner, 'Richard Wentworth: A Sense of Things', in *Richard Wentworth* (London: Thames & Hudson/Serpentine Gallery, 1993), p. 9.

67 Paul Bonaventura, 'Today We have the Naming of Parts: Richard Wentworth Interviewed', first published in *Artefactum*, 20 (1987), 30–5, reprinted in *Richard Wentworth* (Valencia: Sala Parpallo, 1988), p. 158.

68 Geoff Dyer, 'Les Mots et les Choses', in *Richard Wentworth / Eugène Atget: Faux Amis* (London: Photographers' Gallery, 2001), p. 20.

69 Richard Wentworth, 'Magnetic Fields', in Barley (ed.), *Breathing Cities*, p. 54.

70 In 2003, he told Stéphanie Delcroix: 'A lot of photographs I was taking I didn't understand. Walker Evans' work helped confirm what they were' ('Crossing the road', *[a–n] Magazine for artists* (March 2003), 35), while in Anna Dezeuze, 'Richard Wentworth in conversation', *Papers of Surrealism*, 4 (winter 2005), 13–14, he talked of his admiration for Brassaï's photographs of *Involuntary Sculptures*.

71 See note 68.

72 Dezeuze, 'Richard Wentworth in conversation', 16.

73 Jonathan Bayer (ed.), *Concerning Photography* (London; Photographers' Gallery, 1977), p. 40. Among the most delightful explorations of the fundamental surreality of photography were two works by Andrew Lanyon, *The Rooks of Trelawne* (London: Photographers' Gallery, 1976) and *The Vanishing Cabinet* (London: Travelling Light, 1980).

74 For an overview of Parr's life and work, see Val Williams, *Martin Parr* (London: Phaidon, 2002). Some of my comments here are indebted to a discussion with Martin Parr, 13 April 2006.

75 A fellow student was Brian Griffin from the Black Country, whose later commercial work also mixed documentary and surreality, the found and the staged; see his book *Power*, text by Richard Smith (London: Travelling Light, 1981).

76 A portfolio of the 'Beauty Spots' was published in Colin Osman and Peter Turner (eds), *Creative Camera Collection 5* (London: Coo Press, 1978), pp. 113–23. Four images are in Williams, *Martin Parr*, pp. 120–4.

77 See Roberts, *Tony Ray-Jones*, p. 73. In *A Day Off*, no. 33, the Brimham Rock photograph is actually captioned 'Bristol'.

78 Val Williams, 'Jubilee Street Party, Elland, Yorkshire, 1977', in Sophie Howarth (ed.), *Singular Images* (London: Tate, 2005), p. 82.

79 Alan Yentob, 'The World According to Parr' (BBC1, 2003).

80 Martin Parr, *The Last Resort* (Liverpool: Promenade Press, 1986).

81 Yentob, 'The World According to Parr'.

82 Martin Parr, *West Bay* (London: Rocket Gallery, 1997).

83 Martin Parr, *Modern Times: Think of England* (BBC, 1999). Parr's interest in Englishness is also signalled by a book of the same title (London: Phaidon, 2000).

84 Roger Cardinal, 'Collecting and collage-making: the case of Kurt Schwitters', in John Elsner and Roger Cardinal (eds), *The Cultures of Collecting* (London: Reaktion, 1994), p. 69.

85 Martin Parr, *Boring Postcards* (London: Phaidon, 1999).

86 See Chapter 1 for Nash's comment.

87 Richard Ehrlich, 'Changes of Time and Place', in John Davies, *Mist Mountain Water Wind* (London: Travelling Light, 1986), unpaginated.

88 In this context, it is particularly relevant to recall work made by other photographers in marginal or liminal sites – such as Raymond Moore's photographs of the coast of Cumbria or Keith Arnatt's images of rubbish dumps around the Wye Valley.

89 Some of my comments here are based on a conversation with John Davies, Liverpool, 24 March 2006.

90 John Davies, *A Green and Pleasant Land* (Manchester: Cornerhouse, 1987), texts by Michael Wood and Rob Powell. See also John Davies, *The British Landscape* (London: Chris Boot, 2006).

91 Colin Sorensen, *London on Film* (London: Museum of London, 1996), p. 161.

92 Patrick Keiller, 'The Poetic Experience of Townscape and Landscape, and Some Ways of Depicting It', *Undercut*, 3/4 (March 1982), 42–8, reprinted in Nina Danino and Michael Mazière (eds), *The Undercut Reader* (London: Wallflower, 2003), pp. 75–83.

93 Patrick Keiller, *Robinson in Space* (London: Reaktion Books, 1999), p. 230.

94 This was at the conference, *Mass-Observation, Surrealism and the Everyday*, at Manchester Museum on 4 November 2005. Deller is one of a number of young artists whose work has echoed some of the concepts of Mass-Observation; see the project undertaken with Alan Kane, *Folk Archive* (London: Book Works, 2005).

Bibliography

Abbott, C. C. and Anthony Bertram (eds), *Poet and Painter: Being the Correspondence between Gordon Bottomley and Paul Nash 1910–1946* (Oxford: Oxford University Press, 1955; reprinted with an introduction by Andrew Causey, Bristol: Longdunn, 1990).

Abelson, Edward (ed.), *A Mirror for England: An Anthology of the Writings of H. J. Massingham 1888–1952* (Bideford: Green Books, 1989).

Ackroyd, Peter, *First Light* (London: Sphere, 1991; first published London: Hamish Hamilton, 1989).

Ackroyd, Peter, *Dickens* (London: Sinclair-Stevenson, 1990).

Ackroyd, Peter, *Blake* (London: Sinclair-Stevenson, 1995).

Ades, Dawn (ed.), *Dada and Surrealism Reviewed* (London: Arts Council of Great Britain, 1978).

Ades, Dawn, 'Notes on Two Women Surrealist Painters: Eileen Agar and Ithell Colquhoun', *Oxford Art Journal*, 3:1 (1980), 36–42.

Agar, Eileen, *Eileen Agar: A Decade of Discoveries* (London: New Art Centre, 1976).

Agar, Eileen, *A Look at My Life* (London: Methuen, 1988).

Aitken, Ian, *Film and Reform: John Grierson and the Documentary Film Movement* (London: Routledge, 1990).

Aitken, Ian, *Alberto Cavalcanti: Realism, Surrealism and National Cinema* (Trowbridge: Flick Books, 2000).

Alley, Roland, *Graham Sutherland* (London: Tate Gallery, 1982).

Amaya, Mario, 'My Man Ray' (interview with Lee Miller), *Art in America* (May–June 1975), 54–60.

Anderson, Lindsay (L.G.A.), 'Los Olvidados', *Monthly Film Review*, 19 (June 1952), 76.

Anderson, Lindsay, 'Only Connect: Some Aspects of the Work of Humphrey Jennings', *Sight and Sound*, 4 (April–June 1954), pp. 181–3, 186.

Appleyard, Brian, *The Pleasures of Peace: Art and Imagination in Post-war Britain* (London: Faber & Faber, 1989).

Aragon, Louis, *Paris Peasant* (London: Jonathan Cape, 1971), trans. Simon Watson Taylor from *Le paysan de Paris* (Paris: Gallimard, 1926).

'The Architectural Review Competition: Holiday Surrealism', *Architectural Review* (July 1936), 42.

Ashbery, John, 'Tanguy – the Geometer of Dreams' in *Yves Tanguy* (New York: Acquavella Galleries, 1974).

Auden, W. H. and Louis MacNeice, *Letters from Iceland* (London: Faber & Faber, 1937).

J. B., 'Humphrey Jennings', *New Statesman and Nation* (3 March 1951), 246.

Balchin, Nigel, *Darkness Falls from the Air* (London: Cassell, 2002; first published 1942).

Baldwin, Stanley, *On England* (London: Philip Allan, 1926).

Ballard, J. G., *The Unlimited Dream Company* (London: Flamingo, 2000; first published London: Jonathan Cape, 1979).

Ballard, J. G., *A User's Guide to the Millenium* (London: HarperCollins, 1996).

Barley, Nick (ed.), *Breathing Cities* (Basel: Birkhäuser, 2000).

Bartholomew, Michael, *In Search of H. V. Morton* (London: Methuen, 2004).

Batho, John, *Eléments* (Paris: Marval, 1992).

Baxendale, John, '"I had seen a Lot of Englands": J. B. Priestley, Englishness and the People', *History Workshop Journal*, 51 (2001), 87–111.

Bayer, Jonathan (ed.), *Concerning Photography* (London: Photographers' Gallery, 1977).

Beaumelle, Agnès Angliviel de la, Isabelle Monod-Fontaine and Claude Schweisguth, *André Breton: la beauté convulsive* (Paris: Musée nationale d'art moderne, 1991).

Beaton, Cecil, 'Blast of Modern Art! London Bombed into Surrealism', *The Sketch* (13 November 1940), 208–9.

Beaton, Cecil, *History Under Fire*, with a commentary by James Pope-Hennessy (London: Batsford, 1941).

Beaton, Cecil, 'Fashion is Indestructible', *Vogue* (September 1941), 32.

Beaton, Cecil, *The Years Between: Diaries 1939–44* (London: Weidenfeld & Nicolson, 1965).

Bennett, Tony, 'A Thousand and One Troubles: Blackpool Pleasure Beach', *Formations of Pleasure* (London: Routledge and Kegan Paul, 1983), 138–55.

Bertram, Anthony, *Paul Nash: The Portrait of the Artist* (London: Faber & Faber, 1955).

Birch, James, Jonathan Blond and Jeremy Theophilus (eds), *A Salute to British Surrealism, 1930–1950* (Colchester: The Minories, 1985).

Blake, Nicholas, *Malice in Wonderland* (London: Collins, 1940).

Blanch, Lesley, 'Vogue's Spotlight', *Vogue* (May 1941), 41.

Blaswick, Iwona (ed.), *An Endless Adventure ... An Endless Passion ... An Endless Banquet: A Situationist Scrapbook* (London: Verso/ICA, 1989).

Boulestreanu, Nicole, '*Facile*: un nouveau livre dans les années 1930', *Melusine*, 4 (1982), 163–8.

Bowen, Elizabeth, *The Demon Lover and Other Stories* (London: Jonathan Cape, 1945).

Bowen, Elizabeth, *The Heat of the Day* (London: Vintage, 1998; first published London: Jonathan Cape, 1949).

Bowen, Elizabeth, *Collected Stories* (London: Vintage, 1999; first published Harmondsworth: Penguin, 1983).

Brandt, Bill, 'Au cimetière des anciennes galères', *Minotaure*, 6 (Winter 1934–35), 4.

Brandt, Bill, *The English at Home* (London: Batsford, 1936).

Brandt, Bill, *A Night in London* (London: Country Life, 1938).

Brandt, Bill, 'A Chacun son Tombeau', *London Bulletin*, 12 (12 March 1939), 6.

Brandt, Bill, 'Blackout in London', *Lilliput* (December 1939), 551–8.

Brandt, Bill, 'London by Moonlight', *Lilliput* (August 1942), 131–40, with an essay by Tom Hopkinson, 'Bill Brandt – Photographer', 130 and 141.

Brandt, Bill, *Camera in London* (London: Focal Press, 1948).

Brandt, Bill, 'Hail, Hell and Halifax', *Lilliput* (February 1948), 151–6.

Brandt, Bill, *Shadow of Light* (First edition, London: Bodley Head, 1966, introduction by Cyril Connolly and notes by Marjorie Beckett; second edition, London: Gordon Fraser, 1977, additional introduction by Mark Haworth-Booth).

'Bill Brandt: What do you say' (interview), *The Image*, 9 (1973), 42.

Brassaï, 'Du mur des cavernes au mur d'usine', *Minotaure*, 3–4 (14 December 1933), 6–7.

Brassaï, 'Blackout in Paris', *Lilliput*, 36 (June 1940), 509–16.

Breakwell, Ian, *Diary Extracts 1968–1976* (Nottingham: Midland Group, 1977).

Breakwell, Ian, *Continuous Diary and Related Works 1965–1978* (Glasgow: Third Eye Centre, 1978).

Breakwell, Ian, *Ian Breakwell's Diary 1964–1985*, introduction by Nick Kimberley (London: Pluto, 1986).

Breton, André, 'Picasso dans son élément', *Minotaure*, 1 (1933), 4–22.

Breton, André, *What is Surrealism?* (London: Faber & Faber, 1936).

Breton, André, *Nadja* (New York: Grove Press, 1960), trans. Richard Howard from *Nadja* (Paris:

Gallimard, 1928). Reprinted Harmondsworth: Penguin, 2000. (Revised French edition, Paris: Gallimard, 1963, republished 1973).

Breton, André, *Manifestoes of Surrealism* (Ann Arbor: University of Michigan Press, 1969), trans. Richard Seavor and Helen R. Lane from *Manifestes du surréalisme* (Paris: J. J. Pauvert, 1962).

Breton, André, *Perspective cavalière* (Paris: Gallimard, 1970).

Breton, André, *Mad Love* (Lincoln: University of Nebraska Press, 1987), trans. Mary Ann Caws from *L'Amour fou* (Paris: Gallimard, 1937).

Breton, André, *Je vois, j'imagine* (Paris: Gallimard, 1991).

Breton, André and Paul Eluard (eds), *Dictionnaire abrégé du surréalisme* (Paris: Galerie des Beaux-Arts, Paris, 1938; republished Paris: José Corti, 1991).

Briers, David, 'Insignificance', *Art Monthly*, 295 (April 2006), 7–10.

Brittain, Vera, *England's Hour* (London: Macmillan, 1941).

Bryant, Marsha, *Auden and Documentary in the 1930s* (Charlottesville: University Press of Virginia, 1997).

Burgin, Victor, *Some Cities* (London: Reaktion, 1996).

Burke, Carolyn, *Lee Miller* (London: Bloomsbury, 2005).

Byron, Robert, 'The Monasteries of the Meteora', *Country Life* (21 May 1932), 561–4.

Byron, Robert, *The Road to Oxiana* (London: Macmillan, 1937; republished London: Pimlico, 2004).

Cadava, Eduardo, *Words of Light: Theses on the Photography of History* (Princeton: Princeton University Press, 1997).

Calder, Angus, *The People's War* (London: Cape, 1969; reprinted London: Pimlico, 1992).

Calder, Angus, *The Myth of the Blitz* (London: Jonathan Cape, 1991).

Calder, Angus and Sheridan, Dorothy (eds), *Speak for Yourself: A Mass-Observation Anthology, 1937–1949* (Oxford: Oxford University Press, 1985; first published London: Jonathan Cape, 1984).

Calder, Ritchie, *Carry On London* (London: English Universities Press, 1941).

Cardinal, Roger, *The Landscape Vision of Paul Nash* (London: Reaktion, 1989).

Carter, Ernestine, *With Tongue in Chic* (London: Michael Joseph, 1974).

Carter, Ernestine (ed.), *Grim Glory* (London: Lund Humphries, 1941), preface by Edward R. Murrow, photographs by Lee Miller and others. Published in the USA as *Bloody but Unbowed* (New York: Scribners, 1941).

Causey, Andrew, *Paul Nash's Photographs: Document and Image* (London: Tate Gallery, 1973).

Causey, Andrew, *Paul Nash* (Oxford: Clarendon Press, 1980).

Causey, Andrew (ed.), *Paul Nash: Writings on Art* (Oxford: Oxford University Press, 2000).

Caws, Mary Ann, *Dora Maar: With and without Picasso* (London: Thames & Hudson, 2000).

Caws, Mary Ann, *Surrealism* (London: Phaidon, 2004).

Caws, Mary Ann, Rudolf E. Kuenzli and Gwen Raaberg (eds), *Surrealism and Women* (Cambridge, Mass: MIT Press).

Chadwick, Whitney, *Women Artists and the Surrealist Movement* (London: Thames & Hudson, 1991).

Colls, Robert and Philip Dodd (eds), *Englishness: Politics and Culture 1880–1920* (London: Croom Helm, 1986).

Colvin, Clare, *Paul Nash: Places* (London: South Bank Centre, 1989).

'Competition Result: Holiday Surrealism', *Architectural Review* (November 1936), 218–9.

Corbett, David Peters, Ysanne Holt and Fiona Russell (eds), *The Geographies of Englishness: Landscape and the National Past 1880–1940* (New Haven and London: Yale University Press, 2002).

Cork, Richard, *Everything Seemed Possible: Art in the 1970s* (New Haven and London: Yale University Press, 2003).

Courtney, Cathy, 'Interview with Eileen Agar', 8 August 1990, National Sound Archive.

Cross, Gary (ed.), *Worktowners at Blackpool: Mass-Observation and Popular Leisure in the 1930s* (London and New York: Routledge, 1990).

Cunningham, Valentine, *British Writers of the Thirties* (Oxford: Oxford University Press, 1988).

Dalí, Salvador, *The Secret Life of Salvador Dalí* (London: Vision, 1968).

Davies, John, *Mist Mountain Water Wind*, text by Richard Ehrlich (London: Travelling Light, 1986).

Davies, John, *A Green and Pleasant Land*, texts by Michael Wood and Rob Powell (Manchester: Cornerhouse, 1987).

Davies, John, *The British Landscape*, text by Jonathan Glancey (London: Chris Boot, 2006).

Dean, Tacita, *An Aside* (London: Hayward Gallery, 2005).

Debord, Guy, 'Introduction à une critique de la géographie urbaine', *Les Lèvres nues*, 6 (November 1955), 11–15.

Delany, Paul, *Bill Brandt: A Life* (London: Jonathan Cape, 2004).

Delcroix, Stéphanie, 'Crossing the road', *[a–n] Magazine for artists* (March 2003), 34–5.

Deller, Jeremy and Alan Kane, *Folk Archive* (London: Book Works, 2005).

Dennis, Terence, 'Eileen Agar', *Counterpoint*, 1 (1944), unpaginated.

Denton, Pennie, *Seaside Surrealism: Paul Nash in Swanage* (Swanage: Peveril Press, 2002).

Dezeuze, Anna, 'Richard Wentworth in conversation', *Papers of Surrealism*, 4 (Winter 2005), www.surrealismcentre.ac.uk/publications/papers/journal4.

Dodd, Philip, 'Lowryscapes: recent writing about the "the North"', *Critical Quarterly*, 32:2 (1990), 17–28.

Dodd, Philip (ed.), *The Art of Travel: Essays on Travel Writing* (London: Frank Cass, 1982).

Dos Passos, John, *USA* (London: Constable, 1938; republished Harmondsworth: Penguin, 1966).

Dyer, Geoff, 'Les Mots et les Choses' in *Richard Wentworth/Eugène Atget: Faux Amis*, (London: Photographers' Gallery, 2001), pp. 9–21.

Edwards, Steve, 'Disastrous Documents', *Ten.8*, 15 (1984), 12–23.

Einzig, Barbara (ed.), *Thinking about Art: Conversations with Susan Hiller* (Manchester: Manchester University Press, 1996).

Elsner, John and Roger Cardinal (eds), *The Cultures of Collecting* (London: Reaktion, 1994).

Eluard, Paul and Man Ray, *Facile* (Paris: GLM, 1935).

Emin, Tracey, *Strangeland* (London: Sceptre, 2005).

Evans, Myfanwy, 'Paul Nash, 1937', *Axis*, 12 (Early winter, 1937), 13.

Evans, Myfanwy (ed.), *The Painter's Object* (London: Gerald Howe, 1937).

Evans, Walker, *American Photographs* (New York: Museum of Modern Art, 1938; reprinted 1962 and 1988).

Feaver, William, *Pitmen Painters: The Ashington Group 1934–1984* (London: Chatto & Windus, 1988).

Fermor, Patrick Leigh, *Between the Woods and the Water* (London: John Murray, 1986).

Fijalkowski, Krzysztof, 'Objective Poetry: Post-war Czech Surrealist Photography and the Everyday', *History of Photography*, 29:2 (Summer 2005), 163–73.

Fitzgibbon, Constantine, *The Blitz* (London: Macdonald, 1970).

Forster, E. M., *Howard's End* (London: Penguin, 2000; first published London: Edward Arnold, 1910).

Freeman, Judi, *The Dada and Surrealist Word-Image* (Los Angeles: County Museum/Cambridge, Mass: MIT Press, 1989).

Frizzell, Deborah, *Humphrey Spender's Humanist Landscapes: Photo-Documents 1932–1942* (New Haven: Yale Centre for British Art/Paul Mellon Center for Studies in British Art, 1997).

Fussell, Paul, *Abroad: British Literary Traveling Between the Wars* (Oxford: Oxford University Press, 1980).

Gascoyne, David, *A Short Survey of Surrealism* (London: Cobden-Sanderson, 1935).

Gascoyne, David, *Journal 1936–37* (London: Enitharmon Press, 1980).

Gaskell, Elizabeth, *North and South* (London: Penguin, 2003; first published 1855).

Gaskin, M. J., *Blitz: The Story of 29th December 1940* (London: Faber & Faber, 2005).

Germain, Edward (ed.), *English and American Surrealist Poetry* (Harmondsworth: Penguin, 1978).

Gooding, Mel, 'Preface' in *The Imaginative Impulse: Julian Trevelyan 1910–88* (Henley-on-Thames: Bohun Gallery, 1998).

Green, Henry, *Caught* (London: Harvill Press, 2001; first published London: Hogarth Press, 1943).

Greene, Graham, *A Gun for Sale* (London: Vintage, 2005; first published London: William Heinemann, 1936).

Greene, Graham, *The Ministry of Fear* (London: Vintage, 2001; first published London: William Heinemann, 1943).

Grierson, John, 'Propaganda', *Sight and Sound*, 2 (winter 1933–34), 119.

Griffin, Brian, *Power*, text by Richard Smith (London: Travelling Light, 1981).

Grimes, Teresa, Judith Collins and Oriana Baddeley (eds), *Five Women Painters* (Oxford: Lennard, 1989).

Hagen, Charles, 'Bill Brandt's Documentary Fiction', *Artforum* (September 1985), 111–4.

Hall-Duncan, Nancy, *Photographic Surrealism* (Cleveland: New Gallery of Contemporary Art, 1979).

Halliday, Nigel Vaux, *More than a Bookshop: Zwemmer's and Art in the 20th Century* (London: Philip Wilson, 1991).

Hanley, James, *No Directions* (London: André Deutsch, 1990; first published London: Nicholson and Watson, 1943).

Hardy, Bert, *My Life* (London: Gordon Fraser, 1985).

Hardy, Thomas, *The Hand of Ethelberta* (London; Penguin, 1997; first published London: Smith, Elder and Co., 1876).

Harrison, Charles, 'England's Climate' in Brian Allen (ed.), *Towards a Modern Art World* (New Haven and London: Yale University Press, 1995), pp. 207–25.

Harrison, Martin, *Young Meteors: British Photojournalism 1957–1965* (London: Jonathan Cape, 1998).

Harrison, Martin, *Transition: The London Art Scene in the Fifties* (London: Merrell, 2002).

Harrisson, T. H., 'Coconut Moon: A Philosophy of Cannibalism in the New Hebrides', *New Statesman and Nation,* 13:306 (2 January 1937), 12–3.

Harrisson, Tom, *Savage Civilization* (London: Victor Gollancz, 1937).

Harrisson, Tom, 'The Fifty-Second Week of the Year: Impressions of Blackpool', *Geographical Magazine* (April 1938), 387–402.

Harrisson, Tom, 'A World's Brain Trust', *New Statesman and Nation* (10 September 1938), 375.

Harrisson, Tom, 'So This is Blackpool', *Picture Post* (1 July 1939), 26–32.

Harrisson, Tom, *World Within: A Borneo Story* (London: Cresset Press, 1959).

Harrisson, Tom, *Living Through the Blitz* (London: Collins, 1976).

Harrisson, Tom and Charles Madge (eds), *First Year's Work* (London: Lindsay Drummond, 1938).

Harrisson, Tom, Humphrey Jennings and Charles Madge, 'Anthopology at Home', *New Statesman and Nation* 13:310 (30 January 1937), 155.

Heimann, Judith M., *The Most Offending Soul Alive: Tom Harrisson and his Remarkable Life* (London: Aurum Press, 2002).

Henderson, Nigel, 'Photographs', *Ark*, 17 (1956), 48–51.

Henderson, Nigel, *Nigel Henderson: Paintings, Collages and Photographs* (London: Anthony D'Offay Gallery, 1977).

Hewison, Robert, *Under Siege: Literary Life in London 1939–45* (London: Weidenfeld & Nicolson, 1977).

Hewitt, John, *The Shell Poster Book* (London: Profile, 1998).

Highmore, Ben, *Everyday Life and Cultural Theory* (London and New York: Routledge, 2002).

Hiller, Susan, *Rough Sea* (Sussex: Gardner Art Centre, 1976).

Hiller, Susan, *The Muse My Sister* (Londonderry: Orchard Gallery, 1984).

Hinde, John, *Our True Intent is All for your Delight: the John Hinde Butlin's Photographs*, introduction by Martin Parr (London: Chris Boot, 2002).

Hodgkinson, Anthony W., 'Humphrey Jennings and Mass-Observation: a conversation with Tom Harrisson', *Journal of the University Film Assocation,* 27:4 (Fall 1975), 31–5.

Hodgkinson, Anthony W. and Rodney E. Sheratsky, *Humphrey Jennings: More than a Maker of Films* (Hanover, New Hampshire: University Press of New England, 1982).

Hoffman, Dave and Shirley Read, 'Nigel Henderson' (interview), *Camerawork*, 11 (September 1978), 12–13.

Hommage au GPO Film Unit (Paris: La Cinémathèque française, no date).

Haworth-Booth, Mark and David Mellor, *Bill Brandt: Behind the Camera* (Oxford: Phaidon, 1985).

Howarth, Sophie (ed.), *Singular Images* (London: Tate, 2005).

Hubert, Renée Riese, *Surrealism and the Book* (Berkeley: University of California Press, 1988).

Hubert, Renée Riese, *Magnifying Mirrors: Women, Surrealism and Partnership* (Lincoln: University of Nebraska Press, 1994).

Hugnet, Georges, *La Septième face du dé* (Paris: Editions Jeanne Bucher, 1936).

Hugnet, Georges, *Guide Rose: Huit jours à trébaumec* (Paris: Henri Mercier, 1969).

Hussey, Andrew, *The Game of War* (London: Jonathan Cape, 2001).

Hynes, Samuel, *The Auden Generation* (London: Bodley Head, 1976).

Isherwood, Christopher, 'A Berlin Diary', *New Writing*, 3 (spring 1937), 11–26, reprinted in *Farewell to Berlin* (London: Chatto & Windus, 1939).

Jackson, Kevin, *Humphrey Jennings* (London: Picador, 2004).

Jackson, Kevin (ed.), *The Humphrey Jennings Film Reader* (Manchester: Carcanet, 1993).

Jaguer, Edouard, *Les Mystères de la chambre noire* (Paris: Flammarion, 1982).

Jameson, Storm, 'Documents', *Fact*, 4 (July 1937), 9–18.

Jeffrey, Ian, *Photography: a Concise History* (London: Thames & Hudson, 1981).

Jennings, Humphrey, *Pandaemonium: The Coming of the Machine as seen by Contemporary Observers*, ed. Mary-Lou Jennings and Charles Madge (London: André Deutsch, 1985).

Jennings, Humphrey and Charles Madge (eds), *May 12: Mass-Observation Day Survey* (London: Faber & Faber, 1937; republished 1987 with a new afterword by David Pocock).

Jennings, Mary-Lou (ed.), *Humphrey Jennings: Film-maker, Painter, Poet* (London: British Film Institute, 1982).

Keiller, Patrick, 'The Poetic Experience of Townscape and Landscape, and Some Ways of Depicting It', *Undercut*, 3/4 (March 1982), 42–8, reprinted in Nina Danino and Michael Mazière (eds), *The Undercut Reader* (London: Wallflower, 2003), pp. 75–83.

Keiller, Patrick, *Robinson in Space* (London: Reaktion, 1999).

King, James, *Interior Landscapes: A Life of Paul Nash* (London: Weidenfeld & Nicolson, 1987).

Knox, James, *Robert Byron: A Biography* (London: John Murray, 2003).

Krauss, Rosalind and Jane Livingston (eds), *L'Amour Fou* (Washington: Corcoran Gallery/New York: Abbeville Press, 1985).

Kumar, Krishan, *The Making of English Identity* (Cambridge: Cambridge University Press, 2003).

'Lady Penrose', *The Times* (25 July 1977), 14.

Lambert, David, 'Durlston Park and Purbeck House: the Public and Private Realms of George Burt, King of Swanage', *New Arcadian Journal*, 45/6 (1998), 15–52.

Lanyon, Andrew, *The Rooks of Trelawne* (London: Photographers' Gallery, 1976).

Lanyon, Andrew, *The Vanishing Cabinet* (London: Travelling Light, 1980).

Legg, Rodney, *Old Swanage* (Sherborne: Dorset Publishing, 1983).

Levitt, Helen, *In the Street* (Durham NC: Duke University Press, 1987).

Lewer, David and J. Bernard Calkin, *Curiosities of Swanage, or Old London by the Sea* (Swanage: Purbeck Press, 1971, revised 1999).

Lewer, David, *Hardy in Swanage: 1875 and 'The Hand of Ethelberta'* (Wincanton: Dorset Publishing Company, 1990).

Livingston, Jane, *Lee Miller: Photographer* (London: Thames & Hudson, 1989).

Lovell, Alan and Jim Hillier, *Studies in Documentary* (London: Secker & Warburg/British Film Institute, 1972).

Lyle, John, 'Little England: Ian Breakwell's Diary 1964–1985', *City Limits* (17–24 July 1986), 93.
MacCannell, Dean, *The Tourist: A New Theory of the Leisure Class* (London: Macmillan, 1976).
MacClancy, Jeremy, 'Brief Encounter: The Meeting, in Mass-Observation, of British Surrealism and Popular Anthropology', *Journal of the Royal Anthropological Institute*, 1:3 (September 1995), 495–512.
Macdonald, Kevin and Mark Cousins, *Imagining Reality: The Faber Book of Documentary* (London: Faber & Faber, 1996).
MacNeice, Louis, *The Strings are False* (London: Faber, 1966).
MacNeice, Louis, *Autumn Journal* (London: Faber & Faber, 1998; first published 1939).
Madge, Charles, 'Surrealism for the English', *New Verse* 6 (1933), 14–8.
Madge, Charles, 'The Meaning of Surrealism', *New Verse*, 10 (1934), 13–5.
Madge, Charles, 'Anthropology at Home', *New Statesman and Nation*, 13:306 (2 January 1937), 12.
Madge, Charles, 'Oxford Collective Poem', *New Verse*, 25 (May 1937), 16–19.
Madge, Charles, 'Some reflections on popular poetry', *New Writing*, New Series, 3 (Christmas 1939), 65–75.
Madge, Charles, 'The Birth of Mass-Observation', *Times Literary Supplement* (5 November 1976), 1395.
Madge, Charles and Tom Harrisson, *Mass-Observation* (London: Frederick Muller, 1937).
Madge, Charles and Humphrey Jennings, 'Poetic Description and Mass-Observation', *New Verse*, 24 (February–March 1937), 1–6.
Mandler, Peter, 'Against Englishness: English Culture and the Limits to Rural Nostalgia 1850–1940', *Transactions of the Royal Historical Society*, 6:7 (1997), 155–75.
Mass-Observation, *The Pub and The People* (London: Gollancz, 1943; republished with a new preface by Tom Harrisson and photographs by Humphrey Spender, Welwyn Garden City: Seven Dials Press, 1970).
Massey, Anne, *The Independent Group: Modernism and Mass Culture in Britain 1945–59* (Manchester: Manchester University Press, 1995).
Massingham, H. J., *Downland Man* (London: Jonathan Cape, 1926).
Massingham, H. J., *Chiltern Country* (London: Batsford, 1940).
Matheson, Neil, 'The Phantom of Surrealism: Photography, Cultural Identity and the Reception of Surrealism in England', *History of Photography* 29:2 (summer 2005), 149–62.
Matless, David, *Landscape and Englishness* (London: Reaktion, 1998).
Matthews, J. H., '*Diary Extracts 1968–1976* by Ian Breakwell', *TRANSFORMAcTION*, 8 (1977), 38–40.
Mawson, T. H., *The Life and Work of an English Landscape Architect* (London: Richards, 1927).
McDonald, John and Humphrey Spender, *From Worktown to Our Town* (Bolton: Bolton Museum and Art Gallery, 1993).
Mellor, David, 'Mass-Observation: The Intellectual Climate', *Camerawork*, 11 (September 1978), 4–5.
Mellor, David (ed.), *Cecil Beaton* (London: Barbican Art Gallery, 1986).
Mellor, David (ed.), *A Paradise Lost* (London: Lund Humphries/Barbican Art Gallery, 1987).
Mellor, David, *The Sixties Art Scene in London* (London: Phaidon, 1993).
A Midwife, 'Anthropology at Home', *New Statesman and Nation*, 13:311 (6 February 1937), 201.
Montagu, Jemima (ed.), *Paul Nash: Modern Artist, Ancient Landscape* (Liverpool: Tate, 2003).
Morley, David and Kevin Robins (eds), *British Cultural Studies* (Oxford: Oxford University Press, 2001).
Mortimer, Raymond, 'Nature Imitates Art', *Architectural Review* (January 1935), 27–9.
Morton, H. V., *In Search of England* (London: Methuen, 1939; first published 1927).
Mosley, Leonard, *Backs to the Wall: London Under Fire 1939–45* (London: Weidenfeld & Nicolson, 1971).
Mowl, Timothy, *Stylistic Cold Wars: Betjeman versus Pevsner* (London: John Murray, 2000).

Muggeridge, Malcolm, *The Thirties* (London: Hamish Hamilton, 1940).

Murray, Andrew (ed.), *British Surrealism – Fifty Years On* (London: Mayor Gallery, 1986).

Murray, Lynda J., *A Zest for Life: the Story of Alexander Keiller* (Wootton Bassett: Morven Books, 1999).

Murrow, Edward R., *This is London* (London: Cassell, 1941).

Nash, Margaret (ed.), *Fertile Image* (London: Faber & Faber, 1951, with an introduction by James Laver; republished 1973 with an additional introduction by Andrew Causey).

Nash, Paul, '"Going Modern" and "Being British"', *The Week-end Review* (12 March 1932), 322–3.

Nash, Paul, *Dorset Shell Guide* (London: Architectural Press, 1936).

Nash, Paul, 'Swanage, or Seaside Surrealism', *Architectural Review* (April 1936), 151–4.

Nash, Paul, 'Landscape of the Megaliths', *Art and Education* (March 1939), 8.

Nash, Paul, 'Monster Field', *Architectural Review* (October 1940), 120–2.

Nash, Paul, *Monster Field* (Oxford: Counterpoint, 1946).

Nash, Paul, *Outline* (London: Faber & Faber, 1949, with an introduction by Herbert Read; republished, London: Columbus, 1988, with a preface by Andrew Causey).

Newman, John and Nikolaus Pevsner, *The Buildings of England: Dorset* (London: Yale University Press, 1972).

Normandy and Brittany: Guide to the Seaside Resorts (London: Southern Railway Company of England, eighth edition, 1934).

Nowell-Smith, Geoffrey, 'Humphrey Jennings: Surrealist Observer' in Charles Barr (ed.), *All Our Yesterdays: 90 Years of British Cinema* (London: British Film Institute, 1986), pp. 321–33.

Orwell, George, *Coming up for Air* (London: Penguin, 2000; first published London: Victor Gollancz, 1939).

Orwell, George, *The Road to Wigan Pier* (London: Penguin, 2001; first published London: Victor Gollancz, 1937).

Orwell, Sonia and Ian Angus (eds), *Collected Essays, Journalism and Letters of George Orwell, Vol. II: My Country Right or Left 1940–1943* (London: Secker & Warburg, 1968; republished Harmondsworth: Penguin, 1970).

Osborne, Peter D., *Travelling Light: Photography, Travel and Culture* (Manchester: Manchester University Press, 2000).

Panter-Downes, Mollie, *London War Notes 1939–1945*, ed. William Shawn (London: Longman, 1972).

Parr, Martin, 'Beauty Spots', in Colin Osman and Peter Turner (eds), *Creative Camera Collection 5* (London: Coo Press, 1978), pp. 113–23.

Parr, Martin, *The Last Resort* (Liverpool: Promenade Press, 1986).

Parr, Martin, *West Bay* (London: Rocket Gallery, 1997).

Parr, Martin, *Boring Postcards* (London: Phaidon, 1999).

Parr, Martin, *Modern Times: Think of England* (BBC, 1999).

Parr, Martin, *Think of England* (London: Phaidon, 2000).

Parr, Martin and Gerry Badger, *The Photobook: A History, Volume I* (London: Phaidon, 2004).

Paxman, Jeremy, *The English* (Harmondsworth: Penguin, 1999; first published London: Michael Joseph, 1998).

Penrose, Antony, *The Lives of Lee Miller* (London: Thames & Hudson, 1985).

Penrose, Antony, *Roland Penrose: the Friendly Surrealist* (Munich: Prestel, 2001).

Penrose, Antony, *The Home of the Surrealists: Lee Miller, Roland Penrose and their Circle at Farley Farm* (London: Frances Lincoln, 2001).

Penrose, Antony, *The Surrealists in Cornwall* (Falmouth: Falmouth Art Gallery, 2004).

Penrose, Roland, *The Road is Wider than Long* (first edition, London: London Gallery, 1939; second edition, London: Arts Council of Great Britain, 1980, with additional postscript: 'The Road *was* wider than long'; third edition, Los Angeles: J. Paul Getty Trust, 2003).

Penrose, Roland, *Roland Penrose*, text by Norbert Lynton (London: Arts Council of Great Britain, 1980).

Penrose, Roland, *Scrapbook 1900–1981* (London: Thames & Hudson, 1981).
Péret, Benjamin, 'Ruines: Ruine des Ruines', *Minotaure*, 12–13 (May 1939), 57–61.
Phillips, Tom, *Works, Texts to 1974* (Stuttgart: Hansjörg Mayer, 1975).
Piper, John, 'Prehistory from the Air', *Axis*, 8 (early winter 1937), 5–8.
Piper, John, 'A War-Artist on War-Photographs', *The Spectator*, 5898 (11 July 1941), 38.
Pitman, George (Allen Hutt), 'Man in Our Time no. 8: Humphrey Jennings', *Our Time*, 3:12 (July 1944), 12–13.
Plomer, William, 'Surrealism To-Day', *New Statesman and Nation*, 19:488 (29 June 1940), 794.
Potts, Alex, ' "Constable Country" Between the Wars', in Raphael Samuel (ed.), *Patriotism, volume III: National Fictions* (London: Routledge, 1989), pp. 60–86.
Potts, Ian, *Stranger than Fiction*, written by Ian Potts and Angus Calder (London: British Film Institute, 1985).
Priestley, J. B., *English Journey* (London: William Heinemann, 1934).
Pulham, Peter Rose, 'Surrealist Artists', *Lilliput* (October 1943), 323–30.
Pyke, Geoffrey, 'King and Country', *New Statesman and Nation*, 12:303 (12 December 1936), 974.
Raeburn, Michael (ed.), *Salvador Dalí – the Early Years (*London: Thames & Hudson, 1994).
Raine, Kathleen, *The Land Unknown* (London: Hamish Hamilton, 1975).
Ray-Jones, Tony, 'Photographs from England and America', *Creative Camera* (October 1968), 349.
Ray-Jones, Tony, 'Brassaï talking about Photography', *Creative Camera* (April 1970), 121.
Ray-Jones, Tony, *A Day Off: an English Journal*, introduction by Ainslie Ellis (London: Thames & Hudson, 1974).
Read, Herbert (ed.), *Unit One* (London: Cassell, 1934).
Read, Herbert (ed.), *Surrealism* (London: Faber & Faber, 1936; reprinted 1971).
Remy, Michel, *Surrealism in Britain* (Aldershot: Ashgate, 1999).
Renzio, Toni del and Duncan Scott (eds), *Surrealism in England: 1936 and After* (Canterbury: Canterbury College of Art, 1986).
Rimbaud, Arthur, *Complete Works, Selected Letters*, translated by Wallace Fowlie (Chicago: University of Chicago Press, 1966).
Robbins, David (ed.), *The Independent Group: Postwar Britain and the Aesthetics of Plenty* (Cambridge, Mass: MIT Press, 1990).
Roberts, Russell, *Tony Ray-Jones* (London: Chris Boot, 2004).
Robertson, Alexander (ed.), *Surrealism in Britain in the Thirties* (Leeds: Leeds City Art Gallery, 1986).
Roegiers, Patrick, *Magritte and Photography* (London: Lund Humphries, 2005).
Ross, Alan, *Colours of War: War Art 1939–45* (London: Jonathan Cape, 1983).
Rumney, Ralph, 'The Leaning Tower of Venice', *Ark*, 24 (1958), between 20 and 21.
Rumney, Ralph, *The Consul* (London: Verso, 2002).
Sadler, Simon, *The Situationist City* (Cambridge, Mass: MIT Press, 1998).
Samuel, Raphael, *Theatres of Memory, Vol I: Past and Present in Popular Culture* (London: Verso, 1994).
Sansom, William, *Fireman Flower and Other Stories* (London: Hogarth Press, 1944).
Sansom, William, *Westminster at War* (London: Faber & Faber, 1947; reprinted with a new foreword by Stephen Spender as *The Blitz: Westminster at War*, Oxford: Oxford University Press, 1989).
Sansom, William, 'The Making of *Fires were Started*', *Film Quarterly*, 15:2 (winter 1961–2), 27–9.
Seaborne, Mike, *Shelters: Living Underground in the London Blitz* (London: Dirk Nishen, 1988).
Sers, Philippe (ed.), *Atelier Man Ray* (Paris: Centre Pompidou, 1982).
Shields, Rob, *Places on the Margin: Alternative Geographies of Modernity* (London: Routledge, 1991).
Shloss, Carol, *In Visible Light: Photography and the American Writer 1840–1940* (New York: Oxford University Press, 1987).
Sidey, Tessa, *Surrealism in Birmingham 1935–1954* (Birmingham: Birmingham Museums and Art Gallery, 2001).

Simpson, Ann, *Eileen Agar 1899–1991* (Edinburgh: Scottish National Gallery of Modern Art, 1999).
Simpson, J. A. and E. S. C. Weiner (eds), *The Oxford English Dictionary: Volume VI,* second edition (Oxford: Clarendon Press, 1989).
Simpson, Michael, *In the Mind's Eye: Surrealist Works on Paper* (Manchester: Whitworth Art Gallery, 1996).
Smith, I. F., *Windmill Hill and Avebury* (Oxford: Oxford University Press, 1965).
Sobieszek, Robert, 'Erotic Photomontages: Georges Hugnet's *La Septième face du dé*', *Dada/Surrealism*, 9 (1979), 66–82.
Soby, James Thrall, *Yves Tanguy* (New York: Museum of Modern Art, 1955).
Sontag, Susan, *Regarding the Pain of Others* (New York: Farrar, Straus and Giroux, 2003).
Sorensen, Colin, *London on Film* (London: Museum of London, 1996).
Spencer, Robin (ed.), *Eduardo Paolozzi: Writings and Interviews* (Oxford: Oxford University Press, 2000).
Spender, Humphrey, 'Mass-Observation', *Ark*, 23 (1958), 16–17.
Spender, Humphrey, *Humphrey Spender: Worktown* (Falmer: University of Sussex, 1977).
Spender, Humphrey, *Worktown People*, ed. Jeremy Mulford (Bristol: Falling Wall Press, 1982).
Spender, Humphrey, *'Lensman': Photographs 1932–52* (London: Chatto & Windus, 1987).
Spender, Humphrey and Tom Harrisson, *Britain in the 30s* (London: Lion And Unicorn Press, Royal College of Art, 1975).
Stanley, Nick, *The Extra Dimension: A Study and Assessment of the Methods Employed by Mass-Observation in its First Period, 1937–1940* (Birmingham Polytechnic: unpublished PhD dissertation, 1981).
Stansky, Peter and William Abrahams, *London's Burning: Life, Death and Art in the Second World War* (London: Constable, 1994).
Stanton, Gareth, 'In Defence of *Savage Civilization*: Tom Harrisson, Cultural Studies and Anthropology', in Stephen Nugent and Chris Shore (eds), *Anthropology and Cultural Studies* (London: Pluto Press, 1997), pp. 11–33.
Štyrský, Jindřich and Jindřich Heisler, *Na jehlách těchto dní* (Prague: Borovy, 1945).
The Surrealist and the Photographer (Edinburgh: Scottish National Gallery of Modern Art, 2001).
Sussex, Elizabeth, *The Rise and Fall of British Documentary* (Berkeley: University of California Press, 1975).
Sussex, Elizabeth, 'Calvacanti in England', *Sight and Sound*, 44:4 (autumn 1975), 188.
Suschitzky, Wolfgang, *Charing Cross Road in the Thirties*, introduction by Raphael Samuel (London: Dirk Nishen, 1989).
Szarkowski, John and Maria Morris Hambourg, *The Work of Atget: Volume IV: Modern Times* (New York: Museum of Modern Art, 1985).
Tassi, Roberto, *Sutherland: The Wartime Drawings* (London: Sotheby Parke Bernet, 1980).
The Tate Gallery 1972–4: Biennial Report and Illustrated Catalogue of Acquisitions (London: Tate Gallery, 1975).
Taylor, John, *A Dream of England* (Manchester: Manchester University Press, 1994).
Treves, Sir Frederick, *Highways and Byways of Dorset* (London: Macmillan, 1906).
Trevelyan, Julian, *Indigo Days* (London: MacGibbon and Kee, 1957; reprinted with foreword by Raleigh Trevelyan and introduction by Nicholas Usherwood, Aldershot: Scolar Press, 1996).
Ubac, Raoul, *Ubac* (Paris: Editions Maeght, 1970).
'Venise a vaincu Ralph Rumney', *Internationale Situationniste*, 1 (June 1958), 28.
Vaughan, Dai, *Portrait of an Invisible Man: Stewart McAllister* (London: British Film Institute, 1983).
Vaughan, Dai, *Totes Meer* (Bridgend: Seren, 2003).
Walker, Ian, *City Gorged with Dreams: Surrealism and Documentary Photography in Interwar Paris* (Manchester: Manchester University Press, 2002).
Walker, Ian, 'On the Needles of these Days: Czech Surrealism and Documentary Photography', *Third Text*, 18:2 (2004), 103–18.

Walker, Ian, 'Summer of Love: A Photograph by Tony Ray-Jones', *Source*, 40 (autumn 2004), 16–21.

Walker, Ian, 'Between photograph and poem: a study of Štyrský and Heisler's *On the Needles of these Days*', *Papers of Surrealism*, 3 (Spring 2005), www.surrealismcentre.ac.uk/publications/papers/journal3.

Walker, Ian, 'Through the Picture-Plane: On Looking into Photographs', in Martha Langford (ed.), *Image And Imagination* (Montreal: McGill-Queens University Press, 2005), pp. 17–25.

Walker, Ian, 'The "Comic Sublime": Eileen Agar at Ploumanac'h', *Tate Papers* (Autumn 2005), www.tate.org.uk/research/tateresearch/tatepapers/05autumn/walker.htm.

Walker, Ian (ed.), *Contrariwise: Surrealism and Britain*, with a text by J. H. Matthews (Swansea: Glynn Vivian Gallery, 1986).

Walsh, Virginia, *Nigel Henderson: Parallel of Life and Art* (London: Thames & Hudson, 2001).

Walton, John K., *Blackpool* (Edinburgh: Edinburgh University Press/Lancaster: Carnegie Publishing, 1998).

Warburton, Nigel (ed.), *Bill Brandt* (Oxford: Clio Press, 1993).

Watney, Simon, 'Making Strange: The Shattered Mirror' in Victor Burgin (ed.), *Thinking Photography* (London: Macmillan, 1982), pp. 154–76.

Waugh, Evelyn, *Vile Bodies* (London: Penguin, 2000; first published London: Chapman and Hall, 1930).

Waugh, Evelyn, *Put Out More Flags* (London: Penguin, 2000; first published London: Chapman and Hall, 1942).

Wentworth, Richard, *Making Do and Getting By*, music by Ry Cooder (London: Whitechapel Art Gallery, 1985), video, 20 minutes.

Wentworth, Richard, *Richard Wentworth*, texts by Juan Vicente Aliaga and Paul Bonaventura (Valencia: Sala Parpallo, 1988).

Wentworth, Richard, *Richard Wentworth*, text by Marina Warner (London: Thames & Hudson/Serpentine Gallery, 1993).

Wentworth, Richard, *Richard Wentworth*, texts by Michael Bracewell, Roger Malbert, Mark Lythgoe and Simon Groom (Liverpool: Tate, 2005).

Wiener, Martin J., *English Culture and the Decline of the Industrial Spirit 1850–1980* (Cambridge: Cambridge University Press, 1981).

Williams, Val, *Martin Parr* (London: Phaidon, 2002).

Winston, Brian, '*Fires were Started–*' (London: British Film Institute, 1999).

Woods, Alan, *Ralph Rumney: The Map is Not the Territory* (Manchester: Manchester University Press, 2000).

Worsley, Victoria, 'Ian Breakwell (1943–2005)', *Henry Moore Institute Newsletter*, 63 (December 2005/January 2006), unpaginated.

Wright, Patrick, *On Living in an Old Country: the National Past in Contemporary Britain* (London: Verso, 1985).

Wright, Patrick, *The Village That Died for England* (London: Faber & Faber, 2002; first published London: Jonathan Cape, 1995).

Yentob, Alan, 'The World According to Parr' (BBC, 2003).

Yorke, Malcolm, *The Spirit of Place: Nine Neo-Romantic Artists* (London: Constable, 1988).

Yorke, Matthew (ed.), *Surviving: the Uncollected Writings of Henry Green* (London: Chatto & Windus, 1992).

Ziegler, Philip, *London at War 1939–1945* (London: Pimlico, 2002; first published London: Sinclair-Stevenson, 1995).

Index

Note: numbers in *italic* refer to illustrations.